EMERGING TRENDS IN LIBRARY AND INFORMATION SCIENCE
(Library Networking, Library Consortia, Digital Library and Total Quality Management)

EMERGING TRENDS IN LIBRARY AND INFORMATION SCIENCE

(LIBRARY NETWORKING, LIBRARY CONSORTIA, DIGITAL LIBRARY AND TOTAL QUALITY MANAGEMENT)

Edited by:

Parveen Kumar

Librarian S. A. Jain College

Ambala City, Haryana

Ess Ess Publications

New Delhi

Emerging Trends in Library and Information Science (Library Networking, Library Consortia, Digital Library and Total Quality Management)

ISBN: 978-81-7000-703-6

₹1150

First Published 2013

Published by:
Ess Ess Publications
4831/24, Ansari Road,
Darya Ganj,
New Delhi-110 002.
INDIA
Phones: 23260807, 41563444
Fax: 41563334
E-mail: info@essessreference.com
www.essessreference.com

Cover Design by *Patch Creative Unit*

Printed and bound in India at Salasar Imaging Systems.

Contents

Preface

In earlier times, the libraries were having only books and some other printed materials in their collection but today a variety of publications in different forms are coming in the book world or rather in the world of knowledge. In the age of information and communication technology libraries have given rise to revolutionary changes. Today many new trends are emerging in the field of library and information science.

For clarity and understanding of the emerging trends in library and information science, the book, containing twenty three chapters, has been divided into five parts. First part explores the development of library networking in India and at international level as well. Library networking is mounting a fast track route in the age of information and communication technology. Digitization of libraries has diversified the nature of library resources. The term library consortia is getting immense importance to form a cooperative arrangement to use and buy e-information together. The second part is focused exclusively on the concept of consortia. Here, an effort has been made to know how consortia is growing as a phenomenon and a very strong tool for futuristic education. The various issues of consortia are discussed in this part in detail including its use in higher education and its benefits overall. Digitization of libraries has been the area of core concern for the third section. An overview of digital library is presented in this section. Various issues and challenges including the future of this technology have been dealt at a length by various scholars. Digitization of knowledge, being an urgent and prompt requirement, needs a detailed elaboration in the modern era. And the concerned section deals with it in a simple and lucid way. The fourth part encompassed the chapters related to "total quality management" Digitization and networking is all useless if not covered by total quality management. This part focuses on the techniques of application of TQM in various academic libraries. The total quality management undoubtedly enhances the status of libraries but it lacks the applicability part in most of the institutions the scholars are unanimous on the issue that TQM must be applied in academic libraries. The last segment of the book comprises the miscellaneous topics relevant to the main theme of the book. These include the utility of online public access catalogue in related institutes, utility of open access journals and role of language based reference library. The studies in this section are concentrated on the libraries of Kurukshetra University, Panjab University and Punjabi University.

In the accomplishment of this work I have received help from number of individuals. I am indebted to them. Dr. (Mrs.) Ashu Shokeen, Professor, DLIS, KUK deserves the special thanks for her continuous encouragement to complete this work. I am also thankful to Dr. J. N. Gautam, Professor, SOS in LIS, JU, Gwalior for his valuable guidance. A special thank is due to Dr. Suresh Dhanda who has gone through some of the pages of my work and gave valuable suggestions. I am also grateful to all the contributors who sent their papers/ chapters for this edited volume.

I cannot go ahead without putting into words, my deepest thanks from the inner core of my heart, for the moral support and encouragement of my beloved wife, Renu Sharma, who tried her level best in providing whatever I needed, including happy and healthy family atmosphere all the time. The cherry face of my daughter "Akshita" and my son "Anuraag" boosted me up every time to work with a new and high spirit.

With deep sense of gratitude and grateful appreciation, I just cannot limit the depth of love and indebtness to my respected and loving parents Sh. Sat Narain and Smt. Geeta Devi who endured forbearance in my anxious moments and sprayed their love, affection and blessings.

Last but not least my thanks are due to M/s Ess Ess Publications for their untiring effort in bringing out this book well in tlme.

— Editor

List of Contributors

1. **Dr. Chetan Sharma**
   Assistant Librarian
   Guru Gobind Singh Indraprashta University, Dwarka, Delhi

2. **Sandhya Aggarwal**
   Librarian
   MM College, Fatehabad, Haryana

3. **Gurcharan Dass**
   Librarian
   Guru Nanak Group of College, Tohana (Fatehabad), Haryana

4. **Narender Kumar Chauhan**
   Librarian (Senior Scale)
   The Technological Institute of Textile & Sciences,
   Bhiwani, Haryana

5. **Dr Sudhir Narayan Singh**
   Assistant Professor, English & Comm. Skills,
   The Technological Institute of Textile & Sciences,
   Bhiwani, Haryana

6. **Alok Srivastava**
Librarian
D.B.S. College, Kanpur, Uttar Pradesh

7. **Sunil Tyagi**
Library Assistant
Indian Pharmacopoeia Commission,
Rajnagar, Ghaziabad, Uttar Pradesh

8. **Dr. Kishore Kumar Sarmah**
Librarian
Nowgong Girls' College, Nagaon, Assam

9. **Dr. Parveen Kumar**
Librarian
S. A. Jain College, Ambala City, Haryana

10. **Manoj Kumar**
Librarian,
Kendriya Vidyalaya, Air Force Station,
Kasauli, Himachal Pradesh

11. **Randhir Singh Bhaskar**
Senior Librarian
Singhania University, Pacheri Bari, Rajasthan

12. **Mehar Singh**
Deputy Librarian
Deenbandhu Chhotu Ram University of Sci. & Technology,
Murthal, Haryana

13. **Ms. Anita Gaba**
Librarian
G.V.M.Girls College, Sonepat, Haryana

14. **Balvinder Kaur**
Librarian
Darshan Academy, Ambala Cantt, Haryana

15. **Davinder Pal Singh**
Library Restorer
Punjabi University, Patiala, Punjab

16. **Sanjay Gupta**
Librarian
DAV College, Karnal, Haryana

17. **Pankaj K. Bhardwaj**
Librarian
R.D.S. Public Girls College, Rewari, Haryana

18. **Dr. (Mrs.) Nirmal Goyal**
Librarian
Sohan Lal D.A.V. College of Education,
Ambala City, Haryana

19. **Ravinder Kumar**
Librarian
Municipal Corporation, Ambala Cantt, Haryana

20. **Suresh Kumar**
Librarian
Gaur Brahmin Degree College, Rohtak, Haryana

21. **Kulveen Kaur**
Assistant Librarian
Punjabi University, Patiala, Punjab

22. **Rajinder Kumar**
Lecturer
DLIS, Vaish Technical Institute, Rohtak, Haryana

23. Abdul Jalil
Librarian,
Rupahi College, Nagaon, Assam

24. Dr. Sanjay Kumar Singh
Ass. Professor
DLIS, Gauhati University, Guwahati, Assam

25. Gian Singh
Assistant Librarian
Punjabi University, Patiala, Punjab

26. Renu Sharma
M.A., M. Lib., B.Ed.

Introduction

Libraries today are the knowledge hub of information and technology which has given augment to revolutionary changes. As new technologies overwhelm the information field of today better manpower becomes all the more relevant if our libraries have gear at being automated. Libraries are agents of information and as such have a very important role to disseminate knowledge in all the fields of learning because they are basically linked up with the social welfare of people. Both Educational System as well as the library system in our country need to be reformed in order to meet the needs of modern readers of all types. Day by day many new concepts are emerging in the field of library and information science like, digital library, library networking, library consortia, cloud computing etc.

Library networking is comparatively a recent addition to the technology of library and information science. When a group of libraries/information centres is connected together for the purpose of specific requirements, which may be exchange of cataloguing, books etc, is said to be within a library networks. Networking provides a means by which a number of institutions can share equipments, programmes and database using communication lines. During present time, networking, more accurately, refers to those systems which contain elements of computerization with machine readable database capable of being accessed either offline or online. Use of communication between a number of computers and between different terminals in a computer is the result of library network. Networking of libraries is the best way to make resource sharing very effective in order to ensure equitable availability of required information. A library network is broadly describe as a group of libraries coming together with some agreement of understanding to help each other with a view to satisfying the information needs of their users.

Library consortia is a group of *libraries* who partner to coordinate activities, share resources, and combine expertise. The *International Coalition of Library Consortia* is an informal discussion group of such consortia. Consortium of libraries is well known for sharing of resources all over the world. Several libraries in the world have formed consortia to share their human and electronic resources. However, Consortium, now being overheard everywhere, is because of digital form of information. It refers to co-operation, co-ordination and collaboration between and amongst libraries for the purpose of sharing information resources. Currently, university libraries are purchasing materials to respond to the needs of their users. This task is difficult for a single library. By forming a consortium among libraries, it becomes possible to purchase information in stabilized and reasonable prices.

A Digital Library is a *library* in which collections are stored in digital formats (as opposed to print, *microform*, or other media) and accessible via computers. The digital content may be stored locally, or accessed remotely via computer networks. A digital library is a type of *information retrieval* system. The first use of the term digital library in print may have been in a 1988 report to the *Corporation for National Research Initiatives*. The idea of digital libraries is not new, but recent developments have made the realization of this idea more of a practical possibility than ever before. In particular, the availability of tools for easy access to information and for easy production of new information has encouraged traditional publishers to make their information available in digital networked form, but also made it possible for many individual authors to directly publish their own information on the Internet, bypassing traditional publishers and established bibliographic systems

Total Quality Management (TQM) is an *integrative philosophy of management* for continuously improving the *quality* of products and processes. TQM is based on the premise that the quality of products and processes is the responsibility of everyone involved with the creation or consumption of the products or services offered by an organization, requiring the involvement of management, workforce, suppliers, and customers, to meet or exceed customer expectations. The increasing expectations of users for better services have motivated libraries to view quality management as an effective means of incorporating quality improvement into their related services. Effectively implementing quality management in libraries requires an understanding of applying appropriate quality management concepts and techniques. Quality management in libraries and information services has received considerable attention, with a majority of those investigations describing quality concepts, quality management principles, related processes, and limitations. From the perspective of library services, adopting quality programs increases the effectiveness of the library and satisfies increasingly higher customer expectations. Most quality management-related literature is based on experience drawn from industrial organizations, particularly on the manufacturing of tangible products delivered to the end-user at a later stage. Recent years have witnessed the increasing acceptance of quality management into services-related and non-profit organizations, like education. Despite the significant level of adaptation within service organizations and the public sector, there exists missing link between quality management principles/tools and the implementation of quality management in libraries and information services.

The study begins with a discussion on status and prospects of networking in India. Dr. Chetan Sharma feels the urgent need of library networking in India. In the age of globalization, the librares are emerging as a strong source of knowledge having a plethora of literature. To manage such huge literature, resource sharing and library networking can play a very prominent role. It not only strengthens the resource building but checks the expenses also. He is of the opinion that library consortia, resource sharing and networking of libraries are the best means for the maximum benefit of the valuable information resources and literature. The author traces the various levels of library networking with its scope. He categorized the library networking into regional and status level. Regional level networking may occur at local, state, national and international level. While status level networking may be within the public library, academic library, special library and research library. In his attempt to analyze the consortia movement in India he presents a long list of various organizations and associations involved in the porgrammes of establishing the consortia in India. The various efforts taken for library networking in India have also been highlighted by the author in a systemic way.

The development of library networking and consortia at international level has been evaluated by Sandhya Aggarwal with special reference to the services through library consortium and networks. She also highlights the major problems in library consortium and networks along with international efforts for library consortia. She highlights India's initiatives for library consortia. She makes a point libraries in developing countries are working on consortia at national, regional and international level. A huge infrastructure is required for establishing the consortia in the developed countries, no library services can be thought without sharing of resources. Major problems have also been highlighted by the author. Among them, major are- lack of awareness and understanding, lack of speedy decision, budget and funding constraints etc. In the modern age, with the development of science and technology and innovations of techniques and devices, resource sharing has become easier and fruitful due to the availability of databases, information network, and online sharing facilities.

An overview of the development of library network has been presented by Gurcharan Dass in his article entitled "Library networking in India". He elaborated how many libraries and information network are working in India and highlights that the advent of computer networking as an accepted part of the library and information infrastructure had a very significant impact on the way in which library and information systems are perceived. India is thus on the threshold to a new era of computer communication networks both for general purposes and for library and information purposes

Narender Kumar Chauhan and Dr. Sudhir Narayan Singh focused on the library consortium. They elaborated the present scenario and future academic challenges. The paper highlights the major advantages of the consortia and different types of library consortium. They noted that Library consortium is the outcome of meticulous efforts done by the renowned scholars for the present generation and the generations yet to come because library in itself is an unbroken link between the past generation and present generation. In the present era every minute is an information explosion. To satisfy the needs of modern users through manual system are not possible, so the library consortium is need of the hour. In toto, the authors explore the concept, issues and shows how the library consortium is making resources available for its member libraries. They consider the library consortium as an agent of change for futuristic education.

Alok Srivastava pointed out the growth and issues of library consortia and resource sharing in modern era. He discussed the need and functions of consortia with their importance. Library consortia are considered as a coalition between libraries, publishers and vendors. They often provide a reasonable price in a win-win situation for all stakeholders. Thus, libraries have increasingly turned to consortia as a way of brokering better prices and rendering rapid and efficient services to information seekers. However, library consortia are facing new challenges, such as increasing expectations and a static budget, fair use, archiving of information, pricing strategies, measures of effectiveness and licensing e-resources.

Strengthening the academic library through library consortium is the focus of paper authored by Sunil Tyagi. He highlights the evolution of library consortium. He explained the library consortia in Indian context. Today, libraries have to face change management, and they are seeking tools to cope with it, developing strategic alliances with other libraries. Cooperation seems to be the key for libraries to survive. Cooperation efforts vary, depending on geographic areas and on different cultural traditions, but they seem present throughout the world: on one side, nations with libraries used to strong practice in cooperation and sharing have seen a flourishing of new cooperative initiatives and formal consortia; on the other side, nations where this collaborative practice was not within its culture have received a boast towards it.

Dr. Kishore Kumar Sarmah traces the consortial approach as resource sharing in higher education libraries. He mentioned various advantages and disadvantages of library consortia. He explained about library consortium at the national and international level. The creation of the web and networks brought many possibilities for integrating consortia activities at the international and national levels and to share their resources and expand and develop new services. India has been active in consortia activities but due to limitations it is hard to find a successful programme that could be used as a benchmark to replicate in other libraries. The need today is to explore other areas for collaboration to improve the overall situation in terms of services and resources.

Dr. Parveen Kumar strongly stressed on the need to develop library consortia in India. He discussed need, advantages and disadvantages of library consortia. He also explained various challenges and limitations of library consortia. Many library consortia in India are doing well and many libraries are benefited but at the same time library consortia are not free from problems. Consortia are tools, which will aid in exploiting the features of the e-journals as well as in effecting savings. Library consortia, providing for physical and electronic delivery of materials, and integrating the collection-development process are all distinct and crucial steps in moving towards the twenty-first century library.

Manoj Kumar presented an overview of library consortium in India. He pointed out the various factor affecting consortium formation with its challenges. The rapid growth of ICT has enabled Indian libraries to get the maximum out of minimum through Library Consortium. Indian libraries have realized the best way to utilize their limited resources achieved through mutual Collaboration, Joint procurement and Networking. It benefits the libraries to procure more electronic resources in the library with limited library budget and this is what the libraries require in the present scenario. Library Consortiums in India are efficiently managed and are at the same level as some of the best International Consortiums.

Randhir Singh Bhaskar in his article highlighted the library consortia benefits. The study explains the present system of consortia in India. The libraries and information centres are one of the major supporting agencies involved in the process of information transfer and finally the diffusion of information and information technology. Consequently, both the Information Systems and the Information Professionals are adapting to meet the changing needs and growing expectations of the users. The initiatives and development in the areas of automation, networking, resource sharing, consortia, digital libraries, electronic document delivery, etc. have causes to emerge new practices in the operations and management practices of the Library and Information Systems world over. As compared to the research libraries, the university and college libraries in India have shown a slow rate of progress in this direction.

Mehar Singh pointed out the various challenges and issues of digital library, their development and services. He also explained the role of a librarian in digital age. The digital libraries are the result of information explosion. During digitization of traditional library into digital library many problems may appear such as lack of technical knowledge and skill of the information professional, lack of original software package, lack of funds and lack of some other infrastructure facilities. There should be a significant headway to remove the barrier and challenges of digital libraries. Today's information scientists and LIS professionals must give a thought to the establishment of digital libraries.

Anita Gaba wrote on the future of digital libraries. She explained the merits and demerits of digital library. She elaborates various components required for digital libraries. She basically concentrates on these components namely hardware, software and human ware. The emergence of information technology with high resolution capture and sophisticated engines and large storage digital contents continue to ability of conform the digital library and in the future digital library and in the future digital libraries will be common in every institute, Colleges and Universities. Future scenario of digital libraries has also been discussed by the author in detail.

Balvinder Kaur highlights an overview of digital library. She described the role of librarian in digital environment. The initial cost of digitization is high but experiment shows that once digitization is introduced then the cost to manage this collection will be cheaper than that of any traditional library. Day by day the cost of digitization is decreasing, the online publication is increasing, the needs of user are shifting towards a different environment so it's needless to say that after one or two years my library or your library will go to be digitized so it's the peak time to all informational and library professional that they gear themselves to take and face the challenge.

Davinder Pal Singh discussed the challenges and implications of library digitization. He explained the process of digitization of library resources. The digital library permits random access to library materials. This enables the learners to consult wide variations of learning materials at their convenience, thus, making learning easy. Some of the users are not capable of using the existing search technologies, whether manual or electronic and then it becomes the responsibility of the librarian to guide these users, so that they can make optimal use of the library resources. It is the responsibility of librarians to assist library users in their bid to search for materials either manually or electronically. This will encourage the users to relate freely with the librarians and in the library, through some of the users that have problems may not request for assistance.

Sanjay Gupta wrote on the development of digital library in the age of information and communication technology. He also mentioned various challenges in digital development. Library and Information services cannot lag behind and require progress of the civilization. Keeping in view the requirement of time, technological development and global change, librarians are changing their nature from traditional to digital. The target of librarian is not only to provide excellent information services to users but technology has added many new dimensions to this task. All the librarians have to believe in power of Information and take the responsibility to provide effective, efficient, relevant and up to date information to their users. The competencies and skills form the basis for the continual survival and growth of librarianship in this information age.

Pankaj K. Bhardwaj describes how to create a digital library. She explains various tools for building the digital library. Digital libraries are organizations that provide the resources, including the specialized staff, to select, structure, offer intellectual access to, interpret, distribute, preserve the integrity of and ensure the persistence over time of collection of digital works so that they are readily and economically available for use by a defined community or set of communities. We must consider not only the obvious challenges, such as copyright restrictions and finding, but also some less obvious challenges, such as deciding how to organize the efforts and establish partnerships outside the library.

Fundamentally, building a digital library will require a change within the library itself.

The concept of discussed total quality management in academic libraries has been discussed by Dr. Nirmal Goel. She feels an urgent need of ICT based activities required in quality based academic libraries. The library being a service organization, its prime objective is to provide the right documents, information and services to its users. Only the users' satisfaction survey will facilitate the assessment of their satisfaction with products and services offered. Effectively implementing quality management in libraries requires an understanding of applying appropriate quality management concepts and techniques. Nowadays, electronic resources, networks and the World Wide Web represent a large portion of the library services. In this competitive educational environment, most of institutions in India are thriving to establish reputation by way of imparting quality education. Quality means user satisfaction, competitive cost, timely delivery, etc.

Ravinder Kumar conducted an empirical study in libraries of engineering colleges of Kurukshetra to know the application of total quality management. Total Quality Management is a process, the output of which depends upon customer satisfaction and continuous improvement. It provides a way to improve quality by examining the work in a systematic, oriented, consistent and organization wide perspective. There is a need to evolve methodologies and mechanisms for improvement of quality information services. More funds to be allocated for studying the quality of information services on project basis training of staff members in providing quality information services. All the libraries should have good collection of textbooks, journals, reference books and online journals for the implementation of TQM.

Suresh Kumar enquires the total quality management in college libraries. He also described facilities in a good library. This article reviews the quality management tools and techniques developed over the last five decades and, then, categorize them into three broad approaches. In addition, a framework of quality management approaches and techniques is developed and applied to assess and improve the service quality of libraries and information services. The application of total quality management could assist librarians and information officers very well. There are various methods, tools and techniques to measure, control and improve the quality of library services. Quality management provides get the importance and achieve the goal and provide the maximum services to the readers with the help of modern libraries for the benefits of the library as well as user community.

Kulveen Kaur in his article entitled "Electronic age information: an evaluative perspective" discusses the check points for quality information followed by librarians as facilitators etc. The information available in electronic form has grown by heaps and bounds within this decade. But the explosive growth of electronic information poses threats to the quality of information. the librarians and other professionals working with electronic information resources must explicit the protocols and the check points for evaluation on the library websites. Cooperative ventures among librarians should be initiated for safe and reliable search so that the relevance of the library profession can be ensured.

Rajinder Kumar conducted an empirical study in Kurukshetra University and Panjab University libraries to know the usability of online public access catalogue. Now a day, a number of libraries are providing OPAC searching facility to their users to find out the documents. In such a situation, the libraries should observed periodically how much comfort the users feel with this service so that some initiatives could be taken timely to improve this facility. Therefore, a study has been undertaken on the use of OPAC by the users in Kurukshetra university, Kurukshetra and Panjab university, Chandigarh.

Abdul Jalil and Dr. Sanjay Kumar Singh focused on open access journal in their article. They elaborated the need and benefits of an open access journal. They also discussed about the impact of open access journals on libraries. All libraries are unable to subscribe the paid journals, it needs huge amount of money and alternatively open access journals are easily accessible to them. The open access movement is boon to authors, scholars, researchers etc. Moreover, the sharing of each other's work with certain ideas will allow more significant ideas to form. We can safely hope that India as well as the world will march forward towards the ever increasing horizon of anytime, anywhere access of scholarly literature.

Gyan Singh conducted an empirical study in Punjabi University, Patiala to know the subject strengths in Dr. Ganda Singh Punjabi Reference Library collection. He presented the detailed collection of resources in the library from its inception. He also presents a historical description of the library. He used various tables to show the growth and development of purchased and gratis collection year wise. Strength of main subjects has also been depicted through table. Language wise collection has also been presented by the author.

DR. PARVEEN KUMAR

Part A
Library Networking

1

Status and Prospects of Library Networking in India

Dr. Chetan Sharma

ABSTRACT

Information explosion has invented immense range of library resources including print and online. In the era of globalization to get the nascent and relevant information is within the reach of every individual. Particularly university and special libraries are facing the challenges to cope up with this flood of information. To manage such huge literature, resource sharing and library networking plays a very prominent role. Library networking not only strengthens the resource building but check the expenses. Library consortia, resource sharing and networking of libraries are the best means for the maximum benefit of the valuable information resources and literature.

Keywords : Library Networking, Resource Sharing, Information, Library Consortia

INTRODUCTION

Resource sharing is one of the most popular components of the society. Every segment of the society shared what they had since ancient time. Farmers shared their tools of cultivation and it is an elementary culture since early time. A single well was shared by the whole villagers to get water. Resource sharing not only save the money but also establish harmony in the relationship. In every country various services and products has been shared from local to international level. Libraries are also a very good podium of resource sharing. Earlier resource sharing in libraries was called as 'library co-operation.' But in the age of Information Communication and Technology (ICT) term 'Library Networking' is more popular and establish. Digital environment also has diversified the nature of library resources. Though e-journals, e-books, e-thesis, CD-ROMs and DVD etc. are the main components of the library networking in the information period, but the traditional means i.e. books, journals, magazines, handbooks etc. cannot be ignored. As technology is growing with a very high pace and it has established new landmarks in various fields e.g. engineering, medicine, architecture, media etc. Libraries and information centres have also accepted the advancement of technology undoubtedly. Cloud computing is also one of the major components of library networking, two more libraries can rented one cloud to share their data. Even a pool of libraries may also establish their own cloud and a lot of funds it may be saved.

Networks may be classified on the following bases

- Based on Utility standard
- Based on User Group
  - Public Network
  - Private Network
  - Co-Operative Network
- Based on Network Architectures and Protocols
  - Switched Network

- Broadcast Network

- Based on Network Topology
  - Star Network
  - Hierarchy Network
  - Distributed Network
  - Ring Network
- Based on Geographical Area
  - LAN (Local Area Network)
  - MAN (Metropolitan Area Network)
  - WAN (Wide Area Network)
- Based on Mode of Transmission

LEVELS OF LIBRARY NETWORKING

Library Networking may be categorized on the basis of region and status

Regional Level: Library Networking may occur at various levels, it may be at local, state, national and international level.

Status Level: Library Networking is considered as per the status of the library. It may be within the public library, academic library, special library and research library.

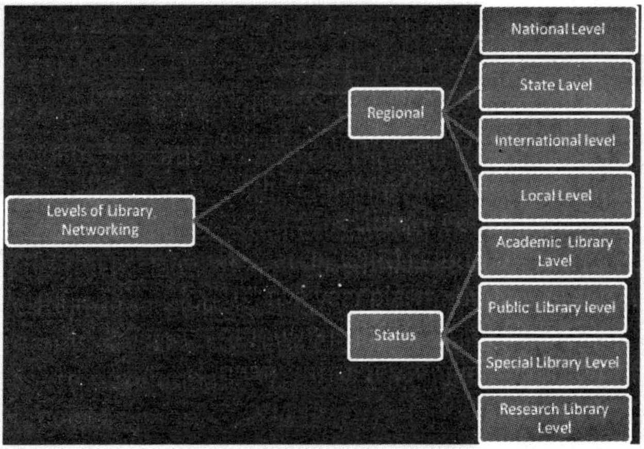

Levels of Library Networking

SCOPE OF LIBRARY NETWORKING

Mainly research and university libraries have a handsome collection of demanding resources. As these libraries remain involve in research, the variety and quality of resources also remain expensive and cerebral. E-resources have drastically overpowered the publishing industry. Due to the electronic nature of the resources it is easy to get the benefit of the networking within the library. As the amalgamators have design the concept of consortia, which is very much successful these days. Some of the most common consortia are as under.

CONSORTIA MOVEMENT IN INDIA

Buoyant by the requirement to contribute the knowledge and innovation an international coalition of Library Consortia (ICOLC) has been formed with Yale University Library as the coordinating center. INDEST and FORSA consortia from India are the members of ICOLC. Some of the prominent Indian programs on library resource sharing are discussed as under:-

INDEST-AICTE Consortium : The Ministry of Human Resource Development (MHRD) has set-up the "Indian National Digital Library in Engineering Sciences and Technology (INDEST) Consortium" on the recommendation made by the Expert Group appointed by the ministry under the chairmanship of Prof. N. Balakrishnan. The Ministry provides funds required for subscription to electronic resources for (58) institutions including IISc, IITs, NITs, IIMs and a few other centrally-funded Government institutions through the consortium headquarters set-up at the IIT Delhi. Besides, (8) Government or Government-aided engineering colleges and technical departments in universities have joined the Consortium with financial support from the AICTE. Moreover, the INDEST-AICTE Consortium, as an open-ended proposition, welcomes other institutions to join it on their own for sharing benefits it offers in terms of highly discounted rates of subscription and better terms of agreement with the publishers. All electronic resources being subscribed are available from the publisher's

Website. The Consortium has an active mailing list and a Web site hosted at the IIT Delhi. The INDEST-AICTE Consortium is the most ambitious initiative taken so far in the country. The benefit of consortia-based subscription to electronic resources is not confined to 38 major technological institutions in the country but is also extended to all AICTE-accredited and UGC-affiliated institutions. (60) engineering colleges and institutions have already joined the consortium on their own. Recently (1242) engineering colleges and institutions joined under self support- new scheme (*http://paniit.iitd.ac.in/indest/*)*UGC-INFONET Consortium:* The UGC-Infonet Digital Library Consortium was formally launched in December, 2003 The Consortium provides current as well as archival access to more than 7000+ core and peer-reviewed journals and 10 bibliographic databases from 26 publishers and aggregators in different disciplines. The programme has been implemented in phased manner. In the first phase that began in 2004, access to e-resources was provided to 50 universities who had Internet connectivity under the UGC-Infonet Connectivity programme of the UGC. In the second phase, 50 more universities were added to the programme in the year 2005. So far 160 Universities out of 181 that come under the purview of UGC, have been provided differential access to subscribed e-resources. These e-resources covers almost all subject disciplines including arts, humanities, social sciences, physical sciences, chemical Sciences, life sciences, computer sciences, mathematics and statistics, etc. The programme is wholly funded by the UGC and executed by the INFLIBNET (Information and Library Network) Centre, Ahmedabad. The benefit of subscription to e-resources would also be extended to the colleges, to begin with the College for Potential with Excellence (CPE) and autonomous colleges. The Consortium has also launched its *"Associate Membership Programme"* wherein private universities and other research organizations are welcomed to join the Consortium for selected e-resources (http://www.inflibnet.ac.in/econ).

FORSA Consortium : The Forum for Resources in Astronomy

and Astrophysics (FORSA) came into existence in the year 1982, for sharing the resources available in astronomy libraries in the country. In 2004, this group has extended its membership to physics and Mathematics libraries in the country who have common interests to carry forward the aim of FORSA and its activities. Currently FORSA has twelve members and it works towards the goals and services which the founder members have started. It shares information among all its member libraries situated at different places in India (http://legacy.icolc.net/FORSA)

DAE Library Consortium : UGC-DAE Consortium for Scientific Research is established for interaction amongst the scientists working in the research centres of the Department of Atomic Energy and the faculty from the universities and other institutions of higher learning, and to enable young students to work on programmes of national importance under the joint guidance of the faculty from universities and the scientists of DAE so as to nurture an organic linkage between the university system and research centres of DAE. Accordingly, the University Grants Commission created an Inter-University Consortium, with its headquarters at Indore for the utilization of the facilities established by the department of Atomic Energy. The inter-university consortium has over the years taken several initiatives to foster the interaction between the university system and the DAE institutions. As per the present MoU, collaboration between the Department of Atomic Energy and University Grants Commission will be expended to cover the disciplines of physical sciences, chemical sciences, life science and engineering sciences (http://www.csr.res.in).

CSIR Library Consortium : Council of Scientific and Industrial Research (CSIR) E-Journals consortium is a network project under 10th five year plan to bridge-up and strengthen the constant decline of journals information base in CSIR labs/institutes. NISCAIR has been entrusted implementation of this projects aims providing access to 4500 world class e-journals to all science and technology personnel of CSIR through pooling and sharing resources. On 10th

June 2002 an agreement was signed with Elsevier Science to access their 1500+ at an odd-on cost of 9% of the subscription for the journal in print form. This initial move met the e-access of 400 unique titles. The project ended its 10th plan period and agreements have been entered into with 19 publishers, facilitating access to 4500+ world class e-journals, patent databases, standard, bibliographic databases etc to all CSIR labs, as against the print base of 20-200 print journals. In the year 2009, autonomous institutions and professional bodies under department of Science technology (DST) are also joined the consortium for accessing information resources. Now consortium has agreement 29 information products including journals, bibliography databases, patents, standards and protocols *(egacy.icolc.net/CSIR).*

IIM Library Consortium : IIM Library consortium is a resource sharing effort among all the Indian Institute of Management in India. The two areas were identified for partnership viz., developing the collection on shared basis and developing the services for exploiting such collection. Six Indian Institutes of Management have formed a consortium and jointly approached the publishers of e-journals and databases in the area of Management, Social Behavioral Science source. They have been giving IP enabled access to e-journals. Well renowned publishers like Elsevier (247 titles), Blackwell (268 titles), Kluwer (33 titles), Wiley (3 titles) provide their resources online to the members of the IIM Consortium. Apart from 25 titles free against print subscription, 2,300 titles as a part of EBSCO databases and 800 titles as part of ABI Inform database have been made available to users of IIM libraries electronically *(Gaudar and Narayana, 2004).*

ISRO Library Consortium : ISRO stands for Indian Space Research Organization which formed a consortium with other space research organizations and institutes to share information on space science. It is having 12 members in its consortium.

HELINET (Rajiv Gandhi University of Health Science) Consortium : HELINET stands for Health Science Library and Information Network conceived by the Rajiv Gandhi University of

Health Sciences and successfully implemented which is first of its kind in the country. University has started the consortium with a vision to improve the quality of education and research in the Health Science institutions of the state through enhanced access to high quality medical information. HELINET goal is to deliver information to users' desk-top, with round-the-clock access. The major benefit of this consortium was expanded access to core international e-journals. Before the launch of the consortium, access to foreign medical journals by each college was limited to around 100. HELINET has made it possible for each college to access and share the contents in more than 600 journals, in effect increasing the access provision by 6-times (http://www.rguhs.ac.in).

ICMR Library Consortium : ICMR stands for Indian Council of Medical Research which shares information in health and medical science. As part of modernization the Indian Council Of Medical research has under taken many new initiatives like subscribing to JCC@ICMR and Full Text Electronic Databases i.e. ProQuest. To keep pace with the rapidly changing information technology scenario, the Council entered into the e-joumal arena through developing an e-journal consortium. The ICMR has identified five core bio-medical journals and subscribes for e-version in consortia mode to all ICMR institutes. These include Lancet, Science, BMJ, NEJM, and Nature. This e-journal consortium will be beneficial for cross sharing of information among the ICMR Institutes (www.icmr.nic.in/library_bull)

ERMED Consortium : Electronic Resources in Medicine (ERMED) Consortium is an initiative taken by Director General of Heath Services (DGHS) to develop nationwide electronic information resources in the field of medicine for delivering effective health care for all. The authorities decided to provide financial support required for the purchase of electronic journals under the ERMED consortium project for Government medical colleges and institutions. For private Medical colleges/institutions the payment per site for e-resources purchased by the consortium will be charged. The Consortium is being coordinated through its headquarter set up at the National Medical Library (NML). NML Started ERMED e-journal consortium in 2008 with 40 members including 28 ICMR+10 DGHS + AIIMS + NTR Health University, Vijayawada, Andhra Pradesh. It provided electronic journals from 5 publishers, which contained 1515 medical journals. The ERMED invested Rs. 2.6 Crore for electronic journals in 2008. The ERMED resources can be searched and browsed through a versatile search platform. In 2009 the ERMED members increased from 40 to 72 Government Medical Colleges/Institutes across the country. NML paid Rs. 7.55 crore for Government Medical Colleges/Institutes. The letter for self payment has been sent to some Private Medical Colleges/Institutes. ERMED is providing over 1600 medical journals in 2009 from 9 leading medical journal publishers (*www.nmlermed.in*).

LIBRARY NETWORKS IN INDIA

A number of library networks have been established in India by the efforts made by NISSAT. Calcutta Library Network (CALIBNET), Developing Library Network (DELNET), Madras Library Network (MALIBNET), Mysore Library Network (MYLIBNET), Hyderabad Library Network (HYLIBNET), Ahmedabad Library Network (ADNET), Pune Library Network (PUNENET), Bombay Library Network (BONET) are the major library networks working in India, which are disused here.

DELNET : DELNET was started at the India International Centre Library in January 1988 and was registered as a society in 1992. It was initially supported by the National Information System for Science and Technology (NISSAT), Department of Scientific and Industrial Research, Government of India. It was subsequently supported by the National Informatics Centre, Department of Information Technology, Ministry of Communications and Information Technology, Government of India and the Ministry of Culture, Government of India. DELNET has been established with the prime objective of promoting resource sharing among the libraries through the development of a network of libraries. It aims to collect, store, and disseminate information besides offering computerised services to users, to coordinate efforts for suitable collection development and also to reduce unnecessary duplication wherever possible. Presently 4589 libraries have the membership of DELNET, out of which 4566 are in Indian and rest 23 are in abroad. DELNET has been actively engaged with the compilation of various Union Catalogues of the resources available in member-libraries. It has already created the Union Catalogue of Books, Union List of Current Periodicals, Union Catalogue of Periodicals, CD-ROM Database, Database of Indian Specialists, Database of Periodical Articles, Union List of Video Recordings, Urdu Manuscripts' Database, Database of Theses and Dissertations, sample databases of language publications using GIST technology and several other databases. The data is being updated in these databases and is growing rapidly. All the DELNET databases have been resident on DELSIS, an in-house software developed on BASIS Plus, an RDBMS, the product of Information Dimensions Inc. of USA which has been provided to DELNET courtesy National Informatics Centre, New Delhi (http://delnet.nic.in).

CALIBNET : The Calcutta Library Network (CALIBNET) was inaugurated on 21 December 1993. CALIBNET, a Government of India Project, has been launched by the National Information Systems for Science and Technology (*NISSAT*), Department of Scientific & Industrial Research (*DSIR*); and managed by the *CALIBNET Society* established under the West Bengal Government's Societies Registration Act 1961. The primary objective of the Project is building access to library and information resources available in the eastern region, through the implementation of a series of Databases, *Bibliographic, Factuals* and Intellectual Assets of West Bengal. This apart, CALIBNET provides its Participating Members and the user community at large with Active links in this Web-Page to access *Indian Library and Network Resources, Overseas Library Resources On India,*

Worldwide Library Catalogues, National Libraries of the World, Newspapers and Journals, Electronic Reference Tools, Factual Information Sources, Document Supply Services, and Varied Programs for *On-Demand Information Services, Consultative Service for Library Automation, Manpower Development Opportunities*, and *Research & Development in IT Applications* (*http://www.calibnet.org*).*MALIBNET:* MALIBNET is a registered society of Tamil Nadu Government (Reg. No.45/1993). It was formed in 1993. Initially six major academic institutions were directly linked to the MALIBNET host system. Nearly 83 libraries are contributing actively to the MALIBNET. 37 major Education/ Research institutions have joined as member institution of MALIBNET. Contents Search Service of MALIBNET allows a search on the contents database existing at MALIBNET. It contains nearly 7747 journals. This database is search able through journal title, year, volume and issue. Users can start availing MALIBNET services after they become registered users of the MALIBNET. After registration, each user is given a unique Login ID and password. MALIBNET provides full text of articles from requested journals. To avail this service, users expected to provide the details of journals, year, volume and issue along with page numbers. The charges for this service are Rs.3 per page for members and Rs.5 per page for Non members (http://www.malibnetonline.com).

MYLIBNET : Mysore Library Network (MYLIBNET) was established at Mysore city in the year 1995 and the Central Food Technological Research Institute (CFTRI), Mysore, being an active member of Mysore City Library Consortium (MCLC), is hosting this network in its premises. CFTRI is one of the premier Sectoral Centres of NISSAT in the area of food science and technology. With this added advantage, MYLIBNET is working closely with MCLC to promote information services in Mysore city. MYLIBNET is also having the same objectives like other library networks in India but with a difference. One of the main objectives of this network is to prepare a union catalogue of periodicals subscribed by the member libraries. Accordingly, most of the library networks have been compiling the catalogue either in hard copy or in electronic form. Due to information technology advancement, this catalogue is now made available on the Internet. MYLIBNET has also compiled this catalogue in the year 1996 in the machine-readable form and developed a software package (floppy disk version) for searching this catalogue either by institution name, journal title or by keywords. This software was released to its members in July 1996 (http://www.dsir.gov.in).

BALNET : Bangalore Library Network (BALNET) is sponsored by JRD Tata Memorial Library. It was established in 1995. There are about 100 Libraries are member of it.

BONET : The Bombay Library Network (BONET) was established at the National Centre for Software Technology (NCST), Bombay, on 6 November 1992, which was sponsored by NISSAT. The major concern of BONET is to fabricate a low cost library information structure and promote cooperation among libraries in Bombay. BONET offered services to its member libraries are On-line catalogue, online document delivery, Information retrieval system, Inter-library loan, dissemination of information etc.

PUNENET : Pune Library Network (PUNENET) is dedicated to the libraries of Pune only. PUNENET provides a number of services to its member libraries i.e. Catalogue of British library's collection in India, Catalogues the books and journals of member libraries, databases of health sciences and biotechnology.

ADINET : ADINET is a Network of Libraries and Information Centers in Gujarat. It was established in 1994 with an initial grant for a few years from National Information System for Science and Technology (NISSAT), Department of Science and Industrial Research, Government of India, New Delhi. It caters to all types of Libraries: school, college, universities, institutional libraries and even public libraries. Hence, access is provided to hundreds of libraries, librarians and organizations through the ADINET Network. The main vision of ADINET is to join Libraries, to enable them to achieve what cannot be done by one library alone. This will help them to harness their limited resources and collective strengths so that Libraries can continue to play their historic role as society's portal to information. ADINET therefore promotes sharing of resources and disseminates valuable information by networking libraries (http://www.alibnet.org).

INFLIBNET : Information and Library Network (INFLIBNET) Centre is an autonomous Inter-University Centre of the *University Grants Commission (UGC)* of India. It is a major National Programme initiated by the UGC in 1991 with its Head Quarters at Gujarat University Campus, Ahmedabad. Initially started as a project under the *IUCAA*, it became an independent Inter-University Centre in 1996. INFLIBNET is involved in modernizing university libraries in India and connecting them as well as information centres in the country through a nation-wide high speed data network using the state-of-art technologies for the optimum utilization of information. INFLIBNET is set out to be a major player in promoting scholarly communication among academicians and researchers in India. The National Centre of INFLIBNET is located in Gujarat University campus at Ahmedabad. INFLIBNET aims to computerizing and networking of university/ college libraries. The selected organizations are provided funds for acquiring computer systems, retro conversion and networking. Application software for data entry and additional library utilities, library standards and formats, etc., are provided by INFLIBNET to the participating libraries. Resource development is a vital part of the programme. Training courses for core library staff engaged in computerized library operations have been conducted since 1992-93(www.inflibnet.ac.in).

CONCLUSION

India has a very rich background of resource sharing and networking among various levels of libraries. With the help of numbers of networks and resource sharing consortia, libraries are benefiting and saving a lot of capital. Resource sharing and networking is welcomed by each kind of library whether it is university or special. Networking is always better for the libraries, as member libraries share the seamless collection of valuable resources at a nominal cost. In an academic library text books have a great importance, with the help of inter library loan, libraries can share whole collection of member libraries. Because each and every document is not available in digital form and importance of print media specially books have a great relevance among academic system, where a variety of students encounter. Alone DELNET is fulfilling the inter library loan demands of 4589 libraries at national and international level. No doubt networking is demand of time and a wonderful concept, but it applies on the libraries having similar interests. The major concern of university and special libraries is to build up collection related to research and development whereas college libraries focus on text books, because college students focus on the material related to their exams. Therefore the interests of the member libraries may not be ignored and there should be the provision for future challenges also.

REFERENCES

- Goudar, I.R.N., and Narayana, Poornima. (2004). Emerging Pricing Models for E-Journals Consortia and Indian Initiatives. In TERI (Ed.) *ICDL* (pp.333-341).New Delhi: TERI
- *http://www.dsir.gov.in* (Access on 12 Jan 2013)
- www.icmr.nic.in/library_bull (Access on 12 Jan 2013)
- http://paniit.iitd.ac.in/indest/ (Access on 12 Jan 2013)
- *http://www.alibnet.org* (Access on 21 Jan 2013)
- *http://www.calibnet.org* (Access on 21 Jan 2013)
- *http://www.csr.res.in* (Access on 21 Jan 2013).
- egacy.icolc.net/CSIR (Access on 21 Jan 2013)
- *http://delnet.nic.in* (Access on 24 Jan 2013)
- *http://www.inflibnet.ac.in/* (Access on 27 Jan 2013)
- *http://legacy.icolc.net/FORSA* (Access on 06 Feb 2013)
- *http://www.malibnetonline.com* (Access on 06 Feb 2013)
- http://www.rguhs.ac.in (Access on 06 Feb 2013)
- *www.nmlermed.in* (Access on 24 Feb 2013)

2

Development of Library Networking and Consortia at International Level

Sandhya Aggarwal

INTRODUCTION

Modern higher education is passing through the phase of information/knowledge revolution. Due to uncontrolled growth of information and financial constraints none of the library or information center can claim to be self-sufficient in terms of finance and collection. In satisfying ever growing information needs of academic community, the concept of library consortia and library networking to aid information resource sharing and support activities in libraries has become a real necessity in anywhere in the world. This phenomenon of sharing of resources was started with Inter Library Loan (ILL), Document Delivery system (DDS), Library Networking (via, LAN, WAN), etc. At present the more accepted system of resource sharing is Library consortia. Main objective of consortia is reducing cost of any type of information to develop a network information environment (via campus systems, campus network and the internet) and can be read anywhere in the world, at any time, by any number of people as long as the readers have an internet connection.

The concept of consortia is based on the basic principle of cooperation as it is a "cooperative arrangement among group or institutions and buying e-information together". Library consortia means to co-operation and collaboration between and among libraries for the purpose of sharing information resources. Libraries in developing countries have been working on consortia at national, regional and international level.

SERVICES THROUGH LIBRARY CONSORTIUM AND NETWORKS

The consortium may be responsible for coordinating, organizing and providing information and literature support at the national and international level. To create awareness among the network members they are organizing workshops and conducting meetings of the networks members on a regular basis. The main activities and functions are as follows:

Acquisition of materials

- Joint purchasing of materials
- Assignment of specialization in material acquisition
- Coordinated subscription
- Exchange of duplicate holdings

Technical services

- Co-operative cataloguing
- Abstracting and indexing services
- Interlibrary loan
- Reciprocal borrowing privileges

- Reference and/or referral services

Publication program/repackaging information

- Union catalogue/list of periodicals
- Mutual notification of purchase through lists of new arrivals or acquisition list
- Bibliography development
- Newsletters
- Joint directories of personnel, projects, consultants, resource persons, etc.
- Manuals

Coordination services

- Clearing house functions
- Retrieval and storage function
- Referral center

Research, training and other special services

- User interest surveys
- Joint research projects
- In-service personnel training
- Workshops and meetings
- Translation services

Databases

- Online/offline databases
- CDROM databases

Budget

- Optimum utilization of funds.
- Facilities to build up digital libraries

Consideration needed to form Consortia

The following issues need to consider before building the consortia:

- Technology infrastructure

- Resources identification
- Budget and funding
- Pricing issues
- Subscription payment issues
- Access related issues
- Licensing and copyright issues
- Archival issues
- Usages and usability issues
- Coordination among partners
- Availability of efficient staff
- Overcoming political objections
- The egos of individuals and institutions
- Adequate professional training on ICT for the LIS professionals
- Sustainability issues

Major Problems in Library Consortium and Networks

Consortia have its inherent benefits but those benefits can be maximized, while minimizing the negative aspects. (Helmer, 1999) express that the benefits of the consortia can threaten by several issues, results the failure of consortia. Sometime it has been found that the consortia initiatives could not materialized, reasons may be the following:

(a) Lack of awareness and understanding : Librarians do not fully comprehend the concept of consortia based subscription to electronic resources and are not very keen to go whole-heartedly for formation of consortia of libraries. Sometimes they do not have good understanding about consortia benefits.

(b) Speed of decision making : Notion that, belonging to consortium the speed of decision making of individual libraries can slow down. Though it depends how centralized or decentralized the consortium is.

(c) Budget and funding : These are always thorny issues. Belonging to a consortium means that part of library budget will be transferred and the issue of loss of control raises again. Lack of initial funds of university libraries may be a barrier to starting library consortium.

(d) Lack of decision making and control : There is a fear that if a library joins a consortium, local decision making, autonomy, and control will be adversely affected.

(e) Technological compatibility and security : The compatibility of the members computing system is critical if a consortium is to achieve the maximum benefit from technology. Different library uses different library software and lbrary tools, so it becomes difficult for the librarian to acquaint with different systems. Security is also another technical issue.

(f) Fear from local identity : Most of the libraries don't want to feel like they are losing their individual identity. They think, if they enter into a consortium they may loss their local identity.

(g) Type of agreements : Agreements between member libraries can have major impacts on the consortium's effectiveness. It has been found that some libraries did not join in the consortia simply because of the agreement that was not of their choosing.

(h) Egos and attitudes : Egos and attitudes of individuals or organizations can have a big impact on the success or failure of a consortium. Each person always makes different strategy and operating models.

(i) Consortial as a legal entity : Consortia of libraries need to have a legal entity with permission and authority to deal with institutions like banks and other institution for collecting subscription amount on behalf of the participating libraries.

(j) Lack of complete automation : A consortia without sharing the resources of the participating libraries is limited to online subscriptions made available from gateway portal. Many libraries are allowed to jump into the band wagon of consortia without considering its automation status. With the availability of some internet connectivity this will allows such libraries to access the resources of other member libraries but their resource remain inaccessible till complete automation is done.

(k) Absence of any culture of interlibrary lending : Generally, no libraries started interlibrary lending activities among them. Traditionally, interlibrary loan facilities or any form of co-operation is functional in the library.

(l) Unavailability of web environment : Unavailability of web environment among the libraries is one of the major problems for accessing in the library consortium. Internet connectivity is still in primitive stages which make online consortia almost unfeasible.

(m) Lack of leadership : Excellent library leadership will begin with the notion of enabling everyone who works in the library to grow in knowledge, ability, and commitment as the primary task. Libraries have lack of creative leader and skilled management body for removing all the barriers for introducing libraries.

(n) Untrained staff : Require training of staffs in handling electronic documents etc.

(o) Decreasing Budget : A consortium requires high initials investments in licensees and information and communication technology. Internet Access ID necessary

(p) Lack of awareness of users : Users are not accepting e-journals as per with the printed Journals.

(q) Lack of appropriate support : from their parent organizations.

INTERNATIONAL EFFORTS FOR LIBRARY CONSORTIA

The development of library consortia is the outcome of the desire for resource sharing and consortia seem to be getting bigger. Library consortia, does not have any remarkable history but the consortia arrangements started with the concept of resource sharing since long back. In 19990's new types of library consortia began to flourish that exploited the advances in information technology. The global development of OCLC in USA is a prime example. Over time the growth of newer consortium like; Colorado's CARL, Georgia's GALILEO, Illinois's IDAL, Maryland's SAILOR, Missouri's MIRACAL, New Zealand's CONZUL, CAUL, Metro Net, North America's CRL, North Carolina's embryonic NCLive, Ohio's Ohio Link, Pennsylvania's PALCI, Portland's PORTALS, Texas's TexShare, Virginia's VIVA, Washington's WRLC, CIC in South Asia , CURL in UK, CALIM in Manchester, Concord in Britain, Metro web in New York etc came into existence in the international scenario (Wikipedia, 2007). In India, major initiatives are regarding consortium is J-GATE form Informatics India, IITS-BARC-TIFR Cooperation, TIFR Libraries Consortium, ISI Library consortia, SNDT consortia of LISA, STI Network, FORSA consortia, INDSET and INFLIBNET consortium under UGC InfoNet. Due to escalating cost of documents, decreasing budgets, inadequate storage area and competent staff, LIS professionals of the world are coming together to form consortia. There are several International efforts for library consortia are:

- The International Association of Aquatic and Marine Science Libraries and Information Centers (IAMSLIC), comprised of 325 members from 86 countries, has a long history of resource sharing based on personal connections among its members.
- Consortium of University Research Libraries (CURL) [http://www.curl.ac.uk]
- Consortium of Academic Libraries in Manchester (CALIM) [http://www.rylibweb.man.ac.uk/calim]
- Colorado Library Information Network, [http://www.aclin.org/]
- Washington Research Library Consortium (WRLC), [http://www.wrlc.org]
- BIBSYS (Shared University, Research and National Library of Norway) [http://www.bibsys.no/english.html]

- Queensland University Libraries Office of Cooperation (QUOLOC) [http://www.quloc.org.au]
- China Academic Library & Information System (CALIS), China, [http://www.calis.edu.cn/calisnew/]
- Takatsu University Library Consortium (YULC), Japan
- [http://www.lib.reitaku-u.ac.jp/limedio/kangai/tulc.html]
- Tokyo Western Regional Academic Library Consortium, Japan, [http://www.tnishi.gr.jp]
- Yamatesen Ensen Private University Libraries Consortium, Japan [http://www.agulin.aoyama.e/info_3.html]
- Korea Resource Sharing Alliance (KORSA), Korea, [http://www.korsa.or.kr/]
- CONsortium on Core Eletronic Resources in Taiwan (CONCERT), [http://www.stie.gov.tw/English/e_CONCERT.htm]
- Ministry of University Affairs (MUA). ThaiLIS, [http://www.uni.net.th/]
- **National Agricultural Information System (NAIS) :** The Agricultural Information Centre(AIC) was taken an initiative to develop a network of agricultural institution.
- **Social Science Research Council (SSRC) :** Social Science Research Council, Dhaka was taken an initiative to develop a social science information network in Bangladesh.
- **Health Literature, Library, and Information Service (HeLLIS) Network :** The HeLLIS network was developed by SEARO (WHO), New Delhi, India and National Health Library and Documentation Centre (NHLDOC), Dhaka. All the health libraries of Bangladesh were brought under this network.
- **Development Information Network on South Asia (DEVINSA) :** The DEVINSA network was organized by CSCD (Committee on Studies for Cooperation for Development in South Asia) through the Marga Institute, Colombo, Sri Lanka. All SAARC countries, except Bhutan, were the

participants of this network. Information Network on Rural Development (INRD): Centre on Integrated Rural Development for Asia and the Pacific (CIRDAP), Dhaka was taken an initiative to develop a regional network on rural development.

- **Women Information Network (WIN) :** Centre on Integrated Rural Development for Asia and the Pacific (CIRDAP), Dhaka was taken another initiative to develop a network on women information.
- **Bangladesh Development Support Information and Communication (BDSIC) Network :** Bangladesh Academy for Rural Development (BARD), Comilla was taken an initiative to launch a network of rural development institutions in Bangladesh
- **National Science and Technology Information Policy (NASTIP) :** Under this policy, a four-tier science and technology information networking system has been recommended.
- The Association of Management Development Institutes in South Asia (AMDISA)
- **Library Network :** The Association of Management Development Institutes in South Asia was launched a library network on management development. The Headquarter of this network was located at the Administrative Staff College of India, Hyderabad. One institute in each
- SAARC country was selected as a focal point. The Institute of Business Administration Library,
- Dhaka University was selected as the National focal point for this network.
- **University Libraries :** Dhaka University Library took an initiative several years' back to develop a network of the university libraries, initially by preparing a union catalogue of the holdings of the university libraries.

- The University Grants Commission of Bangladesh (UGC), in collaboration with the Asia Foundation, took an initiative to compile a union catalogue of the collections of different universities of Bangladesh and to establish an information network within the universities.
- **Bangladesh National Scientific and Library Information Network (BANSLINK) :** Bangladesh National Scientific and Technical Documentation Centre (BANSDOC) was taken an initiative to build up a Network, known as BANSLINK, to develop a resource-sharing network having dial up connectivity with 15 libraries and information centres of the country.
- **Sustainable Development Network Program (SDNP) :** SDNP is a UNDP funded program, which started a union catalog services in 2002 in their virtual library program. The SDNP virtual library prepared this union catalog of 13 libraries, all of which are using CDS/ISIS software for bibliographic record keeping. The SDNP virtual library union catalog is a webbased Online Public Access Catalog.
- **Population Information Network (POPIN) :** The National Institute of Population Research and Training (NIPORT) has taken an initiative to establish an information networking system in the field of health, population, family planning and maternal and child health in collaboration and cooperation with the government and non-government organizations, autonomous bodies, voluntary organizations, and international organizations.
- National Health Library and Documentation Centre (NHLDOC), (Ministry of Health, Government of Bangladesh) and International Centre for Diarrhoeal Disease Research, Bangladesh (ICDDR,B) signed in 1976 an agreement to facilitate library cooperation through an interlibrary loan system and agreed to cooperate with each other to avoid duplication of journal subscriptions. Subsequently, some

other library named, BIDS (1977), BIRDEM (1978), USAID, Dhaka (1992), Aga Khan Community Health Program, Dhaka (1992), and the Bangladesh Rural Advancement Committee (1995) joined this programme by signing interlibrary loan agreements. The system has been working well.

- **United Nations Library Network in Bangladesh (UN L-Net BD) :** In March 2002 United Nations Information Centre (UNIC) Library has taken an initiative to establish the UN Library Network in Bangladesh (UN L-Net BD). Initially the Network consisted of twenty major libraries of different government, NGOs, including the UN agencies in Bangladesh. At present there are 26 members in this network. It was agreed that UNIC library would act as a focal point and secretariat of the network.
- China Academic Library & Information System (CALIS) is a national academic library consortium established in May 1998. CALIS' Union Cataloging System is the largest and first multi-language cooperative online cataloging system in China.
- China Academic Social Sciences and Humanities Library (CASHL, 2008) is to cooperatively acquire, preserve and share foreign and Chinese periodical resources in the humanities and social sciences among member libraries, and to provide a unified online portal for users to retrieve and utilize these resources.
- The National Library of China (*NLC*, 2008), the largest library in China and the fifth largest in world, is the general repository for all national publications. 1 Consortium of National Information Resource Sharing. 2 National Cultural Resources Project (NCRP, 2008)
- Medical Library Association of Chinese Universities and College established in 1985, the primary aim of the Association is to build a national medical information sharing network and coordinate the acquisitions of foreign

biomedical journals among 151 members.

- National Science and Technology Library (NSTL, 2008) as a national special library consortium, NSTL was established in 2000 and funded by the Central Government. Members comprise eight major national science and technology research institutions, covering the fields of science and technology, engineering, agriculture, and medicine. It aims to collect, organize, and preserve cooperatively and comprehensively science and technology information resources, and extend access to these resources through a unified portal.

INDIAN INITIATIVES FOR LIBRARY CONSORTIA

In India at present there are many consortia being run successfully by different organizations. Some of them are as :

- CSIR e-Journal Consortia, [http://www.niscair.res.in/ActivitiesandServices/ MajorProjects/majproj.htm#ejournal consortia]
- INDEST (Indian National Digital Library in Science and Technology) Consortia [http://paniit.iitd.ac.in/indest/]
- FORSA (Forum for Resource Sharing in Astronomy) [http://www.iiap.res.in/library/forsa.html]
- UGC-INFONET [http://www.inflibnet.ac.in]
- IIM Library Consortia, [http://www.iimb.ernet.in/]
- ICICI Knowledge Parк, [http://www.iciciknowlwdgepark.com]
- DAE Library Consortium, [http://www.tifr.res.in/~libws/]
- ICMR Library Consortia, [http://www.jccc-icmr.informindia.co.in/about/about.asp]
- HELINET (Rajiv Gandhi University of Health Sciences, Karnataka) [http://www.rguhs.ac.in/hn/newhell.htm]

when we talk about resource sharing we simply mean collective use of information of all types by various end users from a control coordinating unit or from within a network component at a reduced cost with easy accessibility. In the developed countries, no library services can be thought without sharing of resources and developing country cannot effort to waste its resources. To avoid this, an effective resource sharing and networking system is necessary. In the past, resource sharing was limited to the interlibrary loan system. In the modern age, with the development of science and technology and innovations of techniques and devices, resource sharing has become easier and fruitful due to the availability of databases, information network, and online sharing facilities.

REFERENCES

- Debal, CKar, Bhattacharya, Parha and Deb, Subrata, "Library networking in India for resource sharing: present status and prospects" Available at: *http://www.worlib.org/vol09no1/kar_v091.shtml*
- Dong, Elaine Xiaofen,2009, *"Library consortia in China"*, Libres, issue 1, vol 19, Available at: *http://libres.curtin.edu.au/*
- Jharotia, Anil Kumar and Shukla, Deepak, Development of consortia and library networking in India Available at: *http://librarydotcom.webs.com/apps/blog/entries/show/5844050-library-networking-consortia*
- Karn, Sanjay Kumar and Das, Basant Kumar, "Information library network (INFLIBNET): a boon for higher education in India"
- Sarandha Singh, "Library networking in India" Available at: *http://ncsi.iisc.ernet.in/pipemail/lis-forum/2005-June/002281.html*
- Yernagula, Ramesh and Kelkar, P.K., "Library consortia: benefits and models of e-journals consortia"

3

Library Networking in India

Gurcharan Dass

ABSTRACT

The paper gives an overview of the development of library network in India. It also mentions the efforts made by the planning Commission & Government of India to promote resource sharing amongst libraries in the country. The present scenario of library networking is also briefly presented. A large number of library resource sharing networks like the Metropolitan Area Networks such as DELNET in Delhi, MALIBNET in Madras, BONET in Bombay, CALIBNET in Calcutta, ADNET in Ahmedabad and countrywide ones like INFLIBNET (Universities and Research Institutions), ERNET (Educational and Research Institutions), DESINET (Defence Laboratories) and sectoral ones like BTISNET (Biotechnology Networks) etc. are under various stages of conceptualization, design, development and implementation.

Keywords: Library Network; Information Support System; Information and Communication Technology.

INTRODUCTION

The world has been witnessing a knowledge and information explosion during the past few decades. Over 10 million journal articles are published every year besides news items, increases among the number of users and their different needs and the application of electronic media are forcing libraries to construct and participate in networks. Magnetic tapes, floppy disks and CD-ROMs provide enough data storage capacity. Retrieval through telecommunications networks and access to international databases are available for searching for information on various subjects. With the advent of networks, remote transmission of texts and graphics, video clips and animated clips are also possible.

A library network is broadly described as a group of libraries coming together with some agreement of understanding to help each other with a view to satisfying the information needs of their clientele. According to Martin: "A network is a group of individuals or organizations that are interconnected. The linking must include a communication mechanism and many networks exist for the express purpose of facilitating certain types of communication among their members. In the library world, institutions from network primarily achieve better sharing of resources – resources consisting of bibliographic information and of collection – and better services to patrons. UNISIST II working document defines Information Network as "A set of inter-related information systems associated with communication facilities, which are cooperating through more or less formal agreements in order to implement information handling operations to offer better services to the users." The National Commission on Libraries and Information Science (NCLIS) in its National Programme Document (1975) defines a network as: "Two or more libraries and/or other organizations engaged in a common pattern of information exchange, through communications, for some functional purpose.

OBJECTIVES

- To promote and support adoption of standards in library operations.
- To create databases for projects, specialists and institutions to provide online information services.
- To improve the efficiency of housekeeping operations.
- To coordinate with other regional, national & international network for exchange of information and documents.
- To generate new services and to improve upon the efficiency of existing ones.

NETWORK DEVELOPMENT IN INDIA

Some factors that are responsible for the development of library and information networks in India are:

- The Planning Commission, Government of India, has been taking considerable interest in library resource sharing and library networks. Its efforts in these areas have increased since the Seventh Five Year Plan covering 1985-90. The Commission appointed a working group on modernization of Library Services and Informatics in November, 1983. In July 1984, the working group submitted its report. It recommended among others, interlinking of library systems through library networks. This report was to be considered for the Seventh Plan.
- The Commission appointed another Working Group which submitted its report in May, 1989. It again recommended among others interlinking of library systems in the country.
- The Planning Commission appointed in Feb, 1995, a Core Task Group to prepare an approach paper for enhancing inputs of Science and Technology for library resource sharing.
- The Commission again constituted a working group on Libraries and Informatics under the Department of Culture,

Ministry of Human Resource Development, Govt. of India, which report was to be considered for the Ninth Plan for the period 1997-2002. The report of the Working Group of the Commission includes many important recommendations for the networking and modernization of libraries in the country.

- All these initiatives by NISSAT, UGC, Planning Commission and other departments of Govt. of India have led to increased efforts to the establishment of library networks and library automation in the country.

TYPES OF NETWORKS

Presently, there are three types of computer networks:

Local Area Network (LAN) : A LAN is a number of related computers and electronic devices that share information over a transmission media. A typical use of LAN is to tie together personal computers in an office so that they can all use a single printer and a file server. The LAN can be within a building or a campus wide network.

Metropolitan Area Network (MAN) : Attempts are being made to develop this type of network in metropolitan areas such Delhi, Calcutta, Bangalore, Madras, etc.

Wide Area Network (WAN) : A large-scale network, involving offices in different cities and countries is referred to as WAN, which is specially designed to interconnect data transmission devices over wide geographical areas.

LIBRARY & INFORMATION NETWORKS IN INDIA

Resource sharing in a networked system has been functioning since 1930 in developed countries; while India has concentrated on interlibrary loan. Network activities in India started with the establishment of National Information system for Science & Technology (NISSAT) in 1979. Some of the important and significant networks that exist in India are given below:

General Networks

NICNET: National Informatics Centre (NIC) was established in 1977, and has since emerged as a "prime builder" of e-Government / e-Governance applications up to the grassroots level as well as a promoter of digital opportunities for sustainable development. NIC, through its ICT Network, "NICNET", has institutional linkages with all the Ministries /Departments of the Central Government, 35 State Governments/ Union Territories, and about 625 District administrations of India. NIC has been instrumental in steering e-Government/e-Governance applications in government ministries/departments at the Centre, States, Districts and Blocks, facilitating improvement in government services, wider transparency, promoting decentralized planning and management, resulting in better efficiency and accountability to the people of India.

INDONET: INDONET data Network was established in 1986 and sponsor by CMC Ltd. INDONET presently offers the following information services:

- Database services such as DIALOG
- COMPUSERVE
- IP; SHARP

I-NET(VIKRAM): I-NET was established in 1991 and sponsor by Dept. of Telecommunications, Govt. of India. These are give provide Information exchange through e-mail / FTP; Bibliographic databases services.

Library Networks (Metropolitan)

CALIBNET: CALIBNET, a Government of India Project, has been launched by the National Information Systems for Science and Technology (NISSAT) on 21 December 1993, Department of Scientific & Industrial Research (DSIR); and managed by the CALIBNET Society established under the West Bengal Government's Societies Registration Act 1961.

CALIBNET has adopted a two way system for networking:

1. The networking route with a library automation and networking through its own application software "Maitrayee" and
2. The e-mail route connecting member libraries with on-line access to various databases within network and Internet access.

CALIBNET established a high-tech resource base and provides the following services:

- Online/CDROM based global information search and retrieval services
- Full-text document delivery
- Database services

DELNET : DELNET was started at the India International Centre Library in January 1988 and registered as a society in 1992. It was initially supported by the National Information System for Science and Technology (NISSAT), Department of Scientific and Industrial Reseach, Government of India. It was subsequently supported by the National Informatics Centre, Department of Information Technology, Ministry of Communications and Information Technology, Government of India and the Ministry of Culture, Government of India. DELNET has been established with the prime objective of promoting resource sharing among the libraries through the development of a network of libraries. It aims to collect, store, and disseminate information besides offering computerised services to users, to coordinate efforts for suitable collection development and also to reduce unnecessary duplication wherever possible. DELNET provides access to the central union catalogue for books and monographs, efficient electronic mailing facilities to access databases of member libraries. It also proposes to develop a network for accessing CD–ROM databases available at member libraries in the near future. It also provides CAS and SDI services, consultancy in library computerization, training and assistance to libraries on standardization, local automation, retrospective conversion etc.

DELNET is likely to emerge as a co–operative network incorporating all disciplines of science, technology, social sciences and humanities. DELNET at present has 4288 libraries as its members, of which 241 libraries are in Delhi, 4024 outside Delhi in 32 States and Union Territories and 23 in overseas countries.

ADINET: Ahmedabad Library Network (ADINET) was formally inaugurated in February 1995 when a memorandum of understanding was signed between NISSAT and ADINET at Ahmedabad. ADINET has ten institutional members, five associate institutional members and two professional members. A centralized database has been created at ADINET which contains institute master, journal master and book databases. It also organized six work and training programmes. ADINET provided e-mail connectivity to 30 libraries of Ahmedabad.*MALIBNET:* The need for interconnecting libraries and information centres in Madras was visualized in the Indian National Scientific Documentation Centre (INSDOC) in 1991. Initially six major academic institutions were directly linked to the MALIBNET host system. Two important databases have been created utilizing the resources available in Madras libraries. One is a Directory Database of Current Serials in Madras covering 30 libraries, and the other is a Contents Database covering articles published in 300 journals available in Madras libraries. Both these databases are continuously updated and also expanded. They are available for online- access to any user and the information is also supplied in diskettes and hard copy. Photocopies of articles from member libraries can be supplied within two days.

Madras has about 60 important libraries besides information centres like INSDOC. About 15 of these libraries have a holding of well over 100,000 items. These libraries act as good resource centres on the network. As of December 1993, all the 60 libraries together invest about Rupees 8,000,000 on acquiring journals and books every year. It is estimated that 40% of the information acquired is redundant. With the libraries networked and resource sharing implemented, each user on the network can get access to a vast amount of literature, and redundancy can be brought down significantly. A novel and unique feature of MALIBNET is that the members will be permitted to offer their own innovative information services on the network. A membership in MALIBNET is open to universities, colleges, R&D institutions, industries and individuals.

MALIBNET presently offers the following information services:

- Current serials acquired in about 60 libraries
- Full journal holdings of about 60 libraries
- Contents information of about 500 important journals
- Electronic mail including internet connectivity
- Door delivery system for document photocopies
- It also offers access to about 1000 international databases.

BONET: The Bombay Library Network (BONET) was setup at the National Centre for Software Technology (NCST), Bombay, on 6 November 1992. The Network is sponsored by NISSAT. The aim of BONET is to build a low cost library information system which can possibly be used as a model for future expansion of this service even outside Bombay.

BONET also benefits significantly from the experience gained, and facilities created, by the Education and Research Networking (ERNET) project of the Department of Electronics, Govt. of India, assisted by the United Nations Development Programme (UNDP). BONET is aimed at promoting cooperation between libraries in Bombay. The focus is on inter-library activities, rather than on computerizing individual libraries, which will no doubt computerize their own operations and are likely to share their experiences with each other. BONET offers training related to library computerization and networking, and speed up computerization of Bombay libraries. BONET membership provides for access to its centralized catalogues and for E-mail among BONET members. However, access to library related services outside Bombay in India and abroad would require use of ERNET.

The services offered through BONET include the following:

- Consultation on standards
- Organized training for selected staff of participating libraries
- On-line catalogue of periodicals for the region
- On-line catalogue of books for the region
- On-line catalogue of preprints/reprints
- Inter-library lending of books and periodicals
- Inter-library request for photocopying
- Computer network support for book ordering
- Information retrieval services
- On-line document delivery of items (such as technical reports) made available by participating libraries in machine readable form
- On-line access to foreign databases, subject to the user's willingness to pay the costs incurred
- E-mail interface for inter–library queries
- E-mail facilities to order reprints from abroad, when necessary
- Dissemination of information, on new books etc, using E–mail, Bulletin boards, and SDI techniques
- Courier service for inter–library exchange of materials

Under BONET the following databases were created:

- 25,000 items in a bibliographic database on computers and software technology.
- Union catalogue of journals and other periodicals in libraries in the region.
- Tables of contents of 250 Indian periodicals created by the national centre for information.
- A number of CDROM databases have been mounted on a Novell Server for use to members

MYLIBNET: It is the first library network established in a small city. Mysore Library Network (MYLIBNET) was established at Mysore city in the year 1995 and the Central Food Technological Research Institute (CFTRI), Mysore, being an active member of Mysore City Library Consortium (MCLC), is hosting this network in its premises. It is also unique in a way where one can find information on many areas like food science, sericulture, speech & hearing, pharmacy, dentistry, polymer, medicine, archeology, anthropology, Indian languages and engineering at one place considering this uniqueness. CFTRI is one of the premier Sectoral Centres of NISSAT in the area of food science and technology. With this added advantage, MYLIBNET is working closely with MCLC to promote information services in Mysore city.

BALNET: Bangalore Library Network was established in 1997 and sponsor by JRD and Tata Memorial Library. These are 100 libraries member of the Network

PUNENET: Pune Libraries Network (PUNENET) established by University of Pune in 1986 and Centre for Development of Advanced Computing (C-DAC) and the National Chemical Laboratory (NCL) being funded by National Information System for Science and Technology (NISSAT) of the Department of Scientific and Industrial Research (DSIR), Government of India. There are Database development & other activities:

Database of Books : The database contains 1, 08,853 records from 20 participant libraries of Pune-Net.

Union Catalogue of Periodicals : This database contains 6425 records pertaining to various libraries in the Pune city. Currently data from 60 libraries are available online.

Booksellers database : Pune-Net is trying to provide information on the books available with these booksellers. This will be of great help to librarians and users to locate latest books in subjects of their interest. Currently, Pune-Net has two bookseller's data on its server and more data from other booksellers will be added in near future.

LIS professionals' database : A database of LIS professionals has been created using Microsoft Access. This database provides information about library professionals working in Pune City with their subject expertise.

Pune-Net libraries database : A database of libraries participating in Pune-Net has been created using Microsoft Access. From this database users can find details of each library, viz. name, research area, name of the librarian, rules, timings, etc.

Direct access to libraries : Access to C-DAC and Jayakar Library has been provided on-line through HTML interface.

Data standardization : Data from participating libraries is being collected and stored at the Pune-Net server. Pune-Net is following its own standard, based on the international standard for information exchange - ISO 2709.

Pune-Net Services

1. E-mail and Internet Connectivity
2. CD-ROM Database Services
3. Online Search facility
4. Current Awareness Service (CAS)
5. Photocopy Services: Radio Link between NCL and
6. Bioinformatics Centre
7. Individual Log in and Passwords for Libraries

Library Networks (Wide Area)

INFLIBNET: Information and Library Network (INFLIBNET), a programme of the University Grants Commission, was launched in May 1991. The main aim of INFLIBNET is to establish a national computer-communication network to link libraries and information centres in universities, colleges, universities, UGC information centres, institutions of national importance, R&D institutions, etc., and thereby improve capability in information handling and services. It is a programme for academic excellence to be achieved through establishment of a mechanism for information transfer and access to support scholarship and academic work. It facilitates pooling, sharing and optimization of scarce library resources in the country. As a major programme it helps modernize libraries and information centres in the country through application of information technology.

The National Centre of INFLIBNET is located in Gujarat University campus at Ahmedabad. At present, INFLIBNET aims at computerizing and networking of university/college libraries. Every year, INFLIBNET programme is identifying a number of university libraries for automation depending on the budget allocation. The selected institutions are given funds for procuring computer systems, retro conversion and networking. Application software for data entry and other library functions, library standards and formats, etc., are provided by INFLIBNET to the participating libraries. Manpower development is an important part of the programme. Training courses for core library staff engaged in computerized library operations, have been conducted since 1992-93.

Development of suitable software, standards for various library operations and communication based services (e.g., e-mail, bulletin boards) designing suitable network architecture and preparation of union catalogues of serials, books, non-book materials, and cooperation with other networking organizations like NISSAT, NICNET, etc.,

Information Networks (Sectoral): ERNET (1986), SIRNET, BTISNET, DESINET (1986)

ERNET: It was launched by the Department of Education (DOE), Govt. of India in late 1986 with financial assistance from UNDP (United Nationals Development Programme) to provide academic and research institutions with electronic mail facilities. It is currently used by DSIR Labs, research centres and academic institutions. ERNET India is an autonomous scientific society under the administrative control of Dept. of Information Technology, Government of India having one of the largest nationwide terrestrial and satellite network with 15 points of presence located at the premier academic and research institutions in major cities of the country. Focus of ERNET India is not limited to just providing connectivity, but to meet the entire needs of the academic and research institutions by providing consultancy, project management, training and other value added services such as web hosting, e-mail services, video conferencing, domain registration, CUG services. ERNET India is serving more than 1300 institutions in various sectors, namely, health, agriculture, higher education, schools and science & technology. ERNET was also identified by Govt. of India as the nodal network for India and was connected through high-speed link to the pan-European Education and Research Network (GEANT)during 2006 to 2010. The ERNET-GEANT connectivity is now available through Trans Eurasia Information Network (TEIN3).In tune with the mandate ERNET is providing four types of services, namely, Access Services, Application Services, Hosting Services and Operations Support Services to all Educational and Research Community of India. ERNET provides access to its network through various connectivity options. Application services include E-mail hosting, domain registration, MPLS VPN. It also provides Web Services having state of art of Data Centre and Other services include IT Consultancy and Project Management services for establishment of IT infrastructure & converged Network Projects.

SIRNET: It was established by INSDOC in late 1989 to interconnect all the CSIR laboratories and other R&D institutions in India. Its main objective is to harness the vast S&T information resources available with national laboratories and inculcate the habit of resource sharing among them. Its ultimate aim is to link the entire scientific community of the nation with the national library system and the international links to achieve efficient scientific communication.

BTISNET: The BTISNET programme, envisaged as a National distributed bioinformatics network organization, was launched during 1986-87. The programme has become a very successful vehicle for transfer and exchange of information, scientific knowledge, technology packages, and references in the country involving 10-12 thousand scientific personnel. BTISNET consists of 165 Bioinformatics Centres which include an Apex BTIS Centre at DBT, New Delhi, 5 COEs, 11 DICs, 51 Sub-DICs and 97 Bioinformatics Infrastructure Facility located in universities and research institutes of national importance.

DESINET: Title: Defence Science Information Network (DESINET) was organized by DESIDOC on 17 & 18 February 1987 at Metcalfe House, Delhi

CONCLUSION

During the recent period, quite a large number of Libraries and information centers are forming networks. The advent of computer networking as an accepted part of the library and information infrastructure has had a very significant impact on the way in which library and information systems are perceived. India is thus on the threshold to a new era of computer communication networks both for general purposes and for library and information purposes.

REFERENCES

- Aswal, R. S., ed. Information Networks in India. New Delhi: Ess Ess Publication, 2003
- Baruah, A. Computer Networking in Libraries. Delhi: Kalpaz, 2002.
- Dubey, Y. P. and Menon, V. V. Information Technology and National Development. Agra: Y K Publishers, 1994: 299-308
- http://www.alibnet.org/
- http://www.delnet.nic.in/Del-files/Nacline.htm
- http://www.inflibnet.ac.in/about/biosketch/premchand.html
- http://www.mylibnet.org
- http://www.naclin.org/Brochure.doc
- INFLIBNET : Current Programme. NISSAT Newsletter 12(3) 1993: 19
- Jain, N. K, ed. 50 Years: Library and Information services in India, 1998
- Kaul, H. K. DELNET: An overview. IASLIC Bulletin. 38(3) 1993: 113-122
- Kumar, P. and Arora, O. P. Information and Library Network (INFLIBNET). DESIDOC Bulletin of Information Technology 16(2) 1996: 11-22
- Mitra, A. C. CALIBNET on stream. DESIDOC Bulletin of Information Technology 16(2) 1996: 35-40

- Murthy, S. S. Library Networking in India- An overview. DESIDOC Bulletin of Information Technology 16 (2) 1996: 3-9.
- Padhi, P. Library and Information Networks in India: An Overview, Progress of Library & Information Science, 21(5) 2001:
- Raghavan R, Raghavan J. Notable features of MALIBNET. DESIDOC Bulletin of Information Technology 16(2) 1996: 47-56
- Ramani. Report from the Bombay library network. DESIDOC Bulletin of Information Technology 16(2) 1996: 41-46
- Thakore S R. 1996. Ahmedabad library network - ADINET. DESIDOC Bulletin of Information Technology 16(2) 1996: 57-61
- The National Commission on Libraries and Information Science (NCLIS), USA(1975). National Programme Document
- University Grants Commission (India). Development of an information and Library network: Report of the Inter Agency Working Group, (1988), xxx, 473p.

Part B
Library Consortia

4

Library Consortium: A Revolution in Futuristic Education

Narender Kumar Chauhan
Dr Sudhir Narayan Singh

ABSTRACT

Though the education sector is booming in India, but the quality of education is continuing to be a nagging concern. In the present era of globalization schools, colleges, institute and universities are undergoing a dramatic transformation. In its endeavor MHRD-India has taken steps for implementing e-resources in higher education along with technical education and named the forum as 'Library Consortium'. Moreover there is one consortium dedicated to technical education viz. 'All India Council of Technical Education-Indian National Digital Library in Engineering Science and Technology-Consortium (AICTE-INDEST-CONSORTIUM) and the second one is dedicated to Basic/Physical Sciences and Humanities viz. 'University Grant Commission-Information Library Network' (UGC-INFLIBNET). Noticeable results of both are visible which may further offer drastic changes in the reading habits of the modern users and also enhanced their potential research activities. Consortium can provide a platform to scholars where they can share their research works along with solutions. Library consortium is the outcome of meticulous efforts done by the renowned scholars for the present generation and the generations yet to come because library in itself is an unbroken link between the past generation and present generation. In the present era every minute there is an information explosion and to satisfy the needs of modern users through manual system is not possible, a single Library, however big may it be, is able to satisfy whole needs of its users due to various constraints. Due to such problems the concept of library consortium has come into existence. Consortium is known for sharing of resources all over the world unhindered and in time. It is essential for the 21st century students to have some ideal consortia models for universities libraries to adhere for maximum utilization of their sources and resources. This study tries to elicit the possibilities of information for modern researchers and facilities offered by the library consortium. It also attempts to explore the concept, issues and shows how the library consortium is making resources available for its member libraries. Authors believe that library consortium is a change agent for futuristic education.

Keywords: Resource sharing, Library Consortium, Change agent, e-resources

INTRODUCTION

The prime objective of the Library Consortium is networking people and resources. An emergence of the Library Consortium in higher education, the system of information retrieving, storing and disseminating has become inherent. The new technologies like Information and Communication Technology (ICT), Internet, World Wide Web have become the means of communication and effective ways of transmitting information in a flawless manner. Although, our printed subscriptions are very useful and most of the users those who are beyond the reach of new generation technology 50 years old feel very comfortable with the printed resources because while reading of printed documents he/she doesn't have any requirement of IT applications. Sometimes they also feel that they need more and more updated information on the same topic and then they start realizing the importance of e-contents feel need to switch over to e-resources/contents. E-resources have been very costly, if users are going to purchase them individually. Thus, to cater to the highly specialized needs individual scholars, Government has taken this step and developed 'Consortia' for libraries. In the 18th and 19th century there were very few means available to retrieve and disseminate the information instantly but all means were very costly and very requesting. But with the advent of Consortia, it has become very cheaper (spread information all over the world) and many new opportunities unscrewed due to co-operation among libraries.

At the global level Internet has become the sources of information retrieval and dissemination and at the local level various library networks came in existence and created databases for information sharing. However, this is not feasible for an individual library to cover all knowledge and information explosion and accumulate for the users. Hence to cope up with the situation the concept of library consortium has become very prominent in the last few decades. However, Library Consortium now being overheard omnipresent is because of digital form of information contents. Growth of the digital contents on the internet, and high adoption of online information dissemination methods is making every educational institution to going online with their academic curricula, lessons, lectures, podcasts, audio-visual and animated lessons contents. With the options to digitize printed contents for an academic curriculum becoming very easy and very prevalent in our country, information technology is helping many educational institutions to set up online portals and information networks within the campuses, and helping them establishing infrastructural set up for library consortium which will be like platforms where Library Consortiums are supposed to be working like a network because electronic library of the future is likely to be part of network. This paper attempts to elicit that how Library Consortium(s) has become the revolutionary agent for futuristic education which is mandatory to preserve, protect and promote to nurture the futuristic growth oriented academic environment for the users and learners.

PRESENT SCENARIO AND FUTURE ACADEMIC CHALLENGES

Presently all universities are very much aware in purchasing materials to give answers of the emerging queries of modern users. This is not feasible for a single library collection to cater to the growing research demands. Consortium has become easy or possible to purchase information in stabilized and reasonable prices. Resources accessibility is considered more important than the building infrastructural collections. Consortium provides the more accessibility to library resources and libraries to get the benefit of wider access to e-resources at affordable cost and through this accessibility all e-resources has become the change agent. Consortium provides the navigation to their users in searching the materials. As e-resources are considered as the best among all because it includes all the forms like text, graphics, animation, sound, videos and it makes the program more attractive. A renowned Chinese Proverb says, "A picture is worth a thousand words". Hence the use of e-resources has greatly influenced the technical education in one way or the other. Hence e-resources and communicating means have become able to expand both in functions and numbers over the last decade. Next generation information retrieval methods will be seamless, informal, immediate, personal, simple, minimal, short and this can be happened only through the digital contents or through library consortium.

LIBRARY CONSORTIUM: MEANING AND DEFINITION

Library Consortium is "an agreement, combination or group (as of companies) formed to undertake an enterprise beyond the resources of any one member" (Merriam Webster Dictionary). Library Consortium(s) is varying in their type, goals structure and membership and may be formal and informal licensed based for to achieve a common objective or goal. Consortium is totally based on library collection e.g. academic, medical, engineering, and public. But the objective of all types consortium is common (to enhance the usability of resources with minimum possible time and on affordable cost).

Library consortium is an umbrella terms which covers the concept like inter library loan, library networks, e-library, virtual library etc. Library Consortium is the single solution of these concepts even consortium gives the freedom a library having less collection but they can access any products on nominal price. It has been a growing concern that the size of the library doesn't matter, but the thing that matters is the finance capabilities and quality services offered to its users.

LIBRARY CONSORTIUM: OBJECTIVES

The prime objective of the Library Consortium is networking people and resources. There could be many objectives as per the emergence of the upcoming needs of the users yet so far as The INDEST-AICTE Consortium specifically points out its objectives which targets to meet the following objectives and cater to the need of the users:

a) To provide e-resources through single platform where institutes can get on affordable price and reasonable price which avoids gabbing or bargaining.

b) Networking people and resources.

c) To impart the information regarding usages of e-resources in the members institution to the other engineering and technological institutions where the probability of usefulness and interest is high.

d) To enhance the usability of e-resources among the members institution.

e) To provide the research contents to every scholars of the country whether the contents have been carried in any country of the world.

f) To avoid duplicacy.

g) To improve research and give freedom to any institute during purchasing (they can choose as per their requirement and as per users requirement).

h) To make contents easily accessible, seamless, immediate, interesting, simple etc.

i) To equip with availability, accessibility and accountability.

Though the above said objectives have been specifically visualized for the users of INDEST-AICTE, yet they are applicable for each and every ideal Library consortium in general.

TYPES OF LIBRARY CONSORTIUM

As per the growing need of the time, the emergence of the conceptualization of various types of Library Consortium was pondered over by the academic stakeholders of the society to cater to the need of twenty first century academic users. Consequently, the following types of Library Consortium came into existence which may be nurtured and grow up to the level of giving birth to the new consortium types in near future.

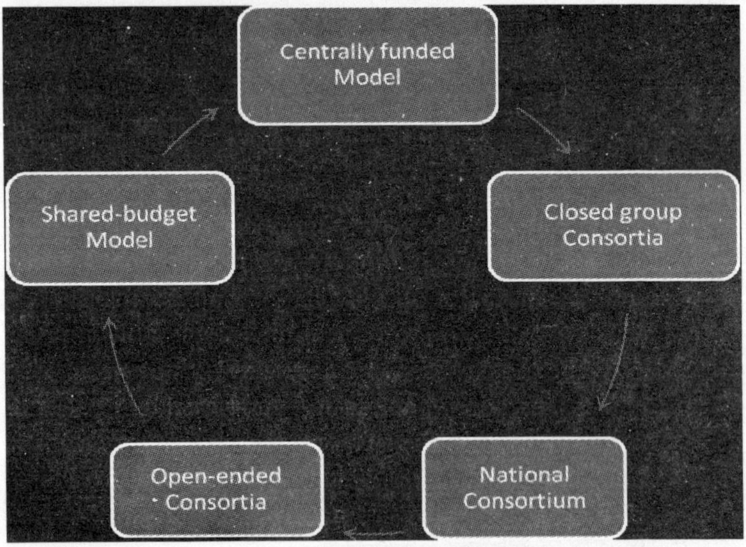

Fig. 1. Types of Consortium

MAJOR ADVANTAGES OF THE CONSORTIA

Library Consortium(s) has been playing a significant role in the higher academic and technical education along with social sciences. Prior to consortium peoples were doing their research work but when they did not get the solution of any problem they feel restricted by the limited resources and restricted accessibilities resulting in irritation and their work held for days, weeks and even months in certain cases because the information and communication mediums were not so sufficient and it was a time consuming process to float the information from one place to another place. Even the compilation and retrieval of data was also a big challenge before the researchers and library users. But with the advent of consortium the academic process has become very easy in terms of floating information throughout the world without wasting a single minute. Moreover, in the age of library consortium researchers feel free to collect the information from any corner of the world at very affordable and reasonable price. The following are the major advantages of the Library Consortium.

a) It's a time saving system because packaging, re-packaging, posting, mailing, receiving of information through hypertext, cyber text, compact disks (CDs' and pen drives) and hard drives are very innate and effortless process in Consortium age.

b) It is the solution of the library budget, building, and space problem.

c) Library consortium can sustain the thrust of information of the modern users with providing the huge amount of data at single platform.

d) Its help in enhancing the reading habit of the users because modern users are interested to read multidimensional materials without wasting time even they require readymade materials as they do not want to go for any calculation and this is possible only through Consortium.

e) It helps in promoting the research of every field and authors personally believe that this is the great achievement of the Library Consortium over the traditional ways of using libraries.

BENEFITS OF ASSOCIATION OF COMPUTING MACHINERY (ACM)

Considering the emerging needs of consortium many users and library consortia developers came under the same umbrella in the name of Association of Computing Machinery. ACM partners with established academic library consortia to provide Direct Library (DL) access to approximately 3,000 academic libraries in over 180 countries around the world. The following is a list of consortia ACM currently partners with. If a user is interested in learning more about how to access the ACM DL via one of these library consortia, s/he may follow the links provided below or reach out to the appropriate consortium administrator.

African Open Consortium	Namibia
AMICAL Consortium	Beirut, Nigeria, Lebanon
ANKOS Consortium	Turkey
Amigos Library Services, Inc	USA
Arabian Advance Systems	Saudi Arabia
B-On Consortium of Portugal (FCCN)	Portugal
C3 - Czech CompSci Consortium	Czech Republic
CAPES Coordenação de Aperfeiçoamento de Pessoal de Nível Superior	Brazil
California Digital Library	USA
California State University	USA
Caul/ Australia	Australia, New Zealand
Chile Consrtium	Chile
CILEA Consortium	Italy
Colombia Consortium	Colombia
Consortia Canada	Canada
Consortium Luxembourg	Luxembourg
Consortium of Academic and Research Libraries in Illinois	USA
Consortium of the Swiss Academic Libraries	Switzerland

Costa Rica Consortium	Costa Rica
CONRICyT (Mexican National Consortium)	Mexico
CVTI - Slovakia Consortium	Slovakia
Couperin/CNRS/INRIA	France
Daneshyar Network	United Arab Emirates
Danish Consortium	Denmark
DRAA (China) Consortium	China
EBSCO Latin America	Mexico, Colombia, Chile
EBSCO North America	USA
EBSCO Ireland	Ireland
EBSCO Latvia	Latvia
EBSCO Poland	Poland
Ecuador Consortium	Ecuador
Federation of Kentucky Academic Libraries (FOKAL)	USA
Finland Consortium	Finland
Greater Western Library Alliance (GWLA)	USA
Higher Education Commission, Pakistan	Pakistan
HeBIS	Germany
Hellenic Academic Libraries Link	Greece
Hong Kong	Hong Kong
Hungary Consortium (EISZ)	Hungary
INDEST (India) Consortium	India
IReL Consortium	Ireland
Iraqi Virtual Science Library	Iraq
Japan National University Consortium	Japan
Japan Academic Open Consortium	Japan
KERIS	Republic of Korea
Kooperation E-Medien Österreich	Austria
Kungl. Biblioteket /National Library of Sweden	Sweden
Lithuanian Research Academic Library Consortium	Lithuania
LOBBI Netherlands Consortium	Netherlands
LYRASIS Consortium	USA
Latin American Consortium	Colombia, Chile, Peru, Mexico, Uruguay, Argentina, Ecuador, Costa Rica

MALMAD - Israel Center for Digital Information Services	Israel
Malaysia Consortium	Malaysia
Maryland Digital Library	USA
Mexico Consortium	Mexico
Midwest Collaborative for Library Services (MCLS)	USA
Middle East Consortium	United Arab Emirates
Midwest Collaborative for Library (MCLS)	USA
MINCyT (Argentina) Consortium	Argentina
Minitex	USA
NEICON	Russian Federation
NERL Consortium	USA
Norwegian Consortium of Academic Libraries	Norway
OhioLINK	USA
PALCI - Pennsylvania Academic Library Consortium, Inc.	USA
Peru Consortium	Peru
Publiciencia Ltda	Colombia, Peru
Robert W. Woodruff Library Consortium	USA
Russian Open Consortium	Russian Federation
SANLic	South Africa
SENAC (Brazil)	Brazil
Singapore Consortium	Singapore
Spain Consortium	Spain
Statewide California Electronic Library Consortium (SCELC)	USA
SWETS Africa	NIgeria
Taiwan Consortium - A.S.	Taiwan
CHE Consortium	Thailand
UGC Digital Library Consortium	Bangladesh
UK Higher Education Institutions (UK HEI)	United Kingdom
University of Puerto Rico Libraries	USA
University of the West Indies Consortium	Trin and Tobgo
VIP Consortium	Philippines
VIVA	USA

Westchester Academic Library Directors Association (WALDO)	USA
Wisconsin Library Services WiLS	USA

E-RESOURCES@UGC-INFONET DIGITAL LIBRARY CONSORTIUM

So far as the authentication of the resources material is concerned University Grant Commission, India has come up with specialized consortia for the users of a specific academic failed in the name of UGC-INFONET Digital Library Consortium which subscribes to the following resources for its member institutions. All electronic resources subscribed are available from the publisher's Web site. Following is the list of E-Resources with link to their brief introduction. List of Journals including Title, URLs are as under.

E-Resources (Full Text)

American Chemical Society	*http://www.pubs.acs.org/*
American Institute of Physics	*http://scitation.aip.org/publications/myBrowsePub.jsp#AIP*
American Physical Society	*http://scitation.aip.org/publications/myBrowsePub.jsp#APS*
Annual Reviews	*http://arjournals.annualreviews.org/*
Blackwell Publishing	*http://www3.interscience.wiley.com/*
Cambridge University Press	*http://journals.cambridge.org/*
Elsevier Science	*http://www.sciencedirect.com/*
Emerald	*http://www.emeraldinsight.com*
Institute of Physics	*http://www.iop.org/EJ/*
J-STOR	*http://www.jstor.org/*
Nature	*http://www.nature.com/*
Oxford University Press	*http://www.oxfordjournals.org*
Portland Press	*http://www.portlandpress.com/pp/journals/default.htm*
Project Euclid	*http://projecteuclid.org/*
Project Muse	*http://muse.jhu.edu/*
Royal Society of Chemistry	*http://www.rsc.org/Publishing/Journals/*
SIAM	*http://epubs.siam.org/*

Springer Link	*http://www.springerlink.com/*
Taylor and Francis	*http://www.informaworld.com/*
SciFinder Scholar	*http://www.cas.org/SCIFINDER/SCHOLAR/index.html*
MathSciNet	*http://www.ams.org/mathscinet/*
ISiD	*http://isid.org.in/*
JCCC	*http://jccc-ugcinfonet.in* or *www.jccc-ugcinfonet.in*
About Open Access	*oaeresources.html*
Open Access E-Journals	*oaeresources.html#ejournals*
Open Access Directories	*oaeresources.html#directories*
IRs@member Institutions	*oaeresources.html#IRs*

E-RESOURCES@INDEST-AICTE DIGITAL LIBRARY CONSORTIUM

So far as the learners of the technical and professional educations are concerned AICTE has come up with another specialized library consortium in the name of INDEST-AICTE Digital Library Consortium which subscribes to the following resources for various categories of institutions. All electronic resources subscribed are available from the publisher's Web site. Local hosting of resources has not been considered at this stage.

E-Resources (Full-Text)

ABI / Inform Complete	*http://search.proquest.com*
ACM Digital Library	*http://dl.acm.org/*
Annual Reviews (Through NME-ICT Project)	*http://www.annualreviews.org*
ASCE Journals	*http://scitation.aip.org/publications/myBrowsePub.jsp*
ASME Journals (+ A M R)	*http://scitation.aip.org/publications/myBrowsePub.jsp*
ASTM Standards & Digital Library	Standards: *http://enterprise.astm.org* Journals: *http://journalsip.astm.org/*
Capitaline	*http://www.capitaline.com/intranet/INDEST_consortium.htm*
CRIS INFAC Ind. Information	*http://www.crisil.com/*

EBSCO Databases	*http://search.epnet.com/*
Elsevier's Science Direct	*http://www.sciencedirect.com/*
Emerald E-books (Business Mgmt & Economics Collection)	*http://www.emeraldinsight.com/*
Emerald Full-text	*http://www.emeraldinsight.com/*
Emerald Management Xtra	*http://www.emeraldinsight.com/*
Euromonitor (GMID)	*http://www.portal.euromonitor.com/portal/server.pt*
IEC Standards	*http://www.igpublish.com/iec-ebooks/main.nsp*
IEEE / IEE Electronic Library Online (IEL)	*http://ieeexplore.ieee.org/*
INFORMS Pub Suite	*http://journals.informs.org/*
INSIGHT	*http://www.insight.asiancerc.com/*
McGraw-Hill's Access Engineering (FKA DEL)	*http://www.accessengineeringlibrary.com/*
Nature (27 titles Through NME-ICT Project)	*http://www.nature.com/*
Optical Society of America (Optics Infobase)	*http://www.opticinfobase.org*
Project Muse (Through NME-ICT Project)	*http://muse.jhu.edu*
Springer Link	*http://www.springerlink.com/*
Taylor & Francis (Through NME-ICT Project)	*http://www.tandfonline.com/*
INSPEC	*http://www.engineeringvillage2.org*
MathSciNet	*http://www.ams.org/mathscinet*
SciFinder Scholar	*http://www.cas.org/SCIFINDER/SCHOLAR/index.html* (access through a Z39.50 Client to be installed on each PC)
SCOPUS Database	*http://www.scopus.com*
Web of Science	*http://isiknowledge.com*
About Open Access	*oaeresources.html*
IRs@member Institutions	*oaeresources.html#IRs*
Open Access Directories	*oaeresources.html#directories*
Open Access E-Journals	*oaeresources.html#ejournals*

SUGGESTIONS AND RECOMMENDATION

a) Awareness campaign is required with regards to library consortium.

b) Spreading awareness will lead to the dream actualization of free and independent learning of those learners who are otherwise deprived from the very basic right of a civilized society i.e. Right to Education (RTE).

c) There is no end to research so the increasing periphery of research will keep expanding day by day and to meet the increasing demands of the individual as well as institutional research the emerging needs of new and specialized pools of consortia will be felt.

d) Every expectation cannot be left at the mercy of concerned government. No government can be capable enough to be assuring to meet out the needs of the requirements of a billions nation. The support from industries, efficient corporate houses, business groups is to be highly appreciated.

e) Considering the ever increasing demand of research in academia, industries and corporate houses private group of colleges, institutes, research organizations and universities should come forward to design and conceptualize the consortia.

f) Considering the highly specialized demands of industrial research the corporate house should also come up with the cutting edged consortia to meet out the demands of spearheading competitiveness. This will not only help them (the corporate houses) in meeting their specific needs but also help them in fulfilling their Corporate Social Responsibilities (CSR).

g) Consortia should take some remedial steps for those institutes who are newly opened because they don't have sufficient funds for subscriptions of e-resources and generally they avoid the same.

h) Some institutions do not have sufficient trained manpower along with IT infrastructure for running these e-resources because they subscribed the same but not able to provide the services of these resources because the uses of e-resources is totally depend up on the capabilities of Library staff.

i) Newly established institutes are not offering permanent job for library staff even they are not hiring qualified staff, thus why Consortia are not getting success in academic colleges as well as technical colleges.

LIBRARY CONSORTIUM: A BOON FOR FUTURISTIC KNOWLEDGE BASED SOCIETY

Ensuring free availability and accessibility of knowledge, information and resources for all has been an unfulfilled dream of human civilization since the time immemorial, but the establishment of Library consortium has been a giant step towards labeling the gap amongst privileged, un-privileged and underprivileged learners. This will also generate a never ending hope in the direction of highly individualized, independent learning for all by opening new vistas in the form of Library Consortium where any user can access relevant study material from anywhere at any time indiscriminately in a highly personalized manner as per his/her own need and requirements which will in turn ensure specific and specialized development for the overall grooming of human personality by offering positive behavioral and academic intervention in a very effective and researched manner. Generations will reap the befitting advantageous crop of this initiative which will yield a futuristic knowledge society.

CONCLUSION

It would be highly relevant to highlight the inferential remarks of Christina Birdie and Vagiswari Alladi which they reflect in their article entitled "The Future of Consortia among Indian Libraries – FORSA Consortium as Forerunner?" where they significantly ponder over the significance of library consortia and its future in the 21st century Academic Society of India. They say that:

> "It is clear that the technology of the web, the increasing importance of electronic resources, and advances in resource-sharing systems have created new opportunities for consortia. Beyond these technological and economic motivations, the instinct of the librarians to work together at a time of uncertainty is very essential at all levels. Combining this approach and support from the government will certainly enhance the chances of forming more consortia models."

Thus, it won't be an exaggeration here, to conceive that the foundation of a society depends on the shoulders of the awakened and enlightened citizens who are supposed to lay down the founding stones of the towering pillars on which the ceilings of the generations rests. Nonetheless, to have the awakened and enlightened generations the healthy arrangements are to be made for satiating the academic appetite as per the individualized learners' need but a single-dimensional library can ensure a unilateral growth and henceforth a rich library consortium becomes the most significant requisites of a growing society. It will become the place where the libraries will be established as the knowledge repositories to making the life of the users fruitful and productive and ultimately enhance the reputation of library professionals.

REFERENCES

- *http://crl.du.ac.in/Infonetresources.htm* browsed as on February 11, 2013.
- *http://librarians.acm.org/academic/members* browsed as on February 11, 2013.
- *http://paniit.iitd.ac.in/indest/* browsed as on February 11, 2013.
- *http://prints.iiap.res.in/bitstream/2248/3919/1/Lisa%20IV_chris.pdf* browsed as on February 11, 2013

- *http://www.librijournal.org/pdf/2003-2pp94-102.pdf browsed as on* February 05, 2013.
- http://www.unak.org.tr/unak08/sunum/AnwarulIslam.pdf browsed as on February 04, 2013.
- ICT in technical education, Proceedings of National seminars September 06-07, 2012, NITTR, Chandigard.

5

The Growth and Issues of Library Consortia and Resource Sharing in Modern Era

Alok Srivastava

INTRODUCTION

No library, however, resourceful, can hope to be comprehensive and self sufficient at any time. No library can hold all the literature which is demanded by the readers. Behavior stands with relationship between ends and scares means which have alternative use. This principle is applicable among human being, economics and also among libraries. There has been tremendous increase in scientific and technical knowledge during the 20th century. We call it 'knowledge Explosion'. The idea of cooperation first stressed by Robert Quon of England in the field of Economics, Libraries follow this principle. Every book in it should be read and every reader should be benefited by a library with the cooperation of other libraries.

A Consortium could be described as a group of organizations who come together to fulfill a combined objective that usefully requires co-operation and the sharing of resources. And need to have a clear mutual goal in order to ensure their success. The aim should be to deliver "more than the sum of the individual parts". A library Consortium formation can be local, regional, state, national and inter institutional level.

By definition a consortium is said to be "a cooperative arrangement among groups or institutions" or "an association or society". Library consortium would be organization of libraries formed to realize the benefit and opportunities of collaborative activity. It is a comparative alliance of libraries to share human and information resources.

(Hirshon, 1999) defines library consortia 'a generic term to indicate any group of libraries that are working together towards a common goal, whether to expand cooperation on traditional library services (such as collection development) or electronic information services. It is now used perhaps too broadly, and encompasses everything from formal legal entitles to information groups that come together solely to achieve better pricing for purchasing electronic information.

CONCEPT OF LIBRARY CONSORTIUM

The emergence of the internet, particularly the World Wide Web, as a new medium of information storage and delivery in the 21st century. In the age of information explosion, the most challenging tasks for the information professionals and information centers all over the world is to supervise the huge information that are being produced and developed in the world. It is impossible for a single library to monitor the entire explosion of knowledge fields and accumulate for the users. To cope up with this situation, the phenomenon of consortia has become very important in the last few years.

Initially the term used for resource sharing activities was library cooperation. Though cooperation theoretically could embrace almost all library activities, practically it was confined to inter-library loan of library documents. But due to physical distance and other reasons even this limited system of cooperation was not being practiced widely. However, with the advent of ICT and its application in library activities, new opportunities opened up for greater cooperation among libraries. At the global level Internet and at the national and local level several library networks came in vogue and databases created for information sharing. In recent years availability of information resources in digital or electronic medium has further facilitated exchange of information resources among libraries, thus creating favorable condition for increased resource sharing. Emergence of library Consortia are a very promising development in this direction.

TYPES OF CONSORTIA

Library consortia function in different ways. During the last three decades, libraries have developed a variety of organizational models. At one end of the spectrum are the loosely affiliated buying clubs where libraries come together primarily to share a discounted rate on electronic journals and databases, while on the other end are consortia that are tightly integrated organizations sharing a variety of resources which require a long term commitment and collaborative decision making at all levels.

Theoretically, consortia may be of following types depending on their characteristics. From the point of view of type of libraries forming the consortium there can be two types of consortia:

Consortia of multi-type libraries : In this type of consortium participating libraries are of different types, such as public, academic and special.

Consortia of same type of libraries : The members of such a consortium are of same type, such as consortium of public libraries, consortium of academic libraries, etc. CSIR E-Journals Consortium is such a consortium.

From the point of view of geographical region of coverage, the consortia may be of following types:

Local level consortia : This consists of libraries situated in a particular city, town of district, e.g. BOSLA (Bombay Science Librarians' Association), which was possibly the first library consortium of the country.

State level consortia : In such a consortium libraries of one particular state participate. There is perhaps no such consortium in the country at present.

National level consortia : Libraries belonging to a country are its members. INDEST is a national level consortium, but covering only libraries of scientific and technical institutions.

Regional level consortia : In such a consortium libraries of a particular region participate.

International level consortia : In this consortium libraries belonging to different countries participate. This may be formed either by individual libraries, such as OCLC, or by bringing different national consortia under one umbrella. Such federation of consortia is known as Meta Consortia, such as International Coalition of Library Consortia, which comprises of nearly 150 library consortia from around the world.

NEED OF LIBRARY CONSORTIA

Electronic publishing has been revolutionizing the format of the recorded knowledge. Electronic information services are attracting readers' attention in today's networked environment. E-journals and E-databases bring new challenges before the library and information professionals to give full text access to scholarly publications both in print and electronic version to its end users. Further subscribing to printed journals by individual libraries is beyond human comprehension. Ever-increasing prices of journals accompanied with the shrinking budget of libraries, management/

parent bodies are forced to resort to the best alternatives like consortia.

FUNCTIONS OF CONSORTIA

It is obvious that the existing consortia are basically serving as buying clubs than consortia in the real sense. But with little initiatives these can be developed into platforms for sharing valuable resources available in different libraries of the country, both in print and non-print media. Not only so, these consortia can also take up several other activities for the mutual benefit of the participating libraries.

(a) Information Resource Sharing : A consortium can undertake the following activities for promoting information resource sharing:

- Cooperative collection development among the member libraries
- Cooperative processing of information resources acquired through the consortium
- Creation of virtual digital library covering all the e-information resources available in member libraries by networking of those libraries
- Compilation of bibliographical and/or full-text database of the holdings of the member libraries, both print and non-print
- Sharing of information resources, both traditional and digital, of member libraries through network or document delivery service as the case may be
- Allowing reciprocal borrowing by the members of all libraries of the consortium
- Digitization of valuable and rare collections of member libraries available in printed format and providing access to such materials to the members of all the libraries of the consortium

- Supporting member libraries for setting up institutional repositories, e-print archives, electronic theses collection, etc.
- Developing common interface to catalogues, databases and e-collection by creating portals
- Creating interoperability among the member systems, databases and services

(b) Other Resource Sharing : A consortium may also share other resources in the following manner for their mutual benefit of the participating libraries.

- Sharing the storage facilities, thereby minimizing expenditure on space
- Sharing of human resources at local, regional and national levels
- Pooling of expert manpower and promoting professional development
- Assist member libraries in creating information technology infrastructure
- Facilitating joint preservation and archiving activities for print and digital materials
- Initiating and supporting research projects of common interest
- Collectively promoting, marketing and publicizing the library services

ISSUES RELATED TO LIBRARY CONSORTIUM

Various factors to be taken for an effective functioning of a successful consortium. The Major issues of consortia approaches are:

- Selecting a coordinating agency to deal on behalf of the entire group of participants and executing and monitoring the work.
- Sources of funding to meet the subscription cost.

- Identifying and negotiating the potential publishers / vendors or aggregators to provide access under consortia purchase.
- Legal issues involved in contracts and usage of material within the consortia.
- Identification of libraries interested in participating and agreeing on common terms and conditions.
- Identifying the necessary infrastructure for electronic access to resources.
- Issues related to backup and archival of database.
- Documentation and training to staff.

IMPORTANCE OF LIBRARY CONSORTIUM IN THE INFORMATION SOCIETY

Access to resources is now considered more important than the collection building. The consortium facilities the libraries to get the benefit of wider access to electronic resources at affordable cost and at the best terms of licenses. A consortium, with the collective strength of resources of various institutions available to it, is in a better position to resolve the problems of managing, organizing and archiving the electronic resources.

The phenomenon of information revolution has posed several problems and this has far reaching implications in the society. The nation or society which possesses more information will lead the world. This is also true in case of individuals. The persons have more information will guide a group or society and they will be superior to others. This power of information has induced the nations and individuals to acquire and control more and more quantities of information. But in this race, the poor nations, societies, institutions or individuals will be back as compared to the others. This has created a big gap in the availability and use of information. The library consortia can be an ideal solution in this context. Perhaps the most important advantages of library consortia would be their enhanced ability to serve the society by giving better library services.

THE ADVANTAGES OF LIBRARY CONSORTIA

The advantages of library consortia may be summarized as following:

1. To leverage resources by sharing existing resources or collection though virtual union catalogue and sharing of:
    - Collections and collaborating on collection development; each library is able to contribute unique titles to the consortium – avoid duplication.
    - Electronic resources including the creation of digital collections-sharing among consortium members need not be just in terms of licensing products- it can also include sharing in the creation of digital collections.
    - Storage of resources – Space is an issue for many libraries
    - Sharing the archiving of resources
    - Sharing staff expertise- a consortium provides opportunities for staff members to develop new skills and interact with a varsity of people who would not have had the opportunity to meet otherwise sharing risk- by sharing risk, members of a consortium can undertake projects that are larger than one institution can safely take on its own.
    - This form of cooperation enables the consortia libraries to borrow books, periodicals, articles, and scientific journals, which are not available locally.
    - Electronic access enables the user initiate their own search of remote catalogues and make requests for information.
    - Sharing catalogues—to enable user's greater access to larger collection
    - CD-ROM union catalogue that provides access to

books, videos and recording for each institution.

- Union List of Serials that provides access to the journal holdings of all member libraries.

2. To reduce the cost of library operations by obtaining a group purchased price for information product.
3. To bring pressure on, providers especially publishers to reduce the rate of rise in the cost of purchasing information.

Thus, library consortium are commonly formed to negotiate joint purchases (e.g. of equipment, software, books, library materials and licensed electronic databases and resources) and to share resources.

GROWTH OF LIBRARY CONSORTIA IN THE WORLD

Libraries, especially academic libraries have long formed consortia for the purpose of sharing existing physical resources—principally books and journals held by member libraries. Library consortia, does not have any remarkable history but the consortial arrangements started with the concept of resource sharing since long back. In 19990's, new types of library consortia began to flourish that exploited the advances in information technology. The global development of OCLC in USA is a prime example. Over time the growth of newer consortium like; Colorado's CARL, Georgia's GALILEO, Illinois's IDAL, Maryland's SAILOR, Missouri's MIRACAL, New Zealand's CONZUL, CAUL, Metro Net, North America's CRL, North Carolina's embryonic NCLive, Ohio's Ohio Link, Pennsylvania's PALCI, Portland's PORTALS, Texas's TexShare, Virginia's VIVA, Washington's WRLC, CIC in South Asia , CURL in UK, CALIM in Manchester, Concord in Britain, Metro web in NewYork etc came into existence in the international scenario (Wikipedia, 2007). In India, major initiatives are regarding consortium is J-GATE form Informatics India, IITS-BARC-TIFR Cooperation, TIFR Libraries Consortium, ISI Library consortia, SNDT consortia of LISA, STI Network, FORSA consortia, INDSET and INFLIBNET consortium under UGC InfoNet.

PRESENT SCENARIO OF LIBRARY CONSORTIUM IN INDIA

India is a vast country with a total of 400 universities and institutes of national importance and about 18,600 colleges that provide higher education in all disciplines. The number of teachers is 3.1 million, and 7.8 million students are enrolled in higher education .

Academic libraries in India are also facing problems such as increasing demands and high expectations from users, budget cuts, high costs of library materials especially electronic journals, and a rise in the amount of information resources in general. It is impossible for a single library to provide access to all materials to meet their users' needs. Library consortia have been initiated in India in order to overcome these problems, and efforts to form library consortia are still in their infancy. At present, there are some networks working at national level (e.g. INFLIBNET and DELNET), some in metropolitan areas (e.g. ADINET in Ahmadabad, CALIBNET in Calcutta, and PUNENET in Pune) and others covering specific topic areas (e.g. HELNET– health libraries, and MANLIBNET– management libraries). Some of these have been in existence since the 1990s – e.g. ADINET started in 1994, DELNET in 1996 and MANLIBNET in 1998. Details of four consortia in India are now described.

UGC: INFONET E-JOURNALS CONSORTIUM AND INFLIBNET

As stated on its web site (www.inflibnet.ac.in/) the Information and Library Network (INFLIBNET) Centre is an autonomous centre within the University Grants Commission (UGC) of India and is involved in creating the infrastructure for sharing library and information resources and services among academic and research institutions.

This is being achieved via the UGC-InfoNet network, which aims to provide high-speed internet connectivity to 150 institutions in its first phase. INFLIBNET functions as a resource centre with an aim to cater for the needs of its members for resources not accessible to them either in electronic media or in print media.

CSIR consortium : The Council of Scientific and Industrial Research (CSIR) in India has 40 scientific laboratories involved in basic and applied research in various disciplines. Many of the laboratories have well equipped libraries, and some of them act as the main information centres for different subjects, functioning as consultant libraries at the national level. Access to e-journals through the use of state-of-the art technology is possible in many of the libraries belonging to these laboratories. Each of the laboratories has a well-established library or documentation centre that is also backed up with strategic information support from the National Institute of Science Communication and Information Resource (NISCAIR), a constituent establishment of CSIR.

INDEST consortium : The Ministry of Human Resource Development (MHRD) has set up the Indian National Digital Library in Science and Technology (INDEST) Consortium. Under this, the ministry provides funds required for the subscription to electronic resources for 38 core institutions including the Indian Institutes of Science (IIScs), the Indian Institutes of Technology (IITs), the National Institutes of Technology (NITs), Regional Engineering Colleges (RECs), Indian Institutes of Management (IIMs) and a few other centrally funded government institutions through the consortium. Besides that, 60 government or government-aided engineering colleges and technical departments in universities have also joined the consortium with the financial support from the All India Council for Technical Education.

FORSA consortium : The Indian Astrophysics Consortium called Forum for Resource Sharing in Astronomy (FORSA) is a typical example of a homogeneous group of members wherein the libraries have a common area of interest and establishing the consortium is slightly easier than in a heterogeneous type of members. The FORSA consortium consists of five members who joined together for negotiating licensing for astronomy journals and identified a subscription agent as a supplier of journals. Subscriptions for both print and electronic format are paid through their supplier.

Several other organizations such as the Indian Council of Agricultural Research (ICAR), State Agricultural Universities, Indian Space Research Organization (ISRO), Defence Research and Development Organization (DRDO), AICTE and some other individual groups of institutions have started working to form different consortia.

CONCLUDING REMARKS

There are many advantages for libraries if they buy their materials, especially electronic resources, through consortia, although there are some disadvantages too. Consortia, in general, are tailored to meet the unique needs of their membership. Consortia purchasing projects have become a basic tool that expand collections and support cooperative technological development for libraries. Library consortia are considered as a coalition between libraries, publishers and vendors. They often provide a reasonable price in a win-win situation for all stakeholders. Thus, libraries have increasingly turned to consortia as a way of brokering better prices and rendering rapid and efficient services to information seekers. However, library consortia are facing new challenges, such as increasing expectations and a static budget, fair use, archiving of information, pricing strategies, measures of effectiveness and licensing e-resources.

It is clear that the creation of the web and networks brought many possibilities for integrating consortia activities both in developed and developing countries. The library consortia are shifting from a peripheral and limited position of resource sharing to an integrated system-wide resource sharing in recent years in the West.

With the help of networks and the internet, libraries in developing countries have also begun to create consortia at national, regional and international level to share their resources and expand access to print and electronic collections and develop new services to meet their customers' needs. However, some barriers such as poor technological and communication infrastructure, inadequate finances, culture and context, attitude toward consortia and multiple efforts are reported to be limitations of consortia activities in developing countries.

While India has been active in consortia activities among developing nations, due to limitations it is hard to find a successful programme that could be used as a benchmark to replicate in other libraries. Francis reported that establishment and maintenance of a separate library consortium for each group of government and government supported institutions in India has led to the duplication of efforts and additional investment. Another issue in Indian library consortia is the fact that almost all the major consortia in India are currently concentrating only on e-resource sharing; therefore the need of the hour is to explore the other areas for collaboration in order to improve the overall situation of libraries in terms of resources and services.

It can be concluded that libraries in developing countries need to battle with the problems that prevent a successful consortia effort, because the advantages of consortia, especially for sharing electronic resources, are much more for these libraries. Membership of international consortia can be recommended for all developing countries as it brings them all together to redefine and re-engineer their consortia efforts.

REFERENCES

- Allen Barbara & Hirshon (1998) Hanging together to avoid hanging separately opportunities for academic libraries and consortia. Information Technology and Libraries,
- Amitabh Chatterjee (2002) Resource sharing among libraries in digital era.
- Bedi & Sharma (2008) Library Consortia : a step forward the information society
- C.K. Sharma (1990) Modern Library System
- Koneru, I. (2004), "E-information service through consortia", in Rao, N.L. (Ed.), Proceedings of the National Seminar on Library Consortia, 22-23 March, Hyderabad, India, pp. 27-37.
- Kumbar (T S). Library consortia: a conceptual overview. *http://*

www.alibnet.org/ Dr.T.S.Kumbhar.pdf (visited on 16.3.2007).

- Kumbar, M.F. (2004), "Consortia for management of college libraries in the e-publishing era: a proposal", Proceedings of the 6th MANLIBNET National Convention, Janakpuri, New Delhi.
- Kumbar, T. S. (2007) Library Consortia : a conceptual overview.
- Mahajan, P. (2005), "Academic libraries in India: a present-day scenario", Library Philosophy and Practice, Vol. 8 No. 1, pp.1-4.
- Mohd. Sohail (2011) Use of E-resources and UGC. Info net consortium by the teachers and research scholars in Aligarh Muslim University.
- Shachaf (Penina) 2003 nationwide library consortia lifecycle.
- UGC (2006) Annual Report of University Grant Commission, Library Consortia in the world.
- Yernagula & Kelkar (2005) Library Consortia: Benefits and Models of E-journals Consortia.

6

Strengthening Academic Libraries through Library Consortium: An Approach

Sunil Tyagi

ABSTRACT

The creation and development of new academic library consortia - or the "resurgence of library consortia" - has characterized the last 10 years, involving the libraries worldwide. The development of library consortia happens in a very complex phase of the academic library life, as: "the decisions libraries face are becoming more complex, the risks are greater, and the resources – both human and fiscal – are becoming scarcer". Library consortia development processes were examined from an ecological approach, combining historical perspective, dynamic developmental approach, and social structure, stressing the issues of permeable boundaries in library consortia and the manifestation of inter-organization relationships. This study aims to explore the concept, issues and facilities offered by the library consortium and shows how the library consortium is making resources available among the member libraries. It believes that establishment of academic library consortium will make academic libraries more productive and effective to their user community.

INTRODUCTION

Academic libraries are at the crossroads of dramatic change, and the pressure to adapt is increasing due to the consequences of the severe economic downturn. Major concerns include ongoing budget stagnation and/or budget cuts and the need to acquire serials materials whose costs rise annually at unsustainable rates. In order to save money and streamline operations, taking advantage of consortial arrangements to eliminate redundant activities among member libraries seems more significant than ever. Fortunately, new Internet-based technologies make collaboration more possible than ever before. Library consortia are uniquely positioned to help their member libraries in this collaborative process.

Electronic publishing and telecommunication have enabled library consortia to expand both in number and functions over the last decade. Library consortium development is rooted in the history of library cooperative efforts and is now also driven by the need to provide remote users with licensed access to electronic resources. Library consortia promote new standards that are helping libraries better manage their usage statistics with Project Counter and SUSHI to standardize the transmission of statistics. Consortia are also promoting the utilization of new standards such as ONIX-PL for the XML transmission of licenses to ease the burden of license management and bring some order to the chaos of electronic resource management.

Library consortia play an important role as promoters of new paradigms. Consortia Excel at promoting collaboration and the most effective library consortia will move beyond being buying clubs for electronic resources and provide significant value in other ways. They might help libraries create institutional repositories, and promote the new models for new forms of publication that move beyond the old print model. Consortia also help libraries collaborate in other ways, including support for digitization and preservation projects and union catalogs for patron-initiated borrowing to reduce ILL costs and to create opportunities for cooperative collection development.

Library consortia play a major role in the world of academic libraries and have been particularly influential in the following areas: -

- Acquisition of electronic resources, with a particular emphasis on pricing and price models;
- Negotiation as a skill to be mastered by librarians responsible for the acquisition of library resources;
- Licensing terms and conditions that are acceptable in the higher education environment;
- The preservation and archiving of electronic journa! and other e-resource information;
- The importance of usage statistics as a metric for the value of acquired information;
- Developing collaborative models of print resource sharing;
- Streamlining and consolidating technical services through a centralized (i.e. union) catalog;
- Professional development and training;
- Collaborative digitization projects, including setting standards for best practices and providing training therein; and
- For those consortia which are statewide or government funded, providing advocacy for libraries and library funding.

HISTORICAL BACKGROUNDS

Cooperation and resource sharing : Cooperation between academic libraries has always been at the basis of library activities. Both Bostick and Alexander report how this concept is strongly rooted in the US tradition, emphasizing how since 1880 this topic has been alive in professional literature (Alexander 2000, Bostick 2001). Many cooperative programs were developed during the past century (Weber 1976); cultural reasons and traditions caused its development particularly in the US area, where many cooperative activities were linked to the Library of Congress (distribution of bibliographic card catalogues; publication of LC subject headings), and where already in 1933 one of the still now most alive academic library consortia arose, the Triangle Research Libraries Network (Bostick 2000).

During the eighties the concept of cooperation, that is "how [libraries] can achieve their objective better by working together" (Sewell 1981) has shifted towards the resource sharing concept. Resource sharing is a richer term, which encompasses also the strategic aspect to link users with the required information or material:

> "The new term appears ... to assume a range of physical, intellectual and conceptual resources on the one hand and a body of people on the other, and covers the activities involved in organizing the one into a set of optimum relationships to meet the needs of the other" (Sewell 1981). The concepts of cooperation and resource sharing have underpinned interlibrary loan arrangements, cooperative acquisition policies within groups of libraries, shared cataloguing projects, also through the organization and administration of national and international programs (Smith 1993). Nowadays the term "resource sharing" best describes also cooperative efforts in managing e-resources (Evans 2002a).

From library cooperation to library consortia : In analyzing the US situation as regards the history of library cooperative initiatives, James Kopp emphasizes the passage from the "cooperation" phase to the "consortium" phase and observes how the term "consortium" begins to appear in the library literature during the 1950s and the 1960s, period in which in the US most of the academic library consortia were created (Kopp 1998).

The debate on the term "consortium" in library science literature is rich. As Giordano points out, the term encompasses a great number of cooperative activities and experiences depending on the contexts and times in which they grew (Giordano 2003). In trying to motivate the use of the term, Reinhardt points out how in Germany "consortium", which originally was linked mainly to legal context, was derived from an Anglo-American background and now assumes a broader meaning than it had, meaning more "partnership", "association" and referring to joint actions of libraries (Reinhardt and Boekhorts 2001) .

The origins and development of library consortia : Kopp, founding his investigation on a series of studies, in particular Patrick's Guidelines for library cooperation: development of academic library consortia (Patrick 1972), stresses how during the 1960s the first important projects in library automations developed, and how consortia supported their activities sharing expertise in this field. Moreover, he reports how, according the Guidelines, the 125 US consortia analyzed can be grouped in four main categories (Kopp 1998):

- Large consortia primarily concerned with computerized large scale technical processing;
- Small consortia concerned with user services and everyday problems;
- Limited-purpose consortia cooperating with respect to limited special subject areas;
- Limited-purpose consortia concerned primarily with interlibrary loan or reference network operations.

As Bostick points out, in this period cooperation library focuses more on access than on ownership to materials (Bostick 2001). Consortia increase rapidly until the 1970s, focusing their activity in:

- Shared acquisition plans;
- Resource sharing (interlibrary loan, document delivery);
- Cost reduction.

But their activity shrinks between 1970s and 1980s, when a new phenomenon occurs: the development of "mega consortia" such as OCLC and RLG, which offer to participating libraries bibliographic utilities: they are catalogue card production and interlibrary loan activities, but, most important and innovative, machine-readable records to be loaded into local systems.

Moreover, during the 1980s libraries concentrate their energies in implementing local integrated library systems and pioneering the use of technology, such as CD-ROMs installed in local networks, thus giving lower priority to consortial activities (Kopp 1998).

In Europe, with the exception of few countries with strong interlibrary cooperation traditions, mostly of the northern area, cooperative activities among libraries begin to bring shape during the seventies and are mainly based on the automation of catalogues processes. The phenomenon of the rise of library academic consortia is relatively new: the same specialised literature pays particular attention to its development in Europe starting from 1998: Spain: (Barrionuevo 2000), Catalonia: (Anglada and Comellas 2000), France (Berard 2001; Chartron 2001; Schmitt 2001), Greece (Xenidou-Dervou 2001; Xenidou-Dervou 2003); UK (Friend 1999; Auckland 2000; Ball and Pye 2000; Bley 2000), Finland (Hakli 2000), Germany (Reinhardt and Boekhorts 2001), Finland (Hakli 2000), Poland (Nikisch 2002), Netherlands (Klugkist 2001), Switzerland (Neubauer and Piguet 2001).

The phenomenon involves even most of the Italian academic libraries, and it assumes different attitudes depending on the different contexts (Giordano 2000; Giordano 2002). As in the other European countries, during these years the first interesting cooperative initiatives are linked to the automation of public library catalogues, through a national automation program, the "Servizio Bibliotecario Nazionale"; to this program most of the academic libraries adhere after the promulgation of Act 168/89, with which the MURST (Ministero dell'Università e della Ricerca Scientifica) is constituted and the financial and administrative autonomy of the University are established (Galluzzi 2001); this new context creates the premises for the organization of the academic library systems from which at the end of the nineties some of the academic library consortial alliances find the basis (e.g. the consortial groups CIPE and CIBER).

LIBRARY CONSORTIA

The factors that have evolved library consortium phenomenon more significant in the second half of nineties are the discovery of mutual interests of publishers and libraries.

A consortium is "an agreement, combination, or group (as of companies) formed to undertake an enterprise beyond the resources of any one member" (Merriam Webster Dictionary), and it "usually involves horizontal collaboration among direct competitors".

A library consortium is a collective activity to provide shared expertise, access to new electronic and print resources, professional development, and new sources of funds. The library consortia could be defined also as the "coming together libraries to achieve a common goal that is beyond what an individual library could achieve on its own".

Library consortia vary in their type, goals, structure, membership, and funding (Woodsworth 1991). A consortium may be a formal or informal agreement between libraries based on a common principle. For example, a consortium may be based on library type – academic, medical, or public. A regional consortium may be based on a geographical principle. A statewide or nationwide consortium may incorporate all its libraries, government-funded and those in private institutions.

Although library consortia form to achieve shared goals, the main goals of cooperation vary. One of the most common goals is resource sharing through union catalogue and interlibrary loan agreements. Electronic resources licensing is another goal, aiming to reduce costs per unit through formation of purchasing consortia.

EVOLUTION OF CONSORTIUM

From an evolutionary stand point, the consortium broadly may be defined as an evolutionary form of cooperation among library/information centre to meet the challenge of constantly declining information resource base with R&D and academic organization. With information resource-base of libraries shrinking particularly in developing countries owing to cost escalation of information resources, library consortia makes it possible to expand information resources through an economically collaborative approach.

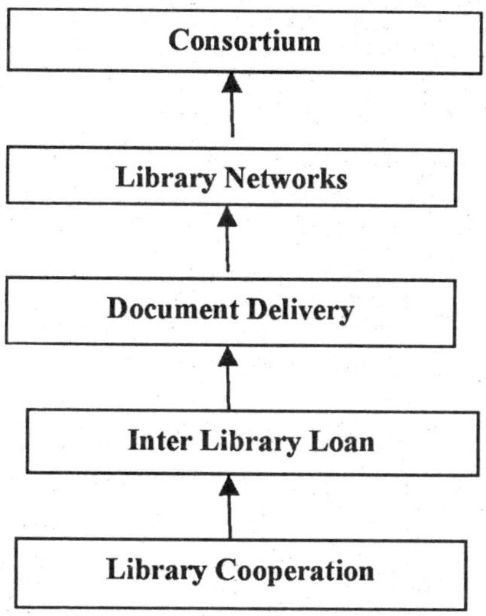

Fig. 1. Evolution of Library Consortium

ECOLOGICAL APPROACH TO CONSORTIA

The ecological approach to library consortia development is influenced by several ecological theories, such as ecological psychology at the individual level (Barker 1968, Bronfenbrenner 1979 and Wicker 1979) and at the group level (Sundstrom, DeMuese and Futrell 1990). In this approach, a consortium is perceived as an organism, and these basic assumptions are made (Wicker 1979):

- A consortium organism cannot be considered to exist or act in isolation. Every consortium is linked with other organisms in a complex network of relationships;
- A consortium organism is affected by internal forces, such as leadership, as well as by external forces of other organisms, such as competitors and customers;
- A consortium adapts to achieve harmonious working relationships in its environment, distinguishing between what is appropriate to its needs and what is not.

ISSUES RELATED TO LIBRARY CONSORTIUM

Various factors to be taken for an effective functioning of a successful consortium. The major issues of consortia approaches are:

- Selecting a coordinating agency to deal on behalf of the entire group of participants and executing and monitoring the work;
- Sources of funding to meet the subscription cost;
- Identifying and negotiating the potential publishers / vendors or aggregators to provide access under consortia purchase;
- Source of funding to meet the subscription cost;
- Legal issues involved in contracts and usage of material within the consortia;
- Identification of libraries interested in participating and

agreeing on common terms and conditions;

- Identifying the necessary infrastructure for electronic access to resources;
- Issues related to backup and archival of database;
- Documentation and training to staff.

Last but not least, designing and launching a library consortium should be long run substance and robust models towards achieving the above goals.

Importance of library consortium in the information society Access to resources is now considered more important than the collection building. The consortium facilities the libraries to get the benefit of wider access to electronic resources at affordable cost and at the best terms of licenses. A consortium, with the collective strength of resources of various institutions available to it, is in a better position to resolve the problems of managing, organizing and archiving the electronic resources (Bedi & Sharma, 2008).

The phenomenon of information revolution has posed several problems and this has far reaching implications in the society. The nation or society which possesses more information will lead the world. This is also true in case of individuals. The persons have more information will guide a group or society and they will be superior to others. This power of information has induced the nations and individuals to acquire and control more and more quantities of information. But in this race, the poor nations, societies, institutions or individuals will be back as compared to the others. This has created a big gap in the availability and use of information. The library consortia can be an ideal solution in this context. Perhaps the most important advantages of library consortia would be their enhanced ability to serve the society by giving better library services.

The advantages of library consortia may be summarized as following:

1. To leverage resources by sharing existing resources or collection though virtual union catalogue and sharing of:
   - Collections and collaborating on collection development; each library is able to contribute unique titles to the consortium – avoid duplication
   - Electronic resources including the creation of digital collections-sharing among consortium members need not be just in terms of licensing products- it can also include sharing in the creation of digital collections.
   - Storage of resources– Space is an issue for many libraries
   - Sharing the archiving of resources
   - Sharing staff expertise- a consortium provides opportunities for staff members to develop new skills and interact with a varsity of people who would not have had the opportunity to meet otherwise
   - Sharing risk- by sharing risk, members of a consortium can undertake projects that are larger than one institution can safely take on its own.
   - This form of cooperation enables the consortia libraries to borrow books, periodicals, articles, and scientific journals, which are not available locally.
   - Electronic access enables the user initiate their own search of remote catalogues and make requests for information.
   - Sharing catalogues-to enable user's greater access to larger collection
   - CD-ROM union catalogue that provides access to books, videos and recording for each institution.
   - Union List of Serials that provides access to the journal holdings of all member libraries.
2. To reduce the cost of library operations by obtaining a group purchased price for information product.

3. To bring pressure on, providers especially publishers to reduce the rate of rise in the cost of purchasing information.

Thus, library consortium are commonly formed to negotiate joint purchases (e.g. of equipment, software, books, library materials and licensed electronic databases and resources) and to share resources.

INDIAN LIBRARY CONSORTIA SCENARIO

Library consortium is a group of two or more libraries which have agreed to co-operate with one another in order to fulfill certain similar needs, usually resource sharing. It usually, refers to co-operation, Co-ordination and collaboration between, and amongst libraries for the purpose of sharing information. Consortia are basically, evolving a form of cooperation among the libraries which come together to share resources electronically. It has gained momentum even in developing countries like India.

Some of the successful library consortia setup so far in India is:

- UGC- INFONET E-Journal consortium. *http://www.ugc.ac.in/* new_initiatives /infonet.html
- Indian National Digital Library in Engineering Sciences and Technology (INDEST) Consortium. http://www.paniit.iitd.ac.in/indest
- Inter University Centers (IUC-DAEF Consortia) (Atomic Energy)
- http://brahma.iuc.res.in/-iuc_cc/iuc_loc.html
- Health Sciences Library and Information Network (HELINET)
- http://www.rguhs.ac.in/hn/ne whell.html
- Forum for Resource Sharing in Astronomy and Astrophysics (FORSA)
- http://www.iiap.res.in/library/forsa.html
- Council of Scientific and Industrial Research
- (CSIR e-journal consortium) http://www.niscair.res.in

- Apart from the mentioned consortia, there have been efforts to setup similar kind of consortia by ICAR, ICMR, ICSSR and other governmental agencies to provide and access to e-resources. Among the above all consortia, UGC-INFONET and INDEST–AICTE Consortium are proving to be a boon for the academic users. These two major initiatives have come to the rescue of academic libraries so that they can cater to the needs of academic depending upon them. These revolutionary steps are providing scholarly resources including peer reviewed journals, databases, abstracts, proceedings etc. These efforts will definitely boost the higher education system of our country.

UGC-Infonet: UGC-Infonet E-Journals consortium initiative was undertaken by the UGC to facilitate free access to scholarly e-journals and databases in all fields and disciplines by the research and academic community across the country through joint partnership of UGC, INFLIBNET and ERNET. This includes interlinking Universities and Colleges in the country electronically with a view to achieving maximum efficiency through Internet enabled teaching, learning and governance. All universities and colleges who are under the purview of UGC have been provided UGC-INFONET Connectivity and access to scholarly e-Journals and Databases. More than 4,500 full text e-journals are available now. As of May 2006, 122 universities are accessing resources from the programme. The access is based on IP range. This effort has had a noticeable impact on the research and academic community.

- Biological Abstracts (BA) http://webspris3.silverplatttter.com/cgi-bin/erl.cgi
- Cambridge University Press Journals http://journals.cambridge.org
- Encyclopedia Britannica http://searcheb.com/
- Institute of Physics (IOP) http://www.iop.org
- JSTOR http://www.jstor.org
- Nature http://www.aip.org

- Project muse journals http://muse.jhu.edu/journals/
- Royal Society of Chemistry http://www.rsc.org/is/journals/jl.htm
- Science Online http://www.sciencemag.org/
- SciFinder Scholar http://www.aip.org

INDEST- AICTE Consortium: The "Indian National Digital Library in Engineering Sciences and Technology (INDEST) Consortium" was set-up in 2003 by The Ministry of Human Resources Development (MHRD). 38 centrally funded Govt. institutions including IITs, Sc, NITs and some other institutions are the core members of the INDESTAICTE Consortium. The Ministry provides funds required for providing access to electronic resources to the core members through the consortium headquarters set-up at the IIT Delhi. The total no. of members through the consortium has now grown to 483 (including 38 IITs, IISc, NITs and other institutes; 63 members from AICTE; 99 self supported Engineering colleges and institutes and 285 institutions have recently joined under the new scheme). The consortium subscribes to over 6500 electronic journals from a number of publishers and aggregators.

E-RESOURCES AVAILABLE THROUGH THE INDESTAICTE CONSORTIUM

- ABI / Inform Complete http://www.il.proquest.com/pqdaeto
- ACM Digital Library http://portal.acm.org/portal.cfm
- American Society of Civil Engineers Online Journals http://www.asme.org/pubs/journals/
- American Society of Mechanical Engineers Journals http://www.asme.org/pubs/journals/
- ASTM International Standard and Journals Standards: http://enterprise.astm.org Journals: http://journalsip.astm.org
- Capitaline http://www.capitaline.com/

- DEL www.digitalengineeringlibrary.com
- Ei Compendex Plus www.engineeringvillage2.org/
- Engineering Science Data Unit (ESDU) www.esdu.com
- Global Market Information Database (GMID) http://www.euromonitor.com/gmid/
- INSPEC on el Village http:www.engineeringvillage2.org//
- IEEE/IEE Electronic Library Online (IEL) http://ieeexplore.ieee.org
- Indian Standards MathSciNet http://www.ams.org/mathscinet
- Nature http://www.npg.nature.com/libraries
- Proquest Science Journals http://www.il.proquest.com/pqdaeto
- Science Direct http://www.sciencedirect.com
- Springer Link http://www.springerlink.com

Consortia for IIMs: Six Indian Institutes Management have formed a consortium and jointly approached the publishers of e-journals and databases in the area of Management, Social and Behavioral science source. They have been giving IP enabled access to e-journals – Elsevier (247 titles), Blackwell (268 titles), Kluwer (33 titles), Wiley (3 titles). Apart from 25 titles free against print subscription, 2300 titles as a part of EBSCO databases and 800 titles as a part of ABI Inform database have been made available to users of IIM libraries electronically.

The usual terms like maintenance of print subscription with the identified base year, 10-15% surcharge over and above print subscription did apply to this consortium. They also provide access to 13 bibliographic databases selectively to different IIMs depending upon their subscription to the titles like ABI Inform, EBSCO, ECONLIT, GMID, Psycinfo, Sociofile etc. IIM Bangalore, alone claims the annual savings of Rs. 16.42 lakhs for accessing bibliographic databases. IIM consortia did not find any difficulties dealing with the publishers as they were able to make payment directly to the publishers individually.

CSIR Consortia: The Council of Scientific and Industrial Research has 40 national laboratories carrying out R&D work in the areas of Engineering, Biological, Chemical, Physical, Environmental and Information Sciences. Put together these laboratories subscribe to about 3100 unique titles by spending about Rs. 25 crores. More than US $ 1.3 million is spent on Elsevier titles alone. Based on the recommendation of the task force and the negotiation committee appointed by CSIR all 1200 Elsevier e-journals have been made available to all 40 laboratories since July 2002. The funding being from single source, CSIR consortia did not face much difficulty to make the payment. However there was a delay in signing the agreement in sorting out the problems concerned to access rights, archiving, fixing the base year etc. Few laboratories like NAL, NCL, IMTECH, NIO, RRLT have been providing access to Elsevier titles since quite some time. The negotiations with other publishers like Kluwer (550 titles) and Springer (450 titles) is in the advanced stage. Attempts have been made to make available the J-Gate Custom Contents for Consortia (JCCC) to all laboratories.

FORSA: The Forum for Resource Sharing in Astronomy and Astrophysics, the consortia of Raman Research Institute, Indian Institute of Astrophysics, Tata Institute of Fundamental Research, Inter University Center for Astronomy and Astrophysics, National Center for Radio Astrophysics and Physical Research Laboratories has given access to 25 e-Journals of Kluwer to their users with the payment of 12.5% over and above the print subscription. This consortium has successfully negotiated with publishers of Nature to provide access to its e-version at a price of almost 1/3 of the list price.

ICICI Knowledge Park, Hyderabad: ICICI Knowledge Park at Hyderabad has signed an agreement with Informatics India Ltd to provide access to J-Gate Custom Contents for Consortia service to four Hyderabad based and one Pune based R&D institutions. Initially this service is free for the members with the objective of making it self-sustaining in the later stage.

ISRO Initiatives: The resource sharing initiative taken by ISRO libraries by avoiding duplicate subscription to bibliographic databases is expected to result in savings of Rs. 41 lakhs per year. Further, the proposed cancellation of duplicate journal titles by its centers is likely to save the surplus amount that could be used to provide access to e-journals for the benefit of the all centers. A move is there to form formal consortia for providing access to e-journals and also J-Gate Custom Contents for Consortia.

CONCLUSION

The development of library consortia has reinforced in academic libraries the spirit of cooperation that is essential in all the library activities, particularly in this period of challenges due to information age and new technologies. This spirit involves for the first time all the stakeholders, who are all concerned owing to the change, but also understand the potentials of the new context, and are trying together to find new models to work together. Disadvantages and difficulties emerge from the different worlds, but the consortial form chosen by academic libraries will help all parts to face the new challenges; it will last in time, owing to the benefits prevailing disadvantages. The explosion of information and the access to e-resources has created new expectations in patrons, which libraries attempt to satisfy creating cooperative alliances that let them share solutions and expertise. It is necessary to find new ways to interpret user needs, which have to remain the main focus of libraries.

Today libraries have to face change management, and they are seeking tools to cope with it, developing strategic alliances with other libraries. Cooperation seems to be the key for libraries to survive. Cooperation efforts vary, depending on geographic areas and on different cultural traditions, but they seem present throughout the world: on one side, nations with libraries used to strong practice in cooperation and sharing have seen a flourishing of new cooperative initiatives and formal consortia; on the other side, nations where this collaborative practice was not within its culture have received a boast towards it.

Consortia are facing new and different challenges. In addition to the traditional goals for resource-sharing and group purchases, they are look at other projects. Consortia can be a great benefit to member libraries in publicizing their collections and services, as well as the consortium's work. Consortia are increasingly involved in political action.

REFERENCES

- Alexander, A. W. (2000). Toward "the perfection of work": library consortia in the digital age. Journal of Library Administration, 28(2), pp.1 – 14.
- Allen, B. M. and Hirshon, A. (1998). Hanging together to avoid hanging separately: opportunities for academic libraries and consortia. Information Technology and Libraries, 17(1), pp. 36-44.
- Ashcroft, L. (2002). Issues in developing, managing and marketing electronic journals collections. Collection Building, 21(4).
- Ashcroft, L. and Langdon, C. (1999). Electronic journals and university library collections. Collection Building, 18(3), pp.105 – 113.
- Ball, D. and Pye, J. (2000). Library purchasing consortia: the UK periodicals supply market. Learned Publishing, 13(1), pp.25 – 35.
- Ball, D. and Wright, S. (2000). Procuring electronic information: new business models in the context of the supply chain. Library Consortium Management, 2(7), pp.145 – 158.
- Barker, R.G. 1968. Ecological psychology: Concepts and methods for studying the environment of human behavior. Stanford, California: Stanford University Press.
- Barrionuevo, M. D. (2000). New strategies in library services organization: consortia university libraries in Spain. Information technology and libraries, 19(2), pp. 96 – 102.
- Berard, R. (2001). Les consortia in France. Liber Quarterly : the Journal of European Research Libraries, 11, pp.60 – 66.
- Bley, R. (2000). NESLI: a successful national consortium. Library Consortium Management, 2(1), pp.18 – 28.
- Bostick, S. L. (2001). The history and development of academic library consortia in the United States: an overview. The Journal of Academic Librarianship, 27(2), pp.128-30.

- Bronfenbrenner, U. 1979. The ecology of human development: Experiments by nature and design. Cambridge, Massachusetts: Harvard University Press.
- Chartron, G. (2001). Electronic resources and documentary consortia: a survey of French scientific institutions. Journal of Librarianship and Information Science, 33(2), pp.85-97.
- Cox, J. (2000). Developing model licenses for electronic resources: cooperation in a competitive world. Library Consortium Management, 2(1), pp.8 – 17.
- Cox, J. (2003). Vendors: extinction or reincarnation? Serials, 16(2), pp.141 – 144.
- Electronic Publishing, 6(2),
- Evans, G. E. (2002a). Management issues of co-operative ventures and consortia in the USA. Part one. Library management, 23(4/5), pp. 213 – 226.
- Evans, G. E. (2002b). Management issues of consortia. Part two. Library Management, 23(6/7), pp. 275- 286.
- Fogg, H. (2001). A review of subscription agency services to law firm libraries: investigating current and future service relationships. Serials, 14(1), pp.57 – 62.
- Friend, F. J. (2001). New intermediaries, or the old intermediaries in a new guise? Serials, 14(1), pp.41- 45.
- Friend, F. J. (2003). Big Deal: good deal? Or is there a better deal? Learned Publishing, 16(2), pp.153-5.
- Giordano, T. (2000). Digital resource sharing and library consortia in Italy. Information Technology and Libraries, 19(2).
- Giordano, T. (2002). Library co-operation on ICT in Italy: an overview. Program, 36(3), pp.144 -151.
- Giordano, T. (2003). Library consortia in western Europe. Encyclopedia of library and information science. New York pp.1613 - 1619.
- Goodman, D. (2000). Where's the fiscal sense? Library journal, 15(June), pp.48 – 49.
- Hakli, E. (2000). Libraries in Finland establish consortia. Liber Quarterly : the Journal of European Research Libraries, 11(1), pp.53 – 59.
- Helmer, J. F. (1999). Epidemiology of the consortial spore. Information Technology and Libraries, 18(3), pp.119 – 120.
- Hirshon, A. (1999). Libraries, consortia, and change management. The Journal Of Academic Librarianship, 25(2), pp.124-126.

- Hunter, K. (1999). Consortia and publishers: a comment. Library Consortium Management, 1(1/2), pp.19 – 22.
- Klugkist, A. C. (2001). Consortium building and licensing by University libraries in the Netherlands. Liber Quarterly : the Journal of European Research Libraries, 11, pp.80 – 86.
- Kohl, D. (2003). Consortial licensing vs. tradition: breaking up is hard to do. Learned Publishing, 16(1), pp.47-53.
- Kopp, J. J. (1998). Library consortia and information technology: the past, the present, the promise. Information Technology and Libraries, 17(1), pp.7-12.
- Landesman, M. and J. Van Reenen (2000). Consortia vs reform: creating congruence. Journal Of
- Morgan, E. L. (1998). Resource sharing and consortia, or, becoming a 600-pound gorilla. Computers in Libraries, 18(4), pp.40-1.
- Neubauer, W. and A. Piguet (2001). The long road to becoming a 'Consortium of Swiss university libraries'. Liber Quarterly : the Journal of European Research Libraries, 11(1), pp. 87-97.
- Okerson, A. (1996). Crazy about consortia? (Some reflections on starting and belonging to one). Meet your new customer: the consortium! Special seminar of the National Federation of Abstractind and Indexing Services (NFAIS), Philadelphia, September 20, 1996.
- Oliver, M. (2000). SPARC: an alternative lifestyle for academic libraries. Collection Management, 25(2), pp.37-49.
- Peters, T. A. (2001). What's the big deal? The Journal Of Academic Librarianship, 27(4), pp.302 – 304.
- Peters, T. A. (2003). Graduated consortial memberships and rogue facilitators. The Journal of Academic Librarianship, 29(4), pp.254 – 256.
- Potter, W. G. (1997). Recent trends in statewide academic library consortia. Library Trends, 45(3), pp.416-34.
- Prior, A. (2001). Acquiring and accessing serials information: the electronic intermediary. Interlending & Document Supply, 29(2), pp. 62 – 68.
- Prosser, D. C. (2004). Scholarly communication in the 21st century: the impact of new technologies and models. Serials, 16(2).
- Reinhardt, W. and P. T. Boekhorts (2001). Library consortia in Germany. Liber Quarterly : the Journal of European Research Libraries, 11 (1), pp. 67 – 79.
- Rowse, M. (2003). The consortium site license: a sustainable model? Libri, 53(1), pp.1-10.
- Sanville, T. (1999). Use levels and new models for consortial purchasing

of electronic journals. Library Consortium Management, 1(3/4), pp.47 – 58.

- Scigliano, M. (2002). Consortium purchases: case study for a cost-benefit analysis. The Journal Of Academic Librarianship, 28(6), pp.393-9.
- Shachaf, P. (2003). Nationwide library consortia life cycle. Libri, 53(2), pp.94 – 102.
- Sloan, B. (2000). Understanding consortia better: what vendors can learn. Library Journal, 15(March), pp.57 – 58
- Smith, M. (1993). "Resource sharing". World encyclopedia of library and information science. Chicago, ALA, pp.715 - 718.
- Stern, D. (2003). Comparing consortial and differential pricing models. Bottom Line, 16(4), pp.154-156.
- Thornton, G. (2000). Impact of electronic resources on collection development, the roles of librarians, and library consortia. Library Trends, 48(4), pp.842 – 856.
- Weber, D. C. (1976). A century of cooperative programs among academic libraries. College and Research Libraries, pp.205- 221
- Wicker, AW. 1979. An introduction to ecological psychology. Belmont, CA: Wadsworth, Inc.
- Wise, A. (2003). Are digital library resources useful for learners and researchers? Serials, 16(1), pp. 23- 26.
- Woodsworth, A. 1991. Library cooperation and networks. N.Y.: Neal-Schuman Publishers.
- www.library.yale.edu/~okerson/crazy.html
- Xenidou-Dervou, C. (2001). Consortial journal licensing: experiences of Greek academic libraries. Interlending and Document Supply, 29(3), pp.120-5.
- Xenidou-Dervou, C. (2003). Moving from print to electronic: a survival guide for Greek academic libraries. Serials, 16(2), pp.145-152.

7

Consortial Approach as Resource Sharing in Higher Education Libraries: An Overview

Dr. Kishore Kumar Sarmah

ABSTRACT

Resource Sharing has been one of the main principles for supporting the library service, but it has changed over the years. The rapid progress of information technology now tries to satisfy the information needs of the users in diverse manner. The expression of information and its explosion has made the libraries to adopt new philosophies and technologies for collection and development, reduce the cost of information and to eliminate duplicity. Not a single library can boast itself of being self sufficient to meet the information needs of the users from its stock to the fullest extent. To overcome this problem, libraries started library cooperation through networks, document delivery services and inter library loan. Library consortia have now come into existence as a more accepted system for sharing of resources. Libraries in consortia have discovered that as a group they have a combined set of information resources which helps them to improve the quality of services offered. There are several international efforts for library consortia and the common examples for consortia in higher education libraries are CALIS, ThaiLIS, GAELIC, RUSLANet, SANLIC, HEAL-Link, ICOLC etc. Some special library and Information centre like the Indian institute of Astrophysics, Physical Research Laboratory, Council of Scientific and Industrial Research, National Medical Library etc have established consortia to share electronic access to journal literature. Common examples are the UGC-INFONET, CSIR, ICMR E-Consortia, INDEST, HELNET and their like. However some barriers such as poor technological and communication infrastructure, inadequate finances can be seen to be the limitations of consortia activities in the developing countries like India.

Keywords: Resource Sharing, Library Cooperation, Consortia, UGC-INFONET, INDEST

INTRODUCTION

The higher education system in India is large and complex occupying the third (3) place behind China and The USA but all education institutions especially the universities face acute shortage of funds to subscribe to international journals. It is estimated that a typical university library subscribes to less than 200 international journals and some of them do not subscribe to any international journals at all. Most colleges do not have financial resources to subscribe to international journals; their subscription list encloses few Indian journals and popular magazines. However, it should be kept in mind that academic and socio economic development is dependent on research which is dependent on the availability of information resources. The rapid progress of IT through R&D activities all over the world tries to satisfy the information needs of the human beings in diverse manner. The explosion of information has urged the libraries to adopt new philosophies and technologies for collection development and reduce the cost of information. Today most of the libraries are faced with economic problems, especially the developing countries to collect all the newly generated information to satisfy the needs of the users. The main task of the librarian is to adjust the input resources with the output by searching various alternatives. To overcome the problem, libraries started cooperation through library networks, document delivery; inter-library loans etc. library consortium has now come into existence as a system of resource sharing among the libraries.

RESOURCE SHARING AND NETWORKING

The term Resource applies to a thing or action to which one resorts to in times of need and sharing indicates contributing that thing to help others. Therefore, resource sharing refers to implying a partnership where each member has something to contribute and each willing to make it available in times of need. Resource sharing is an integral part of library service but in the past it was limited to inter library loan system but now with the development of information technology (IT) it has become easier. Library cooperation and Resource sharing activities can take place in several forms such as interlibrary loan, sharing of expertise, resource and facilities, exchange of publication and reprographic services. The implementation of resource sharing largely depends on library networking which gives a wider access to information. It is a form of arrangement that links a group of organization who has agreed to work together and share resources. Information networking entails the sharing of resources so that information needs of both the parties are met. The benefits of such sharing process results in-

i. Easy access to information materials and improving the quality of service.

ii. Increasing the cost benefit per substance and guaranting local storage of information acquired for continuous use by present and future users

iii. Enables the cooperating institutions to extend the limited resources and promote the rational use of funds

iv. Developing technical capabilities of the staff in operating and using electronic publication databases resulting in better working atmosphere between the staff and the cooperating libraries.

v. Avoid unnecessary duplication and reduces the number of places that one needs to go for services.

When resource sharing is agreed by various institutions following aspects must be kept in mind- like identifying the libraries interested in participating and agreeing to the terms and conditions, sources of funds and identifying the necessary infrastructure for electronic access to resources and selection of database to be hosted at one place followed by training of the staff.

Library cooperation for sharing of resources started a long time ago, at present the more accepted system of resource sharing is the Library Consortia which is one of the many ways of maintaining cooperation and coordinating among the libraries in recent years.

LIBRARY CONSORTIA: THE EVOLUTION OF COOPERATION

Consortium is a Latin word, meaning partnership, association or societies and derives from censors 'partner', itself from con- 'together' and sors 'fate', meaning owner of means or comrade. In simple words it is a resource sharing organization formed by libraries. According to US Federal Communications Commission, "A library consortium is any local, regional or national cooperative association of libraries that provides for the systematic and effective coordination of the resources of schools, public, academic and special libraries and information centres, for improving services to the clientele of such libraries".

It is not a new concept, but no particular date can be cited as the beginning point of library consortium. There are instances of several libraries coming together voluntarily for the mutual benefit of the users. Early examples from the late 1960s include the development of the Ohio College Libraries Centre (OCLC) as a regional computer system for 54 Ohio College libraries to share their resources and to reduce their costs. However, consortia became common in the 1980s. The driving forces for collaboration among the libraries in higher education is due to the number of publication, rise in the cost of these publications, decline in the budgets and increasing information needs of the user community.

Historically, the common form of library cooperation was the sharing of Union Catalogue, information collection development in the US. Later other countries ventured into this cooperative effort. In Europe, with the existence of few countries with strong inter library cooperation traditions, cooperative activities among libraries began to take place during the 70s and are mainly based on the automation of cataloguing process. The development of web in the 1990s imposed new challenges for libraries. Electronic publishing brought many possibilities for resource sharing and consortia activities increased with the advancement of ICT.

The consortia may be formed from on a local, regional, national or international basis; on a functional format or on a subject basis. The salient features for library consortium are:-

- It reduces the problem faced by the libraries in regard to various services to the users
- It helps to meet the information need of the people and is in a position to cope with various form of knowledge both printed and non-printed
- It collects all the documents published at the international and national levels and helps in overcoming the language barrier

ADVANTAGES AND DISADVANTAGES OF LIBRARY CONSORTIA

The role of consortia has increased in the digital environment and for many years the libraries have been working together in various ways such as in document delivery, printed boos and journal acquisition and shared storage of materials. Development in technology have opened a wide range of activities and enabled the libraries to acquire and develop new services. However, both advantages and disadvantages can be seen all the type of consortia and some of them have been given below:-

A. Advantages of library consortia:

- Reduces the manpower by avoiding duplication of works thereby, reducing the cost of storage
- Introduce and discharge new and effective services on time
- Increases the quality of services with possible ability to attract foreign investment
- Enhance online search facilities and site wide access for all involved
- Saves money on the allocation of budget by perfect planning and promotes the rational use of funds
- Provides each institution with the ability to share resources without sacrificing their individuality
- It provides opportunities for staff members to develop new sills and interact with a varsity of people who would not have had the opportunities to meet otherwise.
- To bring pressure on the providers especially on the publishers to reduce the rate on the cost of purchasing information

B. Disadvantages of library consortia:

- Consortia requires a high initial investment in licenses and ICT
- Libraries are not prepared to cash in the savings offered by not handling print edition of the journals
- Copyright problem is always there
- Requires well-trained staff for handling the electronic document and devices
- Insufficient bandwidth and unreliable telecommunication links

- Lack of archiving and back files availability
- Many libraries are reluctant to enter consortia agreements especially where publishers impose payments for off-consortia delivery of document
- Enforcement of licensing agreement is more difficult
- Consortial collaboration and efforts takes a longer period of time and have a high rate of failure

Some Library Consortium at the International and National level

International Level : Library consortia is the outcome of the desire for resource sharing which is due to high cost of information resource, decreasing budget and inadequate storage area and competent staff. There are several international efforts for library consortia and some of them are:-

- ThaiLIS- a national resource sharing system in Thailand formed for THAILNET a network of online catalogue of academic libraries in Bangkok and PULINET, a grouping of provincial academic libraries (*http://UC.Thailis.or.th*)
- Gauteng and Environs Library Consortium(GAELIC)-the largest academic library consortia in South Africa is involved in providing information rapidly and according to the user's need and demand (www. gaelic.ac.za)
- Regional University and Science Library Advanced Network (RUSLANet) in the North West of Russia is a common information space for libraries that is integrating with the world wide information space. (*http://consortium.Ruslan.ru*)
- China Academic Library and Information System (CALIS) is a nationwide academic library consortium formed in 2000 that links services in china (*www.calis.edu.cn/calisnew*)
- Consortium of Academic Libraries of Catalonia (CBUC) is a consortium of the state funded University and the State Library of Catalonia in Spain (*www.cbuc.es*)
- CONSIRAN has been working with the libraries of science,

research and medical university libraries of Iran for online access to licensed resources through networks.

- The department of Science and Technology (DOST),Engineering & Science Education Programme (ESEP) consortium of Philippines is a government sponsored consortium and upgrades the S&T infrastructure in the country via its education programme

South African Academic countries are involved in the library consortia since the 1990s and they are –

- Cape Library Cooperation (CALICO) in 1992
- Gauteng and Environs Library Consortium (GAELIC) in 1996
- Free State Library & Information Consortium (FRELICO) in 1996/1997
- Eastern Seaboard Association of Libraries (eSAL) in 1997
- South East Academic Library System (SEALS)in 1998
- In the year 1999, the South African National Library and Information Consortium (SANLiC) was established
- HEAL-Link is a consortium of all academic and most research libraries in Greece. It was established in 1998 to revive the slow fading away of Greek academic libraries due to lack of adequate budget
- Major breakthrough and recognition in consortia came with the establishment of consortium of consortia in 1990s which changed to International Coalition Of Library Consortia(ICOLC) to discuss various ways to acquire materials and listen to each other's concern

National Level : Academic libraries in India are facing problems such as high demands of the users, low budget and increase in information demands. Library consortia have been initiated in order to overcome some of the problems and it is still at an infancy state. Some of them are as follows-

- UO HYD MATHS consortium was established by the University of Hyderabad in1977 and covers only mathematics literature

- FORSA consortium (Forum for Resource Sharing in Astronomy Astrophysics) was established in 1982 which is a group of five (5) library consortium in the field of Astronomy & Astrophysics with its headquarter at Bangalore
- INDEST consortium (Indian National Digital Library in Science and Technology) was established in 2002 by the Ministry of HRD with its headquarter at IIT, New Delhi. It is the most ambitious initiative taken up so far in India in the area of Engineering and technology
- HELINET (Health Science Library and Information Network) was established in 2002 at Bangalore to cover subjects like health, medical and bio-medical sciences. It was promoted by the Rajiv Gandhi University of Health Sciences, Bangalore (*www.rguhs.ac.in*)
- CSIR consortium (Council of Science And Industrial Research) was established in 2004 with its headquarter at NISCAIR to provide access to more than 4500 international journals to all the S&T personnel of CSIR
- ICMR-E Consortia was started initially in 2007 by subscribing few e-journals for all ICMR institutes. All the scientists of ICMR and its institute can access journals from their desktop
- IGCAR consortium (Indira Gandhi Centre for Atomic Research) was established at Kalpakkam in Chennai to cover 12 units and 14 field stations spread all over the country
- Other consortium are J-CCC (J-gate Custer Content) covering more than 4000 journals, SNDT University is maintaining the Library Information Science Abstract (LISA) in coordination with six (6) other Universities. IIM (Indian Institute of Management) has also formed a consortium with six (6) institutes of Management.

SUGGESTIONS

In the era of global communication, networks and consortia

are very important. It is needed to achieve cost effectiveness and bridging the digital divide. Most of the Indian libraries are showing interest either to form or join the consortia. Certain standards are important for its operation like-

i. India has to modernize its telecommunication and networking system in order to develop its library and information services as no excellence in the education sector can be achieved without the effective and efficient information system. A step should be taken to ensure at least 8-10% of their annual budget for development process
ii. The government and LIS professional bodies should take initiative to conduct some consortia and workshop
iii. Policy makers and Internet Service Providers (ISP) should have a shared obligation to seek ways to achieve wide spread use of the internet
iv. LIS professionals must market their services to private sectors for sponsorship and support
v. Involvement and management by the parent organization is a must for sustainability

CONCLUSION

The unending responsibilities of the information centres are collection, development, preservation and retrieval of information for providing the library services to its users. These responsibilities have become more complex with the introduction of computer and telecommunication technologies. In India, different steps are taken to disseminate information in all the subjects similarly any set of objective will only be achieved if there is a willingness to join together through the efforts of everyone than at the individual levels.

The success and survival of the libraries will depend on how and to what extent they cooperate with each other. Disadvantages and difficulties emerge from different parts but the consortial form chosen by the libraries of higher education system will help all to face new challenges. Information explosion and access to e-resources has created new expectations which the libraries attempt to satisfy by creating co-operational alliances that will lead them to share solutions and expertise. It is very important to find new ways to interpret the needs of the users.

The creation of the web and networks brought many possibilities for integrating consortia activities at the international and national levels and to share their resources and expand and develop new services. India has been active in consortia activities but due to limitations it is hard to find a successful programme that could be used as a benchmark to replicate in other libraries. Another issue that is observed in the Indian library consortia is that almost all of them are concentrating only on e-resource sharing. The need today is to explore other areas for collaboration to improve the overall situation in terms of services and resources.

It can be concluded that libraries of higher education in the developing countries need to battle with the problems that prevent a successful consortia effort because the advantages for sharing electronic resources are more from these libraries as it brings them together to redefine and re-engineer their consortia effort.

REFERENCES

- ARORA, Jagdish and TRIVEDI, Kruti (2010): UGC-INFONET Digital Library Consortium: present services and future endeavours IN: DESIDOC Journal of Library and Information Technology Vol. 30 (2),March 2010: Pp.15-25
- RAMAIAH, LS (2008):Automation, Networking and Consortia: an Indian Development Perspective IN: Changing Library Scenario inn Digital Era ed. by Dhrubajit Das.- Assam College Librarians' Association (ACLA); Guwahati: Pp. 86-97
- RATNAKAR, KV and SATYANARYANA, K (2009): Consortia to Promote Access to Medical Information: some experiences of the Indian Council of Medical Research IN: DESIDOC Journal of Library and Information Technology Vol. 29 (5),Sept. 2009: Pp.7-11
- SHRIVASTAVA, VD (2005): Digital Collection Development and E-journal Management in Libraries IN: PLANNER-2005,INFLIBNET & Assam University, Silchar .-Nov.2005,10-11
- SINGH, Gurudev (2005): Digital Libraries and Digitization.- Ess Ess

Publications; New Delhi

- *www.iitd.ac.in*
- *www.inflibnet.ac.in*

8

Development of Library Consortia in India

Dr. Parveen Kumar

ABSTRACT

Library Consortia or Consortium is now being overheard globally. It is more because of electronic or digital form of information. Consortia are all about sharing resources and improving access to information. These resources are shared among libraries that have common missions, goals and clients (users) and act on those commonalties. Before we are sharing own library resources through inter library loan, but in this Information communication technology (ICT) age it has gained momentum even in the developing countries. When library consortiums are formed, the existing environment about users' preferences and difficulties need to be studied. Initiating such studies would enable to incorporate the findings as the major input in consortium formation.

Keywords: Library Consortia, Consortia management, Networking, E-resources.

INTRODUCTION

No single library can meet the requirements of the users. Libraries since long back are sharing their resources with each other to meet the informational need of their users. Union cataloguing and classification, inter library loan services etc are the example of resource sharing. The introduction of information and communication technology has led to the emergence of networks where all participating libraries are interconnected electronically for exchange or sharing of their information. The libraries all over the world are forming consortia of all types and at all levels with an objective to take advantage of current global network to promote better, faster and more cost-effective ways of providing electronic information resources to the information seekers.

Consortia could be described as a group of organizations who come together to fulfill a combined objective that usefully requires cooperation and the sharing of resources and need to have a clear mutual goal in order to ensure their success. Library consortium is an association of a group of libraries to achieve mutually the common objective. Library consortia primarily aim at fulfilling the educational, intellectual, informational and social aspirations of users, through cooperative provision, superior quality library resources and services are made available to the users. Consortia may be formed at a local, regional, national or international level, on a functional or format basis, or on subject basis. Maximum libraries mainly in developing countries are thinking today about the co-operative purchasing for any group of libraries. Thus, Consortia are constituted for often being useful for establishing a formal structure regarding resource sharing with formal agreement by each participant library.

Library consortium has been successfully implemented in the libraries of developed countries like USA, UK, Germany and France etc. There are many consortia and these consortiums are having one common goal i.e. pooling their collective financial resources to increase greater economic control over their market places.

LITERATURE REVIEW

(Bansode, 2007) in his study concluded that Library consortia are really helping the researchers, faculties and the students to retrieve the information and save their time. It benefits the libraries to procure more electronic resources in the library with limited library budget and this is what the libraries require in the present scenario. India should also take initiatives to establish national archival centers like United States. The mission of the national archival centre could be to build archival collection of important scholarly journal literature and to fill the gap in the library collections of journal back volumes and also help to reduce long term capital costs associated with storage. (Ratnakar, 2009) discussed in his study that Financial crunch and ever rising cost of journals have constrained many scientific/research libraries, especially the medical libraries, to satiate the demands of the users forcing them adopt to new technologies to overcome the challenge of ever rising information demands of the users. In the recent years, library consortium has emerged as a viable solution for resource sharing among libraries. This paper is an overview of the consortia initiated by the Indian Council of Medical Research to share the resources of its medical libraries among its 25 institutes. (Singh and Rao, 2008) discussed in his study that Library Consortia or Consortium is now being overheard globally. It is more because of electronic or digital form of information. Consortia are all about sharing resources and improving access to information. These resources are shared among libraries that have common missions, goals and clients (users) and act on those commonalties. Before we are sharing own library resources through inter library loan, but in this Information communication technology (ICT) age it has gained momentum even in the developing countries. When library consortiums are formed, the existing environment about users' preferences and difficulties need to be studied. Initiating such studies would enable to incorporate the findings as the major input in consortium formation. (Babu and Sivaprasad, 2010) discussed in his study that Libraries in India are facing the problem of shrinking budgets and at the other end exponential rise in the prices of journals. UGC-INFONET, INDEST, CSIR e-journal consortia, IIM Library consortia and HELINET Consortia are five major initiatives that have come to the rescue of libraries so that they can cater to the needs of clients, depending upon them. Library consortium is collaborative activity of a group of libraries to cope up with above mentioned crisis.

NEEDS

Literature Explosion: With the advancement of information technology the form of literature has shifted from printed to digital format. The digital literature grows in such a fast pace that no single library in the world is in a position to keep its holding update.

Limited Finance: Crunching funds is another factor has lead libraries to go for consortia development activities. Libraries are finding it hard to maintain the subscription to even for core journals due to ever increasing cost of the journal subscription especially international ones No library is in a position to acquire each and every published document whether it is in print mode or in digital mode. There is a need of library consortia to cope up with the financial problems.

Users Demand: No library, however big, is in a position to claim self-sufficiency in these multitude and mass sources of knowledge. The demand of the user is changing and ever increasing with newer revolutions and developments. To satisfy the all types of users need library consortia is need.

- Impossibility of self-sufficiency

Advantages/ Features

- Optimum utilization of funds.
- Online accessibility.
- Access multiple e-resources at lower cost.
- Facilities to build up digital libraries.
- Helpful to provide better library services like CAS and SDI.

Disadvantages

- Copyright Problems
- Limitations of IT
- Requires IT skills for handling e-resources.
- Member Libraries: the members may not have the flexibility to join the consortia at any time in the year.
- Internet Access id necessary.

MAJOR LIBRARY CONSORTIA IN INDIA

INDEST: The Ministry of Human Resource Development (MHRD) has set-up the "Indian National Digital Library in Engineering Sciences and Technology (INDEST) Consortium" on the recommendation made by the Expert Group appointed by the ministry under the chairmanship of Prof. N. Balakrishnan. The Ministry provides funds required for subscription to electronic resources for institutions including IISc, IITs, NITs, IIMs and a few other centrally-funded Government institutions through the consortium headquarters set-up at the IIT Delhi. Moreover, the INDEST-AICTE Consortium, as an open-ended proposition, welcomes other institutions to join it on their own for sharing benefits it offers in terms of highly discounted rates of subscription and better terms of agreement with the publishers. All electronic resources being subscribed are available from the publisher's Website. The Consortium has an active mailing list and a Web site hosted at the IIT Delhi. The INDEST-AICTE Consortium is the most ambitious initiative taken so far in the country. The consortium operates through its headquarter at the IIT Delhi.

FORSA: Forum for Resource Sharing in Astronomy and Astrophysics was launched in 1981. It is subscribing to common database full text journals on behalf of all member libraries for their users. Many institutions like, Indian Institute of Astrophysics, National Centre for Radio Astrophysics, Physical Research Laboratory, Tata Institute of Fundamental Research etc. is participating in this consortium. Under this consortium publisher and the library both are benefited. The major objectives of FORSA are collection development in IT environment; facilitate e-access to journals and books; actively participate in resource sharing; to facilitate access to website of each institute library etc.

CSIR E-Journals Consortium: Council of Scientific and Industrial Research was established in 1942. The National Institute of Science Communication and Information Resources (NISCAIR) and other laboratories of CSIR formed a consortia named as consortium for CSIR for accessing e-journals in 2001. In year 2009, autonomous institutions and professional bodies under Department of Science Technology are also joined the consortium for accessing information resources. The consortium is providing access to online journals of many publishers like American Chemical Society, Cambridge University Press, IEEE, Oxford University Press, Emerald, Springer, Taylor and Francis, John Wiley, Elsevier Science Blackwell etc.

UGC INFONET : UGC-Infonet E-Journals consortium initiative was undertaken by the Indian University Grants Commission (UGC) to facilitate free access to scholarly journals and databases in all fields and disciplines by the research and academic community across the country. All universities who are under the purview of UGC have been provided UGC-infonet Connectivity and access to scholarly e- Journals and Databases. University Grant Commission launched a consortium for its member universities to promote the use of e-journals through its network Infonet. The UGC- Infonet Digital Library Consortium was formally launched in December 2003. Tutorials on e-resources subscribed by the UGC-Infonet digital library consortium have been uploaded on INFLIBNET website. The programmme is wholly funded by the UGC and executed by the INFLIBNET centre, Ahmedabad. The UGC provides funds required for subscription to electronic resources for member universities.

HELINET : Health Sciences Library and Information Network is the first medical library consortium in India setup with an objective of networking of libraries affiliated to the university to promote resource sharing, especially with reference to international medical journal and databases. Under this scheme members can access more international and quality e-journals of reputed publishers in the field of biomedical sciences at the lower price. Under this consortium access to e-journals of Elsevier Science, MD Consult, Royal Society of Medicine etc are available. HELINET adopted an indigenously developed and locally available e-journals gateway for its need.

ICMR Consortia : The Indian Council of Medical Research, the apex body in India for the formulation of biomedical research was founded in 1911, and is one of the oldest medical research bodies in the world. As early as in 1911, the Government of India set up the Indian Research Fund Association (IRFA) with the objectives of supporting and coordinating the various medical researchers in India. It was renamed as Indian Council of Medical Research in 1949. ICMR e-consortia was started in 2007. ICMR initially subscribed few e-journals in a consortia mode for all ICMR Institutes. All the scientists of ICMR and its institutes can access these journals from their desktop. Journals can be accessed through IP addresses of the various institutes' libraries including headquarter. Indian Council of Medical Research has been subscribing NML, NEJM, BMJ, Nature etc e-journals in a consortia mode to all IMCR institutes.

IIM Consortia : IIM library consortia is a digital library network system based on internet technology to provided the IIM community an online web enabled access to the information resources available in all the IIMs without any barriers of time and distance. Six Indian Institutes of Management have formed a consortium and jointly approached the publishers of e-journals and databases in the area of management, Social behavioral Science source. They have been giving IP enabled access to e-journals. Well renowned publishes provide their resources online to the member of the IIM Consortium.

ICICI Knowledge Park : The Knowledge Park at Hyderabad has signed an agreement with Informatics India Ltd. Proved access to J-Gate Custom Contents for Consortia service to four Hyderabad based and one Pune base Research and Development institutions. Initially this service is free for the members with the objective of making it self-sustaining in the later stage.

ISRO : The resource sharing initiative taken by Indian Space Research Organization libraries by avoiding subscription to bibliographic databases is expected to result in saving of Rs. 41 lacks per year. Further, the proposed cancellation of duplicate journal titles by its centers is likely to save the surplus amount that could be used to provide access to e-journals for the benefit of all the centers.

UGC DAE consortium for scientific research : To promote interaction amongst the scientists working in the research centres of the Department of Atomic Energy and the faculty from the universities and other institutions of higher learning, and to enable young students to work on programmes of national importance under the joint guidance of the faculty from universities and the scientists of DAE so as to nurture an organic linkage between the university system and research centres of DAE, the University Grants Commission and Atomic Energy Commission have joined hands. The UGC created an inter-university consortium, with its headquarter at Indore for the utilization of the facilities established by the Department of Atomic Energy. The inter-university consortium has over the years taken several initiatives to foster the interaction between the university systems and the DAE institutions.

N-LIST E-consortium : The Project entitled "National Library and Information Services Infrastructure for Scholarly Content (N-LIST)", being jointly executed by the UGC-INFONET Digital Library Consortium, INFLIBNET Centre and the INDEST-AICTE Consortium, IIT Delhi provides for i) cross-subscription to e-resources subscribed by the two Consortia, i.e. subscription to INDEST-AICTE resources for universities and UGCINFONET resources for technical institutions; and ii) access to selected e-resources to colleges. The N-LIST project provides access to e-resources to students, researchers and faculty from colleges and other beneficiary institutions through server(s) installed at the INFLIBNET Centre. The authorized users from colleges can now access e-resources and download articles required by them directly from the publisher's website once they are duly authenticated as authorized users through servers deployed at the INFLIBNET Centre. As on Feb 4 2013, a total number of 3155 colleges have registered themselves with the N-LIST programme including 2881 Govt. / Govt.-aided colleges covered under the section 12 B/2F of UGC Act as well as Non-Aided colleges . Log-in ID and password for accessing e-resources has been sent to the authorized users from these 2881 colleges. All e-resources subscribed for colleges under the N-LIST Project are now accessible to these 2881 colleges through the N-LIST website (*http://nlist.inflibnet.ac.in*)

NTRMEDNET Consortium : The Consortium was started with a vision to improve the quality of education and research in the Medical Colleges of the state through enhanced access to high quality medical literature. One of the goals of NTRMEDNET Consortium is to provide cost-effective services i.e., greater access to information at a minimum cost. The Consortium has successfully accomplished the task of developing an E-journal consortium and a resource-sharing model that networks the health science colleges in the State of Andhra Pradesh.

PROBLEMS/ ISSUES

- The infrastructural disparity among the institutional libraries has created problems for library consortia.
- The publishers and distributors main purpose is to earn profit and for this they may conceal the deficiencies of their products and highlight the deficiencies of other publishers which create problem in selecting the resources.
- Government could not provide the equal infrastructure to all types of institutions of higher learning and there is a big digital divide among the users of very good funded institutes and poor funded institutes.

- Many publishers charge in different currencies which creates confusion.

Resources Identification: Identifying the most suitable product which is agreed upon by all the members of the consortium is more or less a difficult proposition. This is mostly because each and every member will have their own wish list of information products and services, though the overlap between the products will be on the higher side in the case of an ideal homogeneous group.

Technology Infrastructure: Long range planning and sourcing of the appropriate IT and Communication infrastructure conducive for proper delivery of information resources is pre-requisite for every participating library.

Pricing: As discussed earlier, there are no standard practices or processes being followed by majority of the publishers of scholarly literature and hence this is a gray area all together. In most cases cost of the journals are out of reach of many of our libraries and only a consortia approach could provide some meaningful practical solution. Publishers are invited for negotiations and asked to offer their best prices to the consortia. Several methods of pricing are followed, but what is important is that finally the price offered by the publisher should be economically viable for the participating libraries. And it should also ensure uninterrupted and perpetual access to the resources.

Access: Various access methods are offered by publishers towards accessing their resources and it varies from case to case. Access authentication could be User ID / Password based or IP based which are more popular. Uninterrupted and hassle free access to the scholarly content is the ultimate objective of the consortium but varying practices may make access sometimes cumbersome to use consortia approach.

Licensing and Copyright: As against the print paradigm, the e-Journal subscriptions and access models allow only licensing of the content / product for a stipulated period of time which has several restrictions and bindings on the licensee. A number of issues are being debated by librarians, users and publishers which need international attention, deliberations and solution.

Archiving: This needs paramount attention and unfortunately is yet to be attended least in India. Long term preservation of the invaluable wealth of information being accumulated by the consortium is to be archived and preserved for posterity. As the technology is fast progressing and also getting obsolete almost at high pace, it is right time that information resources are carefully archived and preserved on a long term basis through consortia approach and efforts.

Sustainability: Designing and launching a library consortium is perhaps the easier part when compared to its long term sustenance and longevity. The management and the members of the consortium have to strive hard in formulating and establishing robust models towards achieving the above goals.

Usage and Usability: The Return on Investment (ROI) of the consortium is measured in terms of the increased usage, usability of the costly information products which is ultimately reflected in the scientific productivity of the host institutes. It is the earnest efforts of the consortium, the management, the researchers and faculty and the librarians which determine the success or otherwise of any consortium.

Training: Training to the users is another issue that one has to give proper consideration. Usually the users are habituated to handle the traditional resources of information. They are reluctant to sudden change in the handling of information. So, it is the library that has to train the users to face the new media, highlight the benefits through orientation and training programmes.

LIMITATIONS

Following are some of the probable drawback of the consortia:

Membership fee: Organizing body may charge excessive

contribution fee as per their will, and hamper the very objective of the consortium. Besides, there are chances of manipulation of funds.

Potential Conflict: Libraries may join more than one consortium to meet various needs, as each organization has its own bureaucracy culture, level of technology, staff size, budgetary constraints etc. This may give rise to a conflict of vested interests and results in changes and shifts in format and operations of consortia.

User Authentication: Unlike in the print world, electronic information requires validation of the rights of the user. User authentication is regarded as an essential element of electronic resource sharing and may give rise problems of illegal and unethical use.

Preservation and archiving: Electronic information archiving and preservation has barely surfaced as very complex issue. A tension between the two aims exists because as technology changes, software becomes extinct and hardware is replaced. Consequently, resources must be migrated, or transformed, into data readable by new technology. Each time a resource is altered; the newer version strays farther from the original, thereby confounding preservation efforts. The converse is true for preservation's effects on access. As time passes, technology, hardware, and software change, and access to original work is compromised

CONCLUSION

Many initiatives have been initiated in India for the formation of library consortia. Many library consortia in India are doing well and many libraries are benefited but at the same time library consortia are not free from problems. The consortium, with its collective strength of participating institutions, has attracted highly discounted rates of subscription with most favorable terms of agreement. Consortia are tools, which will aid in exploiting the features of the e-journals as well as in effecting savings. Library consortia, providing for physical and electronic delivery of materials, and integrating the collection-development process are all distinct and crucial steps in moving toward the twenty-first century library. It is the case; clearly identified landmarks represent important goals and milestones for measuring our common progress on a journey through a new and unfamiliar landscape. Consortia are tools, which will aid in exploiting the features of the e-resources as well as in effecting savings.

REFERENCES

- Bansode, Sadanand Y. (2007). Library Consortia in India: Issues and Prospects. Trends in Information Management. 3(2), 138-152.
- Ratnakar, K.V. Prerna and Satyanaryana, K. 2009. Consortia to Promote Access to Medical Information: Some Experiences of the Indian Council of Medical Research. DESIDOC Journal of Library & Information Technology, Vol. 29, No. 5, September 2009, pp. 7-11
- Singh, Kunwar and Rao, V Bhaskar. 2008. An Overview of the Library Consortia in India. 6th Convention PLANNER - 2008, Nagaland University, Nagaland, November 06-07, 2008 © INFLIBNET Centre, Ahmedabad. 140-149.
- Babu, V. Nireekshana and Sivaprasad, G. 2010. Library Consortia in India. PEARL - A Journal of Library and Information Science Vol. 4, No. 4, Oct.-Dec, 2010 : 220-223
- *http://paniit.iitd.ac.in/indest/* (Access on 02-02-13)
- *http://nlist.inflibnet.ac.in/about.php* (Accessed on 04-02-13)
- *http://www.ntrmednet.edu.in/ntrmednet.html* (Accessed on 04-02-13)

9

Library Consortium in India: An Overview

Manoj Kumar

ABSTRACT

The paper presents an overview of Library Consortium in India. Libraries in India has witnessed a surge to form consortiums for its information users because of the ever-increasing cost of information and shrinking budget of libraries. FORSA was one of the earliest library consortiums in India and after that many consortiums like CSIR Consortium, HELINET Consortium, IIM Library Consortia, INDEST AICTE Consortium and UGC-INFONET Digital Library Consortium came into existence. Library Consortiums in India are growing at a decent pace and catering to the millions of the users of information.

Keywords: Consortium; E-resources; Library Consortium; India-Library Consortium;

INTRODUCTION

India is a developing economy where resources are limited, hence needed to be utilized in an organized manner with a benefit for all approach. This approach is no different in case of library resources. With the ever increasing cost of information resources, limited budget of libraries, shortage of library staff, information explosion etc., it has become both need and necessity for libraries to cooperate among themselves to procure information resources with a vision to share the burden of expenses among themselves and make the resources available to the end users.

The demand for information by the users through varied types of services has urged each library to go beyond its four walls to cater the endless needs. This reason is quite obvious that no single library can satisfy all the enquiries and reference needs of its clientele. It is rather impossible to purchase all the required information resources by the library all alone. In addition to this the escalation of the prices of the information resources year after years makes it impossible to buy. It is but natural that a librarian has to seek help from other libraries where certain information is available and which he could not acquire himself. This aspect has pressed the librarians to undertake consortium measures, so as to obtain information and make it available to its readers.

LIBRARY CONSORTIUM: MEANING AND DEFINITION

According to ICOLC (International Coalition Of Library Consortia), the library partnership is an important concept leading to consortia formation, which brings about the following activities within the group; Licensing (e-journal, core e-resources, and full-text), Governance (funding, strategic planning, membership), Library & Management system migration, Linked systems projects and virtual union catalogs, with patron-initiated ILL, Cooperative collection and Management, Training, Creation of digital collections and shared storage. The core values of consortia are Collaboration, Joint procurement and Networking (ICOLC guidelines).

The phrase Library Consortium has been used to mean cooperation, coordination and collaboration between and amongst libraries with an intention to share information resources. Library consortia vary in their type, goals, structure, membership, and funding (Woodsworth 1991). A consortium may be a formal or informal agreement between libraries based on a common principle.

A consortium is "an agreement, combination, or group (as of companies) formed to undertake an enterprise beyond the resources of any one member" (Merriam Webster Dictionary).

Allen and Hirshon have explained library consortium as "a generic term to indicate any group of libraries that are working together towards a common goal, whether to expand cooperation on traditional library services or electronic information services. It is now used perhaps too broadly, and encompasses everything from formal legal entities to information groups that come together solely to achieve better pricing for purchasing electronic information."

According to Dong and Zou a "library consortium is an association of libraries established by formal agreement, usually for the purpose of improving services through resource sharing among its members.

There are few models of Consortium available and most of the Library Consortiums fall under one of these models. These Library Consortium models are as under:

1. Open-ended Consortium
2. Close Group Consortium
3. Shared Budget Consortium
4. Centrally funded Consortium
5. National Consortium
6. Publishers' Consortium

FUNCTIONAL AREAS OF LIBRARY CONSORTIUM

Rick Burke has given the following major functions/areas of operations of library consortium:

- Acquisition of electronic resources, with a particular emphasis on pricing and price models.

- Licensing terms and conditions that is acceptable in the higher education environment.
- Developing collaborative models of print resource sharing.
- The preservation and archiving of electronic journal and other e-resource information
- Streamlining and consolidating technical services through a centralized catalogue.
- Professional development and training.
- Collaborative digitization projects, including setting standards for the best practices and providing training therein.
- For those consortia which are statewide or government funded, providing advocacy for libraries and library funding.

Apart from the above points, each library has different needs and goals, hence the area of operations differ for each consortia.

FACTORS AFFECTING CONSORTIUM FORMATION

Various factors to be taken for an effective functioning of a successful consortium like resources identification on the basis of usage and usability, long run planning of the technology infrastructure, access to back runs of periodicals will have to clearly spelt, copyright and licensing, archival issue, price issue should be economically favorable. Last but not least, designing and launching a library consortium should be long term sustenance and robust models towards achieving the above goals. Skilled human resources also affect the formation of a Library Consortium.

LIBRARY CONSORTIUM: CHALLENGES

Libraries have to deal with the following challenges as being a part of any library Consortium:

- Libraries need to manage data and metadata about e-resources which are acquired and accessed.
- Libraries need to select, evaluate, acquire, maintain and

provide informed access to e-resources in accordance with business and license terms.

- To assess usability of e-resource from its trial access or other member feedback.
- Use analysis and then to renew or terminate.
- To deal with restricted access policy and imposed technological control.
- Volatility of content is an issue.
- To monitor product performance and prevent misuse by any user for commercial gain through systematic downloads.
- To have budget control and timely renewal or termination of subscribed resources.
- To ensure right and timely access to right user.
- To deal with built in lack of standardization in various databases with respect to their user interface, search tools, and usage measurement.

LIBRARY CONSORTIUM IN INDIA

Library Consortium has taken different evolution manifestations in India such as library co-operation, inter-library loan, document delivery, library networks etc. The real drive for library consortium was seen after 1980, when more and more libraries started getting automated and used computers for bibliographic processing activities and database searching. Developments in ICT have contributed for accelerating the process of library automation and become responsible for development of mega consortia.

One of the major step in consortia development in India came in the form of advent of different resource sharing networks. A number resource sharing networks that have evolved in India include CALIBNET(1986), DELNET(1988), BONET, MALIBNET(1993), BALNET(1997), and sectoral networks like BTISNET, ENVIS, FOSTIS etc in late 1980's.

Indian Academic, research and technical libraries have started to provide shared web based resources since the turn of 20th century. Some initiatives include FORSA Library Consortium, CSIR Consortium, HELINET Consortium, IIM Library Consortia, INDEST AICTE Consortium and UGC-INFONET Digital Library Consortium.

1. FORSA (Forum for Resource Sharing in Astronomy) : FORSA was established in 1981 and chalked out plans and strategies for library co-operation, resource sharing and developed tools necessary, pertaining to print media. The Indian Astrophysics Consortium is a typical example of a homogenous group of members joined together in order to negotiate consortium licensing for astronomy and astrophysics journals. This consortium is an upshot of an informal network of eight astronomy libraries called FORSA (Forum for Resource Sharing in Astronomy) in India. The homogeneity is based upon the specialized subject area.

Features of FORSA Consortium

- The journal titles for which the consortium license is negotiated are subject focused.
- The publishers find it convenient to negotiate with the members through the agent since the individual invoicing is handled by the agent for the individual members.
- The model is worked out for cross {e-access to the print journals subscribed to by the members of the consortium and hence gives equal access for all the members.
- No additional requirement of budget for the members in terms of subscription to new print journals is required since the currently subscribed titles will be maintained (subject to the normal increase in subscription).
- Institutional usage statistics is provided periodically, viz. weekly, fortnightly and monthly.
- The most important feature is that the members are not burdened with subscribing to peripheral and less important journals, which is a standard feature of 'bundling-together'

by publishers.

2. CSIR e-Journals Consortium : As a result of constant decline of journals information base in CSIR labs, it was decided to setup E-Journals Consortium in 2001. Consequent upon, as a network project of CSIR implementation was entrusted to NISCAIR, New Delhi under its tenth five year plan. It aims at providing access to 4500 world-class e-journals to the CSIR personnel through pooling and sharing of resources. A beginning in this direction was made on 10th June 2002 with CSIR entering into an agreement with M/s Elsevier Science to e-access their 1500+ journals at an add-on cost of 9% of the subscription for the journals in print form. Now the project has been approved in 11th five year plan for continuing access to the large pool of information resources and also to expand the resources base comparable to world's leading institutions. In year 2009, autonomous institutions and professional bodies under Department of Science technology (DST) are also joined the consortium for accessing information resources. Now consortium has agreements 29 information products including journals, bibliographic databases, patents, standards and protocols. CSIR e-Journals Consortium was renamed as National Knowledge Resource Consortium in 2009.

Functions of CSIR e-Journals Consortium:

- Electronic content licensing
- Electronic content loading/presentation
- Interlibrary loan/document delivery
- Training
- Union lists/shared online catalogs

3. INDEST AICTE Consortium : The Indian National Digital Library in Engineering Sciences and Technology (INDEST) Consortium was set up in 2003 by the Ministry of Human Resource Development (MHRD) on the recommendation of an Expert Group appointed by the Ministry. The IIT Delhi was designated as the Consortium Headquarters to coordinate its activities. The Consortium was renamed as INDEST-AICTE Consortium in

December 2005 with major role of AICTE enrolling its approved engineering colleges and institutions as members of the Consortium for selected e-resources at much lower rates of subscription.

Functions/Objectives of INDEST AICTE Consortium:

- To provide electronic resources for the centrally funded and other academic institutions in Engineering, science and Technology of India at highly discounted rates.
- To support and impart training to the users and librarians In the member institutions on subscribed electronic resources.
- To improve scientific productivity of member institutions in terms of quantity and quality of publications.

4. IIMs Library Consortium : The year 2000 was a landmark in the history of IIMs, with the formation of the IIM Consortia. IIMK took leadership in the formation of the IIM Consortia, and had the first meeting in Calicut. The objective was to ensure among the IIMs, optimum utilization and enhancement of the resources, and to minimize the expenditure by consortia based subscriptions to the commonly subscribed databases and journals. The idea was to approach publishers of CD-ROM Databases to begin with, as consortia, for better pricing and services.

The IIM library consortium is a collective activity of all six IIM libraries towards a common goal of sharing resources. With the availability of the state-of-the art information technology solutions and the web revolution, the IIM libraries in India are now better off in terms of easy access to a wealth of information through meaningful co-operation among themselves.

Functions of IIMs Library Consortium:

- Online access to the digital sources of information of all the IIMs.
- Bridging the gap between information resources rich and resources deficient libraries.
- Users of all IIMs are provided equal access to all the information at all time.

- Transaction costs and time of sharing information resources among IIMs.

5. HELINET Consortium : The HELINET Consortium started with the efforts at different institutional levels. The Digital Library at The Rajiv Gandhi University of Health Sciences(RGUHS) piloted the Health Sciences Library and Information Network(HELINET), it was the first such initiative of a University consortium in the field of Health Science which covered initially 25 medical libraries in the state of Karnataka in the year 2003, currently the membership has grown to 650+ with the coverage of other faculties i.e. Dentistry, Pharmacy, Nursing, Physiotherapy, Ayurveda, Homeopathy, Unani, Naturopathy and Yoga. The consortium witnessed serious involvement and commitment from the Institutional and University managements, and a novel method of participative funding was evolved to make the consortium self-sustained.

6. UGC- INFONET Digital Library Consortium : This Consortium was launched by Honorable Dr. APJ Abdul Kalam, the then President of India in the year 2003. It is a national initiative for providing access to scholarly electronic resources including more than 5000 core and peer reviewed full text journals and bibliographic databases in the all the subjects from different publishers for the benefit of academic community of selected universities in India. The access to e-resources was given to 50 universities in the first phase in 2004, and at presently it has been extended to 156 universities in the country.

Objectives of UGC INFONET Digital Library Consortium:

- To subscribe electronic resources for the universities at a highly discounted rates of subscription and at the best terms and conditions;
- To extend the benefit of consortium-based subscription to all Indian universities and colleges;
- To extend the benefit of consortium to associate members of this Consortium;

- To impart training to the users, librarians, research scholars and faculty members of the institutions on the electronic resources with an aim to optimize their usage;
- To have increase interaction amongst the member libraries;
- To increase the research productivity of the institutions both in terms of quality and quantity of publications;
- To evaluate the usage of the resources subscribed; and
- To identify new resources that are required to be subscribed under the programme based on the availability of resources and funds.

7. NKRC (National Knowledge Resource Consortium : NKRC was formerly known as CSIR e-Journal Consortium. It was in 2009 the NKRC was established. It was the mutual collaboration of Council of Scientific and Industrial Research (CSIR) and Department of Science and Technology (DST). It is a network of libraries and information centers of 39 CSIR and 24 DST institutes. Today, NKRC facilitates access to 5,000+ e-journals of all major publishers, patents, standards, citation and bibliographic databases. Apart from licensed resources, NKRC is also a single point entity that provides its users with access to a multitude of open access resources. The Consortium envisions emerging as a leader to serve the R&D sector with much needed information to strengthen the research and development system in the country.

CONCLUSION

The rapid growth of ICT has enabled Indian libraries to get the maximum out of minimum through Library Consortium. Indian libraries have realized the best way to utilize its limited resources can be achieved through mutual Collaboration, Joint procurement and Networking. It benefits the libraries to procure more electronic resources in the library with limited library budget and this is what the libraries require in the present scenario. Library Consortiums in India are efficiently managed and are at the same level as some of the best International Consortiums. It is clear that the technology of the web, the increasing importance of electronic resources, and advances in resource-sharing systems have created new opportunities for consortia. Beyond these technological and economic motivations, the instinct of the librarians to work together at a time of uncertainty is very essential at all levels. Combining this approach and support from the government will certainly enhance the chances of forming more consortia models.

REFERENCES

- Allan B M and Hirshon A, Hanging together to avoid hanging separately: oppurtunities for academic libraries and consortia, Information Technology and Libraries, 17(1)(1998) 36-44.
- Bansode S Y, Library Consortia in India: Issues and Prospects. Available at: ojs.uok.edu.in › Home › Vol 3, No 2 › Bansode (Accessed on 25 December 2012).
- Birdie Ç and Alladi V, The Future of Consortia among Indian Libraries – FORSA Consortium as Forerunner?, In B Corbin et al (Eds), Library and Information Services in Astronomy IV, July 2-5, 2002, Prague, Czech Republic.
- Birdie C, Library Consortia and Open Access Initiatives: Collaboration at Different Level. In SLib 2005 : Positioning Information Services Towards Organisational Excellence, 15-17 May 2005, Nikko Hotel Kuala Lumpur.
- Burke R, Library Consortia and the future of academic libraries. Available at: www.neal-schuman.com/academic/Burke2010.pdf (Accessed on 23 December 2012)
- Chand P and Nishy P, Strengthening R & D information systems through library consortium: a case of CSIR laboratories, Annals of Library and Information Studies, 55(1)(2008) 45-51.
- Dong E S and Zou T J, Library Consortia in China, LIBRES Library and Information Science Research Electronic Journal, 19(1) (2009)1-10.
- Harrod L M, Harrod's Librarians' Glossary, 7th edn (Hants:Gower) 1990, p. 164.
- Jambhekar A, Pandian P and Gupta DK, Partnership for Success: A case of IIMs libraries' consortia model. Available at: www.tifr.res.in/~libws/paul-paper1.htm (Accessed on 23 December 2012).
- National Knowledge Resource Consortium. Available at: ejournal.niscair.res.in/
- Sahoo B B and Aggarwal G P, INDEST-AICTE Consortium: A decade of service for engineering, science and technology community of the

country, Annals of Library and Information Studies, 59(3)(2012) 170-180.

- Shachaf P, Nationwide Library Consortia Life Cycle, Libri, 53(2003) 94-102.
- UGC-Infornet Digital Library Consortium. Available at: http://www.inflibnet.ac.in/econ/
- Walmiki R H, Ramakrishnegowda K C and Prithviraj K R, Awareness and use of UGC-Infornet digital library consortium by the faculty members of Karnataka state universities, Annals of Library and Information Studies, 57(1)(2010) 33-43.
- Yalaburgi S V, Compilation and Study of Health Sciences e-Resources subscribed under Helinet Consortium. Available at: 119.82.96.198:8080/jspui/.../Helinet%20Consortia%20ejournals.pdf (Accessed on 23 December 2012).
- Yernagula R and Kelkar P K, Library Consortia: benefits and models of E-journals Consortia. Available at: www.isical.ac.in/~serial/consortia/CBSOR-11.pdf (Accessed on 23 December 2012).

10

Library Consortia Benefits

Randhir Singh Bhaskar

ABSTRACT

The present approach towards partnership, networking, consortia and resource sharing adopted by Indian libraries need radical changes to evolve responsive partnerships in order to achieve best performance in service. The current practices of journal acquisition in most of the libraries in the colleges and universities in India are print based, in which each library is an island with regard to access of information. Moreover, there is wide disparity in the availability and use of information among different universities and colleges. But, consortia based acquisition and electronic desktop delivery of information can eliminate this gap and increase the access and use considerably.

Keywords: Library consortium, resource sharing and Interface, library consortia benefits, University libraries

INTRODUCTION

The Library and Information Systems (LIS) and services are being transformed by the modern Information and Communication

Technologies (ICTs). The ICTs have the potential to transform both the processes and products of the entire economic sphere–as well as all types of market transactions, institutional linkages, and human interactions and learning. Since nearly all economic activities rely on information acquisition, processing, and transmission, the scope for the use of this technology is unbound. Information is the "lifeblood" of competitive markets, and improvements in information technologies are transforming the whole economies into fast-moving information-intensive economies and globalizing production and competition in many industries and services. The libraries and information centres are one of the major supporting agencies involved in the process of information transfer and finally the diffusion of information and information technology. Consequently, both the Information Systems and the Information Professionals are adapting to meet the changing needs and growing expectations of the users (Jalloh, 2000). The initiatives and development in the areas of automation, networking, resource sharing, consortia, digital libraries, electronic document delivery, etc. have causes to emerge new practices in the operations and management practices of the Library and Information Systems world over. As compared to the research libraries, the university and college libraries in India have shown a slow rate of progress in this direction. Now, these libraries also have shown increased interest in the inevitable refinement of their management processes.

LIBRARY CONSORTIA: BRIDGING THE GAP IN THE AVAILABILITY OF INFORMATION

The phenomenon of information revolution has posed several problems and this has far reaching implications in the society. The nation or society which possesses more information will lead the world. This is also true in the case of individuals. The persons have more information will guide a group or society and they will be superior to others. This power of information has induced the nations and individuals to acquire and control more and more quantities of information. But, in this race, the poor nations, societies, institutions or individuals will be back as compared to others. This has created a big gap in the availability and use of information. A study by the author in 1997 revealed that while 77 per cent (total no. 2,31,510) of the higher education faculty in India were engaged in the affiliated colleges, only 23 per cent (total no. 69,283) of the faculty were engaged in the Universities (Francis, 1997). Though the salary and other emoluments given for the faculty in colleges and universities are same, there is much difference in the scientific productivity and research out contributed by these two classes of the faculty. A major reason for this difference is the lack of availability and use of research information. As compared to the university libraries, only a meager amount was allotted for college libraries in India. Over the time, academic institutions typically have spent a decreasing percentage of their educational and general budgets on their libraries. Nonetheless, academic institutions and library clients expect their libraries to obtain new electronic resources while simultaneously maintaining or growing traditional print collections until the electronic resources are fully stable. Libraries also are expected to do this with no additional funding. Academic libraries and information providers must use information technologies to facilitate increased information delivery and to make information more generally, readily, and flexibly accessible than its print counterpart. The current practices of journal acquisition in most of the libraries in the colleges and universities are print based, in which each library is an island with regard to access of information. The digital libraries expected to increase information access. They will allow for greater standardization of data, multiple and remote access to information resources, easy sharing, etc. (Aregu, 2001). The Library Consortia can be an ideal solution in this context, if that has been established and managed at the wider interests of the society and the mankind in total. The activities and operations of the library and information centres are being influenced and drastically changed with this new approach to information management. The pattern of common acquisition, subscription or licensing for access by the consortia will benefit more to the poorer group. The conventional practices of journal acquisition are grounded in the legacy of a print-bound world in which each library is an island of access for its own patrons. But with electronic desktop delivery of information, the increased ease of access allows far greater information use than previously possible (Sanville, 1999). Experiences of the several libraries show that the improved ease of access has demonstrated the high elasticity in information usage. Libraries in consortia benifits of purchase of electronic journals can seek this desirable outcome that provide for expanded journal access. A study in the Ohio University Library System reveals that the use of journal titles has increased by three times than they previously held in print. Even the small and new colleges were also the beneficiaries through access to scholarly journals. As the evolution to broad scale electronic access continues, libraries and consortia must take advantage of the opportunities to adopt sustainable economic benefits of information purchase that maximizes information use. There are several efforts to operate library consortia at regional, national or international levels. The Washington Research Library Consortium (WRLC, 2004)) is a good regional resource-sharing organization established by several universities in the Washington, D.C. metropolitan area to expand and enhance the information resources available to their students and faculty. The International Coalition of Library Consortia (ICOLC, 2004) is an informal organization that began in 1997. Comprising about sixty library consortia in the United States, Canada, the United Kingdom, the Netherlands, Germany, Israel, and Australia, the Coalition represents over 5,000 member libraries worldwide. The Coalition serves primarily higher education institutions by facilitating discussion among its members on issues of common interest.

PRESENT SYSTEM OF CONSORTIA IN INDIA

Several working benefits of library consortia are prevailing in different nations and among different groups of institutions. In India, we have seen some library consortia such as UGC Infonet of the University Grants Commission, the INDEST (The Indian National Digital Library in Engineering and Science and Technology) of the Indian Institute of Technologies (IIT) and similar institutions, Consortium of the Council of Scientific and Industrial Research (CSIR), etc. Several other organizations such as the Indian Council of Agricultural Research (ICAR), State Agricultural Universities, Indian Space Research Organisation (ISRO), Defence Research and Development Organisation (DRDO), All India Council of Technical Education (AICTE) and some other individual groups of institutions have started working to form different consortia.

All consortia are formed on the basis of memorandum of understanding and agreements between the publishers, database vendors, user institutions, libraries, etc. Since the basic responsibility of providing infrastructure for education and research in India is vested with the Union and State Governments and the fund required for this is meeting from the government exchequer, the present system of formation and maintenance of different library consortia for each group of academic and research institutions is unscientific. The contradiction is that all educational and most of the research institutions in the country are getting full or partial financial support from the government. All universities, colleges and poly techniques in India are funded either by UGC, ICAR, AICTE, Indian Medical Council (IMC) or similar government agencies. All major research institutions directly run by the Government of India. There are some such institutions under the state governments also. This situation has posed a major question, "Why separate consortia for each group?". Potter (1997) argues as follows. "The fact that a group of libraries shares a common funding source is it directly through elected officials or through a board of regents or oversight agency is an important reason to build statewide cooperative systems. There is great appeal in efforts to pool resources and in cooperating to control costs". GALILEO in Georgia, the Louisiana Library Network, Ohio

LINK, Tex Share in Texas, and VIVA in Virginia were some of the consortia functioning in USA in 1997 with state wide operation.

CONSORTIA FOR COUNTRYWIDE ACCESS: A FUTURE BENEFITS

The present system of consortia has lot of merits over the earlier pattern of individual subscription to journals and databases. Such benefits can be maximized by establishing consortia for nationwide access. Instead of establishing separate library consortia by different groups of educational and research institutions, it is better to form one consortium for all educational and government research institutions with country wide access to all online journals and databases. Such a consortium in India may be named as, *"Indian Library Consortium"* (ILC). Here, the unnecessary duplication of efforts for the establishment and maintenance of separate consortia within a country can be avoided. Moreover, wide disparity existing in the availability, accessibility and use of information among education and research institutions can be eliminated to a large extent by this system. This disparity will be minimized on establishing high speed Internet connectivity with uniform per user bandwidth to all academic and research institutions. The publishers and database vendors also will be benefited in this venture because their efforts for marketing and providing services and technical support will be less. Access to electronic journals and online databases are now controlled by the database vendors either by authenticated I. P. (Internet Protocol) Numbers of the Proxy Servers or by User Name and Password. In a single consortia, they can adopt the Gateway based Access Control. The vendors can establish Mirror Server Centres in each country. This has several benefits in database maintenance, backup and service. So, it is high time to consider the benefits for a single consortium and a real network at country level. Several experts and users have felt the need for such a network or consortium of all LIS. But, it is difficult to include the commercial organizations and industrial houses in the consortia visualized for academic and government research institutions.

ROLE OF INFLIBNET

The established task of the INFLIBNET (Information and Library Network) of the UGC is to interconnect all educational and research institutions in the India for pooling and sharing of library and information resources and there by ensure easy availability and speed access of information resources for all academic and research programmes in the country (UGC, 1988). The service purview of the INFLIBNET covers all types of educational and research institutions and government organizations and hence, it has the primary responsibility to plan and establish a single consortium for the whole country. This should not be limited to serve only the conventional universities and colleges, but include agricultural, veterinary, medical and engineering universities, all types of colleges, government research institutions engaged in the fields of defence, space, industry, agriculture, medicine, atomic energy, etc. The fund required for establishing and maintaining the proposed Indian Library Consortium should be set apart either centrally in the Union Budget or by individual controlling institutions such as

UGC, ICAR, AICTE, DRDO, ISRO, IMC, etc. In order to establish an integrated information system in India, increased administrative, financial and technical support by the government is essential (Francis, 1998). Though the role of the INLIBNET is clearly defined, more dynamic and strong actions are needed to achieve target.

NEED FOR RE-ENGINEERING UNIVERSITY LIBRARIES

In reaping benefits of the modern ICTs, the library and information centres in India are far behind as compared to those in the developed nations. Inadequate fund, infrastructure, manpower training, unscientific rules and management policies, etc., are the reasons for this situation. Uneven distribution of the available resources causes wide disparity in information availability, access and use. Gaur (2003) indicated the need for proper management benefits suitable for the modern ICT environment as follows. "It is important to find out why Indian Libraries and Information Centres have not been able to benefit to the extent expected by the computer revolution in spite of huge investments, and with so much of hue and cry. ... But, in reality all these effort have gone as waste. Why is it so?. Are these efforts not in proper direction?. Or is there something wrong in our planning?. In this process there will be a need for benefits and frameworks that help us to understand and identify specific problems". The advent of electronic journals and online databases coupled with high speed data communication facilities has paved the way for the present form of library consortia. The benefits of single library consortia, proposed for the whole country, can bring an ideal situation of information availability and use, which provide maximum economy and service efficiency. Consortia based information acquisition, processing and servicing warrant a total re-structuring of the entire processes of the university libraries. The principles of centralized and co-operative operations as advocated by Dr. S.R. Ranganathan can be effectively implemented in the consortia mode. Maximum benefits of such a system can be reaped in a single consortium for country wide access of information resources.

MAJOR AREAS OF RE-ENGINEERING

A study conducted mainly in the Kerala Agricultural University reveals that a thorough re-structuring of the University Library and Information System is needed to suit the requirements warranted by the modern ICTs. In has felt that the modern ICTs warrants total changes in the processes of acquisition, technical processing, user education, services, human resource development (HRD), financial management, etc. of the university libraries. It is visualized that, the consortia based operations and electronic document delivery services of the libraries will enhance this need for thorough restructuring. In comparison, it is revealed that similar situation prevails in almost all universities in India and the findings are relevant to them also.

i. Re-engineering the Acquisition : The activities of

document suggestion, selection, approval, order placing, passing of bills for payment, releasing payment, etc. can be done through the local area network and or Internet. The work of accessioning can be done using computers. Due to some audit regulations, it may not be possible initially to replace the paper form of Accession Register by computer form. So, till the audit regulations are getting revised, the libraries can prepare Accession Register by printing the document details from the OPAC (Online Public Access Catalogue) in Loose Sheaf. This will avoid a lot of duplicate and unnecessary work of accessioning. Moreover, multiple copies of accession registers can also be printed easily.

ii. Re-engineering the Classification and Cataloguing : It is ideal to centralize globally the work of classification and cataloguing. The Library of Congress (LC) is already doing such work efficiently. Few libraries in India are availing the service of LC for downloading the classification and catalogue data. The ILC can either subscribe the service of the LC or the ILC itself can start such service for all libraries in India. It is ideal to collaborate with the National Library, Calcutta in this venture. Here, the work of preparation of Indian National Bibliography also will be automatically supplemented.

iii. Re-engineering the User Services : The work of user services has to be thoroughly re-engineered on the lines of consortium and electronic document delivery. The procedures for all user services such as compilation of bibliographies, current awareness service, selective dissemination of information, photocopying, other documentation services, CD based and online database services, etc. has to be re-defined and need total revision.

CONCLUSION

The possibilities of ICTs, Digital Information, Electronic Document Delivery, Library Consortia and Web based operations, etc. have helped to provide better services to the users. But, wide disparity in the availability and use of academic and research information still prevails among different universities and research institutions in India. Moreover, establishment and maintenance of separate library consortium for each group of government and government supported institutions in a country has lead to the duplication of efforts and additional investment. Since the present pattern of higher education and research is inter-disciplinary, clear cut demarcation of areas of subject interest and information requirement is difficult. That means, the information requirements are cross-disciplinary and also at micro-level. This underlines the need for providing access of information in all subject areas to the students, teachers and researchers in all branches. This justifies the establishment of National Library Consortium which automatically will bring economy, efficiency and equality in information availability and use.

REFERENCES

- Aregu, Raphael (2001). Digitizing agricultural data for rapid agricultural modernization in Uganda: strengthening Ugandan NARS issues. In Digital libraries: Dynamic Landscapes for Knowledge Creation, access and Management. The fourth International Conference of Asian Digital Libraries, Bangalore, India, December 10-12, 2001, organized by University of Mysore and Indian Institute of Information Technology, edited by Shalini R. Urs, TB Rajashekhar and KS Raghavan. Bangalore: ICADL. 404-415 pp.
- Francis, AT (1997). Regional Information Networks: necessary thrust area for INFLIBNET to establish Integrated Information System in India. In Information Technology Applications in Academic Libraries in India with emphasis on Network Services and Information Sharing. Fourth National Convention of Libraries in Education and Research (CALIBER – 97), Patiala, India, March 6-8, 1997, organized by INFLIBNET Centre and Thapar Institute of Engineering and Technology, edited by AL Moorthy and PB Mangala. Ahmedabad: INFLIBNET Centre. 102-106 pp.
- Francis, AT (1998). Integrated Agricultural and Rural Information System (IARIS): an evaluation of the existing Information System in Kerala. In Towards the new Information Society of Tomorrow: Innovations, Challenges and Impact. 49th FID Conference and Congress, New Delhi, India, October 11-17, 1998 edited by Malwad NM et al. New Delhi: INSDOC. III- 153 pp.
- Gaur, Ramesh C (2003). Reengineering library and information services:process, people and technology. Mumbai: Allied Publishers. 112-114 pp. 5. ICOLC (International Coalition of Library Consortia) (2004):

Statement of current perspective and preferred practices for the selection and purchase of Electronic Information. *http://www.library.yale.edu/consortia/* icolcpr.htm. (Accessed on 04-10-2004).

- Jalloh, Brimah (2000). A plan for the establishment of a library network or consortium for Swaziland: Preliminary Investigations and Formulations. Library Consortium Management: An International Journal. 2(8) 165-176.
- Potter, William Gray (1997). Recent trends in Statewide Academic Library Consortia - consortia - consortia discussed include Georgia's GALILEO, Louisiana Library Network, OhioLINK, TexShare, and Virginia's VIVA - Resource Sharing in a Changing Environment. Library Trends. Winter. 45(3). Accessed through htth://www.findarticles.com).
- Sanville, Tom (1999). Use levels and new benifitss for consortial purchasing of electronic journals. Library Consortium Management: An International Journal 1(3). 47–58.
- University Grants Commission (1988). Development of an Information and Library Network, Report of the Inter Agency Working Group. New Delhi: UGC. 488 p. A.T. Francis is a post graduate in Library and Information Science and also in Commerce. Presently he is working as Assistant Librarian in the Kerala Agricultural University. He has worked as a Library Professional for more than 15 years in organizations, like DRDO, Lakshadweep Administration, etc. His areas of interest are Information and Communication Technologies, Library Automation, Networking and Resource Sharing, Re-Engineering and Management of Library and Information Systems, HRD and User Education and Training.

Part C
Digital Library

11

Digital Library: Issues and Challenges

Mehar Singh

ABSTRACT

The 21st century in which we are living today is the information and communication technology age. With the advent of digital publishing the libraries are going from traditional to digital. At present, the demand of digital information is increasing on their desktop. This article focuses on digital library and highlights the objectives, development, components and advantage of a digital library. Some issues and challenges are also discussed, which are faced day to day. Most of the libraries are moving to digitization resulting which the entire LIS professionals ready to face the challenges.

Keywords: Digital Library, Informational Technology, Digital Collection, Issues and Challenges.

INTRODUCTION

Today, we are living in the information and communication technology age, where libraries known as Digital Library. But there are so many different views on nature of digital library. There are number of terms which are used about the digital libraries. These terms are electronic library, desktop library, online library, virtual library, cyber library etc. The origin and development of a digital library has become a very common source for information seekers. It provides the remote access at worldwide level at a very faster rate. The fast growth of information and communication technology digital library and particularly digital library has changed the traditional methods of research, storage, retrieval and communication of information. In fact, modern libraries are moving traditional to digital environment. The library which is provides digital information to their users, which is consisted text, images, digitized material, video and audio. The digital library is an organised collection of digital material which can be accessed through internet around the world.

Numerous terms are used to signify the concept of digital libraries. For example: - Larsen defines, "A digital library as a global virtual library-the library of thousands of networked electronic libraries". Michel Lesk defines, "digital library is a collection of information that is both digitized and organised and which offer capabilities beyond those of the traditional library". Digital library foundation defines, "digital library organizations that provide the resources, including the specialized staff to relate the structure, offer intellectual access to interpret, distribute and preserve the integrity of and ensure the persistence over time of collection by a defined community or set of communities".

WHY WE REQUIRED DIGITAL LIBRARY

- Explosion of information and knowledge.
- Demand of high information.
- For save the time of the users.
- To solve the space problem in the library.
- To improve the quality of service in traditional libraries.

DEVELOPMENT OF DIGITAL LIBRARY

The traditional libraries were located as close to users and services not available to another place. They were organised the information uniquely with the librarians. But the digital library movement in India is swiftly increasing and the traditional libraries are now on their way to digitization in a phased manner. Today, libraries are being changed with the development of technology and their librarian has become information scientists, who keeps the library on a click of mouse and retrieve the required information to the users. The photo shows the main changes.

Change from a traditional library to digital library

The digital libraries are providing easy access to collections through the use of computerized library catalogue such as On-line Public Access Catalogue (OPAC) as shows in figure. Digital libraries differ significantly from the traditional libraries because they allow users to gain an on-line access and work with the electronic forms of full text documents and their related images. Many digital libraries also make available an access to other multi-media content like audio and video.

When the users search the required information or document with manual system in the traditional library it was taken more time to search the information but in digital the library the users search such required information or document in a second. The example of catalogue from traditional to digital shows the current development in library. The traditional libraries are changing to themselves in to digital library system due to the dramatic changes in technology.

DIGITAL LIBRARY SERVICES

(Kulshrestha and Singh, 2012) Digital library provide a wide array of services to assist members of the library. The following services are offered by the by the digital library:

- Audio and Video communication
- Electronic publishing
- Bulletin Board Services
- CD-ROM database
- Subscription of e-books and e-Journals
- Remote information service
- Electronic document delivery services
- Electronic mail
- Internet Access
- Access to online catalogue within the campus
- Current Awareness Service and Selective Dissemination of information service through e-mail alert.

COMPONENTS OF DIGITAL LIBRARY

The following components are very essential to create a

digital library for access of huge digital collection in a network environment.

Software requirement

- Operating system Linux/Window.
- Web designing software for example Java, front page etc.
- Adobe acrobat reader.
- Digital Library software for example DSpace, Greenstone, E-print and fedora etc.

Hardware requirement

- PCs.
- High Speed Processor.
- Server.
- Internet connectivity – LAN or WAN.
- Scanner
- Printer – Laser and ink jet.
- Hard disk with large space.
- Wi-Fi access point.
- UPS for backup.
- Multimedia interfaces
- Anti virus
- Digital camera
- CDs (Read and Write) and DVDs

OBJECTIVES OF DIGITAL LIBRARY

The objectives of digital library as mentioned below (Sharma and Kushwah, 2012).

- To collect, storage and disseminate the information in digital form via communication channels
- To save the time of library users and library staff
- To reduce cost concerned in various library operations
- To minimize the space problem of large library

- To provides access to very large collection of digital information
- To meet the requirements of users in the I.T environment
- To provide the facility of networking and resource sharing

FEATURES OF DIGITAL LIBRARY

- It provide user-friendly interface
- It supports advanced search and retrieval
- It supports multimedia content
- It save the library man power and funds
- It provide help in Inter Library Loan (ILL)

ADVANTAGE OF DIGITAL LIBRARY

1. No physical boundary : The users of digital library need not go to the library physically, people from all over the world can access to the same information where internet connection is available.

2. Round the clock availability : The users of digital library can be accessed the digital information at any time, may be 24 hours a day or 7 days of the week.

3. Multiple access or Remote access : The same resources can be used at the same time by a number of users.

4. Information retrieval : The users are competent to use and search the information of the whole collection. Digital libraries can provide very user friendly interfaces.

5. Easily accessible : It can be easily access within a short period of time.

6. Space : The digital libraries have store much more information because digital information requires very little physical space to keep them.

7. Dissemination and retrieval : the digital library can disseminate their information via internet and the users can retrieve information in the same way.

ROLE OF LIBRARIAN'S IN DIGITAL AGE

Long ago the duty of librarian's was mainly to preserve the library collection and make them available to the users whenever required. But in this digital environment the librarians have to change themselves due to a dramatic growth technological development. Digital library needs digital librarians who leads to produce, manage, maintain and services the digital information. The modern librarians in digital age have to plan, implement and support to digital services. So a librarian in this information communication and technology and digital age should have extra skills for efficiency and adopting to change, as and when required.

Dr. S. R. Ranganathan stated "Librarianship" is a noble Profession. A librarian derives his joy by seeing the dawn of joy in the face of the readers, helped by him to find the right book at the right time. (Muqueem, 2007) Concept of librarian ship has changed with the change of time. Currently librarians equipped themselves with the skill of handling the new technologies. Electronic media such as CD-ROMs and DVD etc is replacing physical form of books and Journals. The information experts working in digital information environment requires balance combination knowledge, expertise.

DIGITAL LIBRARY–ISSUES AND CHALLENGES

The Challenges of Creating
a Digitial Library

(Jagtap and Kapade, 2012). In this IT environment the online publications are increasing day by day. More issues and challenges are facing during digitization of traditional libraries to digital libraries.

1. Technical architecture : Technical architecture is the first issue in creating of any digital library system. The technical architecture will include gears such as:

- High speed internet connection
- FTP and Web Server
- Selection of digital material
- Bibliographic database in printed or digital form

2. Building digital collections : One of the major issues in creating digital library will be the building of digital collections. There are three methods of building digital collections:

- Digitization of existing collections to digital form
- Acquisition of original digital collection like e-books, e-Journals etc.
- Access to external materials

3. Digitization : It is the Conversion of any printed analogue media such as books, Journals, articles, photos, paintings, microforms and etc into digital form through scanning. An observable barrier to digitization is that it is very expensive. The infrastructure cost is generally very high. Digitization is one of the issues and challenges in creating digital libraries.

4. Metadata : Metadata is another issue in the development of digital libraries. Metadata is an important in digital library because it is the key to search and use of any document.

5. Copyright/rights management : The copyright has become the most difficult barrier to the development of digital library. The digital document can be easily copied without the permission of the author and remotely access by the multiple users at the same time. The information scientists and LIS professionals will have to develop mechanisms for managing copyright and the system allow to them provide information without violating copyright.

6. Preservation : Preservation is one of another issue to the development of digital library. Most of the storage devices have a short life span. The digital information which is preserved in PDF form and another file can be moved from one to another medium of storage, in this process the containing digital information become obsolete. So the preservation of storage medium, preservation of access to content and preservation of fixed –media material through the digital technology in considering the type of preservation. The preservation of digital material is an important part for making a digital library (Verma and Dominic, 2009).

CONCLUSION

The digital library is continued to attract the digital information seekers that could lead us to a highly structured collection. The digital libraries are the result of information explosion. During digitization of traditional library in to digital library many problems are appear such as lack of technical knowledge and skill of the information professional, lack of original software package, lack of funds and lack of some other infrastructure facilities. There should be a significant headway to remote the barrier and challenges of digital libraries. Today's information scientist and LIS professionals must give a thought to the establishment of digital libraries.

REFERENCES

- Ganguly, Shantanu (2012). Creating Digital Library in Globalized E-Society, 88-93. New Delhi: DPS Publishing House.
- Lal, C. & Kumar, K. (2007). Descriptive Questions in Library and Information Science, 521-523. New Delhi: Ess Ess Publication.
- Prof. Seadle, Michael (2012). World Digital Libraries: An international Journal. 5 (1), June 2012, 51-73. New Delhi: TERI Press.
- Prasad, ARD and Devika P. Madalli (2007). International Conference on Semantic Web and Digital Libraries. DRTC.

- Verma, Naresh Chandra and Dominic, J. (2009). Journal of Library Information & Communication Technology. 1 (1), 2009, 44-55.
- Kataria, Sanjay (2012). Future of Libraries in Digital Age, 312-320. New Delhi: KBD Publication.
- *http://www.google.co.in/imgres/* visited on 20.03.2013.

12

Digital Libraries: The Future

Ms. Anita Gaba

INTRODUCTION

Digital libraries are an information system providing network access to organized digital collections containing primary documents. Digital Libraries are where the library resources available in digital form. They may also referred to as a new type of online public access catalog (OPAC). Online public access catalogs have been around for many years and have served libraries well; however, with the arrival of the "virtual library"- remote, dispersed information resources accessible primarily via some form of telecommunications network- existing forms of OPACs,. Digital libraries basically store materials in electronic format and manipulate large collections of those materials effectively.

"Digital libraries are organizations that provide the resources, including the specialized staff, to select structure, offer intellectual access to interpret, distribute, preserve the integrity of and ensure the persistence over time of collections of digital works so that they are readily and economically available for use by a defined community or set of communities." Don Waters "A digital library is a machine readable representation of materials which might be found in a university library together with organizing information intended to help users find specific information. A digital library service is an assemblage of digital computing, storage, and communicating machinery together with the software needed to reprise, emulate and extend the services provided by conventional libraries based on paper and other material means of collecting, storing, cataloging ,finding and disseminating information," Edward A. Fox "The digital library as "an electronic information access system that offers the user a coherent view of an organized, selected and managed body of information" Clifford Lynch

These definitions are recognized the more traditional role of a library in the digital world: at the very least a digital library should offer services along with information such as indexing & cataloguing. Users of digital library resources may come to expect more sophisticated functions, such as information and knowledge management services, resource discovery mechanisms and personalization of access and monitoring of new and existing digital resources. Digital Libraries have received wide attention in the recent years allowing access to digital information from anywhere across the world. They have become widely accepted and even preferred information sources in areas of education, science and others. The rapid growth of internet and the increasing interest in development of digital library related technologies and collections helped accelerate the digitization of printed documents in the past few years.

CHARACTERISTICS/ FEATURES OF THE DIGITAL LIBRARY

Digital Library has a number of advanced browse and search features

Searching

- By title, keywords, issue or volume number, or author name plus click on an author name in the article abstract to perform a search.
- By inspect classification codes or indexing (thesaurus terms) save any search query as your own dynamic RSS feed.
- Browse by publication type, or a particular journal title.
- Buy Articles: purchase articles online with a credit card via the Document Store order print articles from our document delivery service info retrieve.
- E-first: view abstract of advanced articles as soon as they are published with the 'E-first' feature.

Register

You can register for access to these useful personalization features:

a) Customization : Personal table of contents email alerting service save links to articles in your my articles collection bookmark your favourite titles in my Publications list

b) Information Sharing : Download citations in Endnote, Bib Tex or plain text format. Email an abstract or collection of article links to your colleagues. In addition, subscribing users will be able to take advantage of these features:

Usage Statistics

- Counter complaint customer usage statistics available monthly
- Linking: To inspect (or other bibliographic database) abstract of cited articles via cross Ref DOI to cited full- text From an article to those that have cited it to a related article (e.g erratum, or comments)
- Different patrons are permitted different actions and to see different parts of each collection.
- To find specific information, each user must understand the catalog structure.

- The catalogue may describe items not actually held as part of the collection at hand.
- The catalog and the collected items are used differently and not necessarily housed in the same place.
- Documents are catalogued with text descriptions and also with conventional properties such as author names.
- Documents contain cross-reference to other documents.
- Documents identifiers are different from document names.
- Translations of a document may express essentially the same information, e.g. versions of classic literature in different languages.
- Each stored item is valuable, often with part of its residual value assigned by its authors originally or authors assignees.
- Part of the value provided by a library is the provenance information it hold for each item.
- Item are put into libraries because, while each is thought valuable for futures reference, the specific individuals who will read it and the times when this will occur are not known.

COMPONENTS OF DIGITAL LIBRARY

Digital library requires well-established and proven information technologies by accessing the database or servers through networks. The following components are very essentials to create digital library.

Hardware requirements

- 24 hours internet connectivity
- Computer servers
- LAN or WAN
- Scanners
- Storage media: high power hard disk
- Wi fi tower and CDs
- Digital Camera

- High power Ups
- Converters
- Networks
- Multimedia interfaces

Software

The software requirement of the DL as indicated below:

- Linux operating systems
- Digital library software like Greenstone and D-Space
- Editing software

Humanware

The key skills are required for digital library staff as indicated below:

- Management skills
- Technical skills
- Subject skills

Objectives of Digital Library

The objectives of digital library as mentioned here in:

1. To collect, store, organize and access information in digital form via communication channels.
2. To meet the requirements of patrons by providing better services
3. To provide personalized and retrospective services in efficient way.
4. To have large digitized databases.
5. To save time of library staff by avoiding routine jobs.
6. To provide coherent view of all information within a library in any format.
7. To serve widely dispersed communities throughout the network.
8. To minimize massive storage and space problem of large libraries.

9. To reduce cost involved in varies library activities.

SERVICES OF THE FUTURE

- **Cataloguing :** not much left, all done centrally
- **Acquisitions :** mostly becomes large and bundled
- **Circulation :** largely automated, replaced by on-line access
- **Reserve shelf :** almost certainly gone
- **Reference :** perhaps more complex, and different remote clients
- Emphasis on electronic searching & delivery
- **Special collection :** increase its importance: A collection service, which performs selection against defined criteria, tailored and specialized catalogues or other resource discovery aids and administrative process.
- Children's material, or "study hall" function at college: same?
- **Data services :** more of a struggle, but might centralize.
- The libraries are access rather than holdings: they are accessible from far away.
- In a world where every bookstore, video store, hardware store and drugstore are now branches of national chains, is an independently run library an anomaly.
- **Must emphasize personal services :** just delivering books is not going to be enough.
- Distance learning will be a online learning means online libraries.
- Repository service, where digital objects can be deposited and stored, and to which the digital library provided access.
- A naming service, which ensures that each digital object has a globally unique name and that this can be resolved into at least one physical location.
- An index service, which enables sets of digital objects to be

described and queries to be resolved into result sets containing unique names.

MERITS OF DIGITAL LIBRARY

The main advantage of the DL as indicated below:

- Helps in Resource sharing facilities.
- It saves the library manpower and funds.
- Helps in inter-library loan.
- Helps to reach information of their users at faster rate through ontime communication.
- It minimizes the duplication of new invention.
- Helps the libraries to get recent publications from the publishers.
- Researches! Information scientists will get information with minimum time.
- Helps to get bibliographical information, retrospective search, union catalogue, Abstracting and indexing of periodicals.
- On-line library catalogue through internet gives access to bibliographic records of millions of books and details of holding of academic and research libraries, e-journals and newsletters.
- E-publications provide aids for connectivity, audio visualization, customizability, creation and revision of documents, interactivity and rapid information retrieval.
- E-publications may help in overcoming the restrictions on the length of the paper imposed by many scholarly journals.
- The E-publications data can be maintained up-to-date so hat the buyer will be able to purchase the latest version of the publications. This enables on demand publishing and allows retrospective searching and SDI.

DEMERITS OF DIGITAL LIBRARY

Digitizing of information does help a great deal. However, there are problems for handling and using these large volumes of digitized information. Digital and Electronic libraries are also not without their limitations, Few of these are.

Compatibility and standardization problems are likely to be faced due to the use of a variety of hardware, software, information collection and storage and retrieval methods.

- A problem frequently encountered and difficult to overcome will be the one of copyright and intellectual property issues.
- This phenomenon is faced because electronic information is more easily manipulated and reproduced and the identity of the author or changes affected to original data is harder to establish.
- The unrelenting invasion of the viruses will pose another ethical risk.
- Changing habits in the arena of learning and teaching is also another problem browsing on the digitized form is difficult when compared to printed form remote access to documents are uncomfortable when compared to spot accesses a disappearance of nascent information in internet.
- Problems in the scholarly publishing.
- Some documents are used only when it is seen.
- Inadequacy of the libraries to predict the future use of documents, irrespective of its type i.e. printed or digital.
- Locating the information on the internet requires good skills.
- Problems of intellectual property rights of the author and publisher, etc.
- There is the problem of health hazards associated with the use of computers e.g. eye and back problems as well as the exposure of radiation from monitors.
- There will be a necessity to be proficient in computer usage and keep abreast of the state-of-the art in the field, if they

wish to retain an edge in the provision and utilization of information services.

- Librarian like professionals perceive a threat to their jobs posed by computers which can presumably takeover their functions with greater efficiency and will resist the move towards complete computerization.
- The emphasis on consistently upgrading skills and the yawning gap between information rich and poor will give way to such new social problems as technophobia and this will initiate a new battle in the users.

GUESS FUTURE

Libraries becoming increasingly virtual, the librarian becoming a knowledge navigator? Or will libraries disappear as the world goes wifi – will Google become the future library? Or will place remain central, as libraries become anchor tenants in co-located in commercial and public transit-orientated developments? Or is social justice what libraries are really about – a place for empowering, for creating a better society, finding spaces for young and old, for books and digital media?

The library, while appearing to be stable has changed throughout history. It has moved from being elite based, for the few that could read, to being a public space, and funded by the public has well, instead of by wealthy benefactors. And while the advent of the printing press changed the nature of the library, moving it from the monastery and the painstaking efforts of monk scribes, the recent digitalization of the world is leading to even more dramatic transformations.

The library has entered a contested domain – their definitions, its bundle of services are up for grabs – who defines it, which pays for it, what are its basic purposes. And with the onset of edutainment and as the peer-to-peer knowledge revolution, might libraries become places not just for receiving knowledge but for directly creating knowledge.

Few challenge a stable future for libraries include:

- Local and state governments dramatically decreasing their funds for libraries- other financial models- user pays, Mclibrary.
- Users changing from young to the aged OR from the aged to the young.
- Libraries building as examples of green and even developing cradle to grave green technologies for books and for facilities design.
- The library as a place for escape from a chaotic world, eg the slow movement: slow time, slow learning –slow everything-as the world quickens and moves to hyper time and culture, libraries find niches by providing places of quietness and calm.
- The librarian becoming a digital avatar, interacting with users, learning about their changing needs, and even in the longer term, organizing our memories.
- The off-shore Call Centre Library.
- Death of the book-continuing emergence of new media formats.

The impact of these emerging issues point to libraries changing dramatically from today – particularly in the areas of funding and location; purpose and skill sets for librarians and core activities. But would libraries be more digital or slow; for the young or the aged; in suburbs or co-located in denser cities? Which future?

SCENARIOS OF THE FUTURE

There are four possible futures. The first is the "Lean, Mean, and Information Machine." This future would arise from concern about the costs of buildings, space becoming too valuable and libraries moving down the list of core priorities for funding. A library is the future would need to seek funding through philanthropy to supplement government funding. The choices would be: from the user, from community groups, from federal and Global grants and from corporate sponsorship. With the expected rise in triple bottom line reporting, it was anticipated that corporate sponsorship may become more attractive as libraries would be an easy and safe way to show that they were good corporate citizens-helping young & old. The role of some librarians would shift, becoming entrepreneurial, a broker of services and entities (community groups, corporations, city, state and federal authorities).

The second scenario is the opposite of this. Civilizing the world, civilizing ourselves is the foundational purpose of the library. No corporation should fund it, as over time market values would poison human values. The purpose of the library is that of community builder–providing ideas to all, those who can and those who cannot afford. Books cannot be overlaid with digital sponsorship, purity must be kept. However, the best way to serve as community builders is to go to the community. "Co-location for Community Capacity Building" is the title of this scenario. Libraries move to areas of intersection–of young and old, poor and rich, information savvy and digitally challenged. Among possible areas could be transport hubs. Libraries could continue to develop as anchor tenants, co-existing with other government service providers, with coffee shops and commercial tenants. As passengers stepped out of light city rail carriages, they would enter the library. In front to them would be transparent glass, the lighting illuminating knowledge.

Libraries would have multiple shifting rooms, focused on the needs of different groups. Or libraries could segment, based on citizen travel patterns. Some libraries would be more classical-more focused, other edutainment, others as places for social community groups to meet or libraries could change during the day-shifting who they were from noon to three pm to evening time. The librarian would need to be multi- skilled; understanding the diverse needs of different age groups-engagement with the community would be primary. The library in this future would model what it meant to be civilized: deep & diverse democracy.

In a third scenario, the library and the librarian becomes a "Knowledge Navigator". Users would see and then create – use information to create new knowledge, new communities learn and recreate. Libraries would be a hybrid of physical and virtual space with cutting edge technologies, cultural maps of the world, to help users develop their interests, find connection to each other and find their place in the changing digital world. The library would be an 'experience'. For those new to the digital world and for emerging technologies they would , it could train them, ensuring democratic and enabling access for all; for those adept, it would create games for them to learn, indeed, gaming may become a metaphor for the library. Users would find their knowledge treasures through clues left by the knowledge navigator or other users engaged in knowledge sharing and production – the division between the fun of electronic gaming and the seriousness of the library would breakdown. Public space would become an open and porous, local and global public space.

The last scenario takes the knowledge navigator future but makes the tough observation - given the billions of dollars Google and other web engines have to play with, and given the skill sets of their employees and owners, what makes us think libraries can survive. Aren't they the "Dinosaurs of the Digital Knowledge Era". The globalization of the coffee shop eats up one market; digital search portals eat up another market, until through continuous dis-aggregation there is very little left. The future of the library is easy to predict – there won't be any. Funding will move to other core areas for cities – traffic, water, and dealing with global warming, competing for young people in an aging society; post-oil energy problems. Libraries will slip down the priority radar as they will not be seen as a response to these issues.

Many librarians as well are unable to meet the challenge of the skills shift. They are unable to be relevant with the new world dis-order. As the library monopoly dies, other competitors enter the fray and foundationally change the nature of the library. A few survive as some still want to see and touch books, but with the virtual book about to include physical senses, the writing is already on the virtual wall

CONCLUSION

The emerging of information technology with high resolution capture and sophisticated engines and large storage digital contents continue to ability of conform the digital library and in the future digital library and in the future digital libraries will be common in every institute, Colleges and Universities.

REFERENCES

- Ane's Encyclopedia Dictionary of library & Information Science: Amjad Ali.
- Arms, Williams Y., "Digital Libraries", Cambridge
- Articles: Which future for Libraries? : Metafuture.org.
- Digital library: Suresh Chandra dwivedi
- Electronic media & the library services: R.S. Khochar.
- Empowering Knowledge for all: Roll of Digital Library : Anil Kumar Jharotia
- Future of digital libraries in India: T.B.Rajashekhar
- Model of digital library: J sridevi & Vijaylakshmi
- The digital library of India project: process, politics and Architecture: Vamshi Ambati

13

An Overview of Digital Library

Balvinder Kaur

INTRODUCTION

We are in the age of a networked society where IT in addition to its use in all spheres of human activity has been used extensively to record, store, and disseminate the information in the digital form. IT has almost converted the world into a global village. The revolution in the IT sector is influencing the information industry also. Libraries are also changing to meet the demand put on them. The new generation whose demand for information is never met is always demanding that traditional libraries should be developed as a well equipped and interconnected as digital libraries. If we consider that the information is for use and for all then why not libraries for all? Why not libraries become universal' open for all those who seek for information. By considering this view a number of large organizations in USA and Europe have already more or less switched over to digital mode. They are making digital images of periodicals which are not available in electronic form and there after no new procurement are being made on print media if a digital version is available. Examples of such organizations are University Micrographic Inc. (UMI of USA), National Institute of Scientific and Technical Information (INIST of France) etc.

The term Digital Library has a variety of potential meanings, ranging from a digitized collection of material that one might find in a traditional library through to the collection of all digital information along with the services that make that information useful to all possible users. As there are many definitions of a "digital library," terms such as "electronic library" and "virtual library" are often used synonymously. A digital library is nothing but a large database for the people who are working on hypertext environment. It is an environment, which supports the full life cycle of creation, storage, preservation, dissemination and use of data, information and knowledge.

According to Arms a digital library is a managed collection of information with associated services where the information is stored in digital format and accessible over a network. The digital library federation in the USA defines the digital library as: Digital libraries are organizations that provide the resources, including the specialized staff, to select, structure, offer intellectual access to, interpret, distribute, preserve the integrity of, and ensure the persistence over time of collections of digital works so that they are readily and economically available for use by a defined community or set of communities. A digital library is an organized collection of digitized material or its holding in the digital form, which can be accessible by a computer on the network by using TCP/IP or other protocol.

The Digital Library is:

1. Organized collection of multimedia and other types of resources.
2. Resources are available in computer process able form.
3. The function of acquisition, storage, preservation, retrieval is carried out through the use of digital technology.

4. Access to the entire collection is globally available directly or indirectly across a network.
5. Support users in dealing with information objects
6. Helps in the organization and presentation of the above objects via electronic/digital means etc.

REQUIREMENT FOR DIGITAL LIBRARIES

The Internet and World Wide Web provide the impetus and technological environment for the development and operation of a digital library. The Internet provides the TCP/IP and or its associated protocol for accessing the information and web provide tools and technique for publishing the information over Internet. In the digital environment it is reasonable to say that a central back up or archive should be created at the national level, which will store information output of the region as well as information from outside the country. Some of the requirements for digital libraries are:

1. Audio visual : Color T.V., V.C.R., D.V.D., Sound box, Telephone etc.

2. Computer : Server, P.C. with multimedia, U.PS. Etc

3. Network : LAN, MAN, WAN, Internet etc.

4. Printer : Laser printer, Dot matrix, Barcode printer, Digital graphic printer etc

5. Scanner : H.P. Scan jet, flatbed, Sheet feeder, Drum scanner, Slide scanner, Microfilming scanner, Digital camera, Barcode scanner etc

6. Storage devices : Optical storage device, CD-ROM, Jukebox etc.

7. Software : Any suitable software, which is interconnected and suitable for LAN and WAN connection.

RESOURCES OF A DIGITAL LIBRARY

The resources of a digital library are those, which the

computer can store, organized, transmit and display without any intervening conversion process. It includes both print and electronic or digital material. The digital material may be of multimedia types or any other i.e. only digital audio, video, full text information, photograph, drawing, digitized sound, e-book, v-book, electronic tax, map, image, 3D representation etc. The collection may also include structured /unstructured text, scanned images, graphic audios, video recording etc

ON LINE RESOURCES

1. Local database of traditional books in machine-readable form.
2. E-book, v-book, electronic tax, map, image, sound, video, and multimedia etc.
3. E-journal
4. LAN, MAN, WAN for web browsing, e- mail etc.
5. Well trained manpower for online help

OFF LINE RESOURCES

1. C.D-ROM, Jukebox etc.
2. Audio visual aid etc.

A SHIFT FROM TRADITIONAL LIBRARY TO VIRTUAL LIBRARY

The development is already taking place. The traditional closed access libraries are shifting towards open access library. The open access libraries are shifting towards automated library, the automated one towards the electronics, the electronics to digital and finally end in Digital library and its different aspect/ Badan Barman virtual library. Is it really true? The truth is that nobody knows what will be the future of libraries. In the following Para an attempt has been made to categorized the different types of libraries based on the technology used. It's the best time to mention that there is no strict line of demarcation between the latter four types of libraries.

1. Traditional library : The collection of the traditional libraries is mostly print media, manuscripts etc and are not well organized. The document are deteriorating at a rapid rate, the collection information is not easy to locate and so does not easily reach to user, Again the traditional libraries are confined itself within a physical boundary.

2. Automated library : A library with machine-readable catalog, computerized acquisition, circulation and OPAC are called as automated library. The holding of this type of libraries are same as that of traditional libraries.

3. Electronics library : When automated libraries goes for LAN (Local Area Networking) and CD-ROM networking and started procuring E-journal and other similar kind of publication then it is known as electronic library. The resources of the electronic libraries are in both print and electronic form. The electronic Medias are used for storage retrieval and delivery of information.

4. Digital library : It is a later stage of electronic library. In digital library high speed optical fiber are used for LAN and the access is over WAN and provide a wide range of Internet based services i.e. audio and video conferencing and like other. The majority of the holding of a digital library is in the computer readable form and also acts as a point of access to other on line sources.

5. Hybrid library : The libraries, which are working both in electronic or digital and print environment, are known as hybrid library. Actually it is a transitional state between print and digital environment. It is estimated that in near future libraries will be of hybrid nature, some of the very strong point in favor of this view are centuries old reading habit of paper, convenience of handling and reading a paper document then the digitized one (in case of digitized some equipment are must needed to read the document), incompatible standard of electronic product, different display standard of digital product and its associated problem etc.

FACTORS OF CHANGE TO DIGITAL LIBRARIES

The limited buying power of libraries, complex nature of recent document, storage problem etc are some of the common factor which are influencing to change to digital mode, some other factors are-

1. Information explosion
2. Searching problem in traditional libraries
3. Low cost of technology: When we consider the storage capacity of digital document and its maintained then it can be easily realize that the cost of technologies is much more less than that of traditional libraries.
4. Environmental factor: the use of digital libraries is the cleanest technologies to fulfill the slogan "Burn a CD-ROM save a tree"
5. New generation needs

ADVANTAGES OF THE DIGITAL LIBRARY

A digital library is not confined to a particular location or so called building it is virtually distributed all over the world. The user can get his/ her information on his own computer screen by using the Internet. Actually it is a network of multimedia system, which provides fingertip access. The spoken words or the graphical display of a digital library is again having a different impact from the words that are printed. In the new environment owing a document will not be problem for the library because the user will pay for its uses.

1. No physical boundary : The user of a digital library need not to go to the library physically, people from all over the world could gain access to the same information, as long as an Internet connection is available.

2. Round the clock availability : Digital libraries can be accessed at any time, 24 hours a day and 365 days of the year

3. Multiple accesses : The same resources can be used at the same time by a number of users.

4. Structured approach : Digital library provides access to much richer content in a more structured manner i.e. we can easily move from the catalog to the particular book then to a particular chapter and so on.

5. Information retrieval : The user is able to use any search term bellowing to the word or phrase of the entire collection. Digital library will provide very user friendly interfaces, giving click able access to its resources.

6. Preservation and conservation : An exact copy of the original can be made any number of times without any degradation in quality.

7. Space : Whereas traditional libraries are limited by storage space, digital libraries have the potential to store much more information, simply because digital information requires very little physical space to contain them. When the library had no space for extension digitization is the only solution.

8. Networking : A particular digital library can provide the link to any other resources of other digital library very easily thus a seamlessly integrated rêsource sharing can be achieved.

9. Cost : The cost of maintaining a digital library is much lower than that of a traditional library. A traditional library must spend large sums of money paying for staff, book maintains, rent, and additional books. Digital libraries do away with these fees.

DISADVANTAGES OF THE DIGITAL LIBRARY

The computer viruses, lack of standardization for digitized information, quick degrading properties of digitized material, different display standard of digital product and its associated problem, health hazard nature of the radiation from monitor etc. makes digital libraries at times handicap.

1. Copyright : Digitization violates the copy right law as the thought content of one author can be freely transfer by other without his acknowledgement. So One difficulty to overcome for digital libraries is the way to distribute information. How does a digital library distribute information at will while protecting the copyright of the author?

2. Speed of access : As more and more computer are connected to the Internet its speed of access reasonably decreasing. If new technology will not evolve to solve the problem then in near future Internet will be full of error messages.

3. Initial cost is high : The infrastructure cost of digital library i.e. the cost of hardware, software; leasing communication circuit is generally very high.

4. Bandwidth : Digital library will need high band for transfer of multimedia resources but the band width is decreasing day by day due to its over utilization.

5. Efficiency : With the much larger volume of digital information, finding the right material for a specific task becomes increasingly difficult.

6. Environment : Digital libraries cannot reproduce the environment of a traditional library. Many people also find reading printed material to be easier than reading material on a computer screen.

7. Preservation : Due to technological developments, a digital library can rapidly become out-of-date and its data may become inaccessible.

ROLE OF LIBRARIAN IN DIGITAL ENVIRONMENT

Though the digital environment is built as a system, which can be used by its ultimate end user directly from their desktop pc, the role of librarian cannot be overlooked. In digital environment also the librarian and information scientist will be needed for packaging and repackaging of information, for electronic publishing, for reference purpose, to advise the user about the strategy to identify relevant electronic sources etc. thus the librarian will be more or less a hypertext engineer. In the new environment it will be very difficult for the librarian to decide what should be organized? How to give citation? How to organize the collection? Etc because the new environment will be really challenging one for the librarian to decide who are author who are publisher and who are user? . In the new environment anyone who has access to the network of digital libraries can be a publisher by merely posting messages to an online discussion group or by other means. A virtual environment is really open for all. In some cases, librarians have the opportunity to digitize unique material in their libraries' collections, which can then be made accessible to users of the World Wide Web at large. Some US libraries have done this with local history collections; see, for example,

CONCLUSION

Digital libraries are not going to replace the physical existence of document completely but no doubt to meet the present demand, to satisfy the non local user digitization must be introduced so that at least libraries becomes of hybrid nature. The initial cost of digitization is high but experiment shows that once digitization is introduced then the cost to manage this collection will be cheaper than that of any traditional library. Day by day the cost of digitization is decreasing, the online publication is increasing, the needs of user are shifting towards a different environment so it's needless to say that after one or two years my library or your library will go to be digitized so it's the pick time to all informational and library professional that they geared themselves to take the challenge.

REFERENCES

1. Ansari MEhtab Alam (2003) Digital Libraries, needs technology and benefit, IIA Belletin, 38 (3), pp 22-26
2. Banerjeem Swapna and Chakrabarty, Biplab (1999) , Digital libraries, some issues and perspective, II A Belletin 34 (3-4) October1998 to March 1999, pp 60-63
3. Cyric, Jiji, Deshmukh, GR and Rajalakshmi (2002) Digitalization of Libraries, in modern era, IIA Bulletin 38 (3) Pp 68-73
4. Dhaka, R.P.S and Arora, Kamlesh (1995) Electronic libraries, in A myth or a reality, Ambala of library science and documentation , 42(4) pp 152-59

5. *http://en.wikipedia.org/wiki/Digital* library

6. *http://scholar,lib.vt.edu/DL12/define DL.html*

7. *http://www.clir.org/pubs/issues/issues* 04.htm/#dlt

8. *http://www.dlib.org/metrics/public/papers/dig-lib-scope.html*

9. *http://www.firstmonday.org/issues/issue6 6/lynch/#12*

10. *http://www.kmentor.com/socirtech-info/archives/000694.html*

11. *http://www.wwwp.org/final-posters/poster17.html*

12. Khan, shaked Ahmad, Khayat, Roshan and Yunus, Mohad (2003), Digital libraries , the present scenario , ILA Bulletiin 39 (2) pp 3-7

13. Koteswara Rao, M (2003), Digital Libraries; Challenges, opportunities and Implimcations, paper presented at SIS 2004 conference 22-23 January 2004, Madras

14. Kumar, Bhuvan and Reddy, V.Sreencecias (2203) Digital library use; a case study of NIT library, Warangal, ILA Bulletin 39 (2) pp 40-45

15. Ravi Chandra RAO I.K and Suma P. (1996) Digital libraries challenge and issues, Digitized information paper presented at the SIS-96, 18-20 January 1996, Bangalore, (Eds) T.B Rajasethar, IK Ravi Chandra Rao and N.V Satyanarayana, pp 185-95.

14

Library Digitization: Challenges and Implications

Davinder Pal Singh

ABSTRACT

Digitization implies conversion of documents and art works into digital images. Digital images here mean electronic copies of documents. Digitization is a process in which materials are converted from the hard copies to electronic copies. The major purposes of digitalization are to enhance access and improve preservation of library materials. A number of challenges are encountered in the process of digitizing library materials. These challenges include human and technical problems, which have implications for planning and policy. Digitization is an essential task in modern day libraries, because of the current challenges, and the need to go digital, that is, provide online services.

INTRODUCTION

The invention of computer and the internet facility seems

to have posed new challenges to the practice of librarianship. The application of computer to librarianship tends to be gaining momentum all over the world. It has led to the development of a separate field of study, virtual library, which is now offered in some universities as a course of instruction, even up to doctoral degree level. Library digitization has a lot of influence on the librarianship profession. Library digitization has become part of the work of librarians. Most libraries are involved in digitization. Digitization can involve simple data conversion from catalog cards or paper to digital form, video and audio migration to digital form, and so on. Digitization which is also called computerization refers to the shift to a society where computers are everywhere. Digital refers to the language used by computers. To paraphrase, digitization means that computers are becoming more and more integrated into all parts of the society that is, moving towards a society where computers will be involved in most, if not all, aspects of everyday life.

Several users can use the same library material the same time and in different locations, without disturbing each other. The use of the digital library is also very flexible. Library users are not restricted to the official library hours of a conventional library. The digital library permits random access to library materials. This enables learners to consult wide variations of learning materials at their convenience, thus making learning easy Some of the users cannot use any of the existing search technologies, whether manual or electronic. It is the responsibility of the librarian to guide these users, so that they can make optimal use of the library resources. It is the responsibility of librarians to assist library users in their bid to search for materials either manually or electronically. This will encourage the users to relate freely with the librarians and in the library. Some of the users that have problems may not request for assistance. It is the duty of the librarian to detect their problems and offer assistance.

PURPOSES OF DIGITIZATION OF LIBRARY RESOURCES

There are three major reasons for digitization:

1. There is a need to preserve endangered library resources.
2. For the improvement of the efficiency of information search mechanisms.
3. It improves access to library resources.

Most libraries are digitizing materials which might be lost in the future, such as old manuscripts, research projects, photo images, analogue maps, non-live musical recordings, government official gazettes and several other historical records. Digitization is useful in preserving precious materials. Making high-quality digital images available electronically will reduce wear and tear of fragile items. However, digital copy should not be seen as a replacement for the original piece, therefore original document should be cared for even after digitization. Preservation remains a secondary benefit of digital projects.

The search mechanisms for information in the traditional library set-up are very slow and inefficient. If the libraries become digitized, such library resources can be assessed online without stress. Online links can be made to existing digital libraries; this will enable users to use materials that are not available in the local library. By digitizing library collections, information will be accessible to all instead of a group of researchers. Digital projects allow users to search for collections rapidly and comprehensively from anywhere at any time. Several users can access the same material at the same time without any hindrance. It also removes the problem of distance, as users do not have to travel to libraries that possess the hard copies of library materials before they can access and use such materials. A digital library can be made to serve a region.

THE PROBLEM

The manual system of searching for information and materials in the traditional library does not permit multiple use of the same material by different library users unlike the online library services. It is inefficient and time consuming, hence the need to exploit the advantages of the digital library which enables provision of online library services. However, there are a lot of challenges facing the setting of a digital library or conversion to digital status. Digitization is time consuming and it is also a very expensive endeavour which requires adequate planning and monitoring. Creating a digital library is a very good solution to these problems. There is a need to undertake a psychological preparation of the employees, so that they will not resist digitization of the library resources. There is also a need to retrain the workers. The major problem is lack of technical-know-how; hence most digitization projects often run into problems. There is a need to design flexible and compatible programs. In addition, the interface should be user friendly, so that users can search for information with ease. It is not all electronic copies of documents that will suit the application format, hence the need to take this into consideration during conversion or digitization exercises. Data entry can be very rigorous and expensive, hence it is easier and cheaper to provide online links to existing digital libraries, rather than start a digital library afresh. This has its own limitations. It does not take care of local materials. Developers need to bear in mind copyright laws, while digitizing or scanning. There is a need for permission from the publishers of materials to be digitized. This paper addresses this problem and also examines the implications for policy and planning.

PROCESS OF DIGITIZATION OF LIBRARY RESOURCES

The setting up of a digital library entails the following stages:

(i) Policy enactment : A policy is a guiding statement. The top management should enact a policy on the project. Such a policy will serve as a reference point and guide for implementing the project. The policy should contain the goals of the digitization project. Good goal setting is important for any new initiative, and digitization is no exception. The goal 'To make our materials more accessible on the web' is not specific enough. There is a need to be specific, particularly on the categories of users that will access the collection, the type of material they may be interested in, how they will use it, how many people are envisaged to use it, the planned procedure for its advertisement, and the benefit of the material to users and institutions. Contacting current and potential users is an excellent way of having clues to all these issues. One may consider sending out a survey to the project's intended audience in order to learn how they are currently using the material, and how they might use it differently if it was digitized. It may be helpful to contact other institutions that have digitized similar collections and learn from their successes and failures.

(ii) Policy approval : The policy should be approved by appropriate authorities before project implementation. For instance, a university library may need the approval of the university management and other funding agencies before any digitization project can be embarked upon.

(iii) Planning, budgeting and monitoring : This is a very essential stage. It is desirable to set up a planning committee that will draw the plan and budget for the digitization exercise. Budgets for digitization projects should include the following categories:

(a) Salaries, wages and benefits (likely to be about 50% of the project cost);

(b) Staff training;

(c) Equipment and supplies;

(d) Services, contracts and legal fees;

(e) Overhead and indirect costs (including offices and workspace);

(f) Maintenance, licenses, and communications charges; and

(g) Contingency (setting aside about 10% of the total project budget for unexpected expenses).

The purposes of the digitization project, the source of fund and the amount available for the project should also be taken into consideration. At the regional or national level, effective planning for digitization can bring together all types of libraries, museum, academic/professional societies, historical societies and archives to take advantage of the exercise.

(iv) Acquisition of appropriate technology : The plan drawn for the project will determine the appropriate technology to acquire. Technology here refers to all the equipment/hardware and software that are needed.

(v) Administrative decision on the procedure to be adopted: Decision has to be made on the mode of operation, whether to just establish links with existing digital libraries or to digitize in-house or to contract it out. There is a need to establish time limit for the project.

(vi) Sensitization, psychological preparation and retraining of staff : In most places the staff will like to resist the digitization project. It is a common thing for people to resist change, just for the fear of the unknown. The library staff may fear that the success of the project may affect their jobs adversely. Those who are not computer literate may not be willing to adjust. All these categories of people have their genuine reasons to resist. It is the responsibility of the library management to educate them and allay their fears.

(vii) Copyright permission : Violation of the copyright laws should be avoided. It is not necessary to obtain copyright permission for materials published before 1922. Copyright permissions have to be obtained for materials to be digitized, particularly those that are not available in the government domain. When the copyright permission is granted, it is essential to enter the date of approval and the name of the person who granted the permission into the database. If an item is still under copyright, it can be digitized for in-house use only. Usually, copyright statements permit educational and non-commercial usage. Seeking copyright permission may even be another way of establishing collaborative and cooperative relationships. An introductory note should be inserted in the database for this showing the source of the material and the person who granted the permission.

(viii) Implementation and trial testing : At this stage it good to start with trial testing, using a few materials as samples. This will enable us to know whether the format and fields are flexible and suitable. Adjustments can be made. A pilot digitization project should start with a manageable collection. Focusing on items with consistent or standard formats (photographs of all one size or type, documents from one collection, etc) provides the best chance of success. If the trial testing is successful, the project can be commenced. Data entry is rigorous, time consuming and very expensive. Existing materials can be scanned. Modification of scanned and digitized documents is very essential, so as to minimize errors. This will enable developers to put them in appropriate formats.

(ix) Evaluation of the project : The top library management needs to be making periodic evaluation of the project. This will reveal lapses that have to be addressed. Evaluation is an often neglected aspect of digitization projects. Project evaluations should not just be easily quantifiable figures or an attempt to determine program's impact on the user. Several digital projects are judged by the number of items they digitize. This is really one of the least useful measures of a project's success. The number of images digitized means nothing, if they are of low quality, hard to locate in a database, or not interesting to the public. Assessing how users are using digital materials provides a more effective evaluation tool. At the bare minimum, projects should be formally evaluated based on the set goals.

The Benefits of Digital Access for Collections

- Can be viewed from anywhere, at any time of the day
- Can be printed from the web
- Viewers can find what they are looking for quickly and independently

- Can save staff reference time by answering frequently asked questions on the web
- Can enhance images electronically so that they can be viewed with greater legibility
- Increases use of collections and facilitates learning and scholarship

The Preservation Benefits for Collections

- Objects do not have to be re-shelved or located by staff
- Objects are not handled frequently which reduces wear and tear

CHALLENGES OF DIGITIZATION OF LIBRARY RESOURCES

Digitization of library resources poses a great deal of challenge to the major stakeholders, that is, the library management, employees and library users. The library management has to source for fund for the digitization project. It is often easy to get sufficient fund for the project, as the required fund can be enormous. Most academic libraries face unmanageable budgetary demands. The financial constraints have to be taken into consideration. This is essential so as to be able to continue with the digitization exercise after the conversion program. Clear cut decisions have to be taken on the form of digitization to adopt. Where the fund available is grossly inadequate, the library can be linked to existing digital libraries. It is also possible for t library to select and digitize additional materials. The proportion of the additional materials to be digitized will therefore depend upon the available fund. The problem of most digitizing efforts is that of inadequate fund and not that of technology. There should also be continuous flow of fund so that the project can be functional. The academic libraries are often located in research environments, where students, faculty and other researchers will depend on the library for timely information. Management of the digitization project entails policy initiation, setting priorities and planning. These are challenging tasks for the management. The library management needs to consult libraries that had digitized their materials so as to learn from their experiences. This will guide a lot while formulating policies on the digital project. A planning committee has to be set up. It is the responsibility of this committee to draw plans and budget for the project. The library management will also need to prioritize the different activities involved and assign each task to a committee. Time limits should be assigned for completion of each task. The task of carrying along all the staff and guiding library users can be challenging. Some of the staff will like to resist change, particularly those that are not computer literate. It is essential for the library management to explain the essence of the project to them and arrange to retrain the employees so that they can participate in the project and remain functional in a digital library. Some of the library users will definitely find it difficult to search for materials in the digital terrain. It is good for library assistants to be available to render assistance. Orientation programs can be organized for these library users from time to time. This is very essential in academic libraries where the users can be many and are also regular users.

IMPLICATIONS FOR POLICY AND PLANNING

This paper has a lot of implications for policy and planning. In view of the importance of digitization, a special annual vote or financial allocation ought to be made for it. This is necessary, because it is not a onetime activity. Libraries keep on acquiring materials, some of which have to be digitized. Orientation programs should be organized for the staff. This will enable them to understand the purpose and importance of the exercise. Those of them that lacked the required computer skills should be retrained. The services of appropriate technical personnel should be employed. This will reduce the flaws in the exercise. If there is inadequate fund for digitization, the library authority can manage the available fund to create digital links with existing digital libraries. This will enable library users to access library resources in such digital libraries.

Digitization has to be treated as an emergency situation in libraries that are just starting the conversion of their library resources to digital form. Huge allocations of fund, time and personnel have to be devoted to the exercise, as it is very expensive, tedious and time consuming. Special policies and plans have to be formulated to guide the exercise. It is advisable to adopt the committee system for its execution, so as to guarantee efficiency. A committee ought to be assigned to each aspect of the exercise. There should also be a monitoring committee to monitor and evaluate performance.

CONCLUSION

This paper has established that digitization is an essential task in modern day libraries. If a library is to live up to current challenges, it has to go digital, that is, provide online services. This will enable it to preserve endangered library resources, improve the efficiency of information search mechanisms and enhance access to library resources. It is essential for the library management to provide policy guidelines and articulate plans for the exercise.

REFERENCES

- Balakrishnan, N. Reddy, Raj. Ganapathiraju, Madhavi. Ambati, Vamshi (2006), Digital Library of India: a testbed for Indian Language Research TCDL Bulletin, 3 (1).
- Bekele, S. (2002) The role and impact of the digital library on capacity building in the developing world- a case study of the OSSREA Digital Library, International
- Digital Library Federation. (2001), Registry of Digitized Books and Serial Publication, Available at http://www.digilib.org/collections
- http://www.idealibrary.com
- Information and Library Review, 34, 129-137. Retrieved December 12, 2006 from
- Krishnamurthy, M. (2005) Digital Library Services at the Indian Statistical Institute, Electronic Library, Vol. 23, No.2.

- Liu, Y.Q. (2004) Best practices, standards and techniques for digitizing library materials: a snapshot of library digitization practices in the USA, Online Information Review, 28, 338-345. Retrieved September 21, 2006 from *www.emeraldinsight.com/1468-* 4527. htm
- McCook, K. (2004) A digital library to serve a region: The Bioregion and the first nations collections of the Southern Oregon Digital Archives, Reference and User Services Quarterly, 44, 116-121.
- Radford, M. (2001). Encountering users, encountering images: Communication theory and the library context, Journal of Education for library and information science, 42, 27-41.
- Radford, M. (2006). The reference encounter: Interpersonal communication in the academic library, Chicago: ACRL International Journal of African & African American Studies Vol. V, No. 2.
- Smith, Abbey (2001), Strategies for Building Digitized Collection. Washington, D.C. Digital Library Federation, Council on Library and Information Resources. Available at *http://www.clir.org*
- Varatharajan, N. Chandrashekara, N.M. (2007), Digital Library Initiatives at Higher Education and Research Institutions in India, Library Philosophy and Practice, Vol.9, No.2.

15

Digital Library Development in ICT Era: An Overview

Sanjay Gupta

ABSTRACT

ICT has brought dramatic changes in every sphere of modern library era. Many kind of technology is available now and technology innovations are the future. These innovation including artificial intelligent, robotics, speech, synthesis, email, CD/DVD, networking, barcode system, e-publishing, hypermedia, multimedia, tele-facsimile, radio data paging etc share common technology revolving around electronics, computers, telecommunication, printing and reprography popularly known as ICT. The project aims to give an overview on digital library is purpose, a planning of digital library, DL initiatives in India, challenges in digital environment, role of librarian in digital development and some advantages mentioned.

INTRODUCTION

Digitization of the library material has become the need of today. However the transition of the traditional libraries to the most modern and effective digital library is not an easy process. In note only involves conceptual as well as a practical understanding of the concepts of digital libraries as this is the age of the ICT (Information and Communication Technology) so it is very necessary to run with the time and should use all the latest technology so that we should not leg behind wit the world. The advancement of the science and technology has made a tremendous improvement and changed almost in very walks of life. This service rendered with the help of ICT is faster and more effective. Digital library is the electronically library in which the information is store in the digital form.

William Arms - "An informal definition is a managed collection of the information, with associated services where the information is store in digital formats and accessible over a network. A crucial part of this definition is that information is managed. A stream of data sent to part from a satellite is not a library. The same data, when organized systematically, become a digital library collection. Digital library is a collection of electronics resources that provides direct or indirect access to systematically organized collection of document. According to IAN Witten and David Bainbridge, "Digital library is a focus collection of digital objects, included text, video and audio along with methods for access and retrieval, and for selection, organization and maintenance of the collection".

PURPOSES

The purpose of the digital library is to facilitate access to electronic information, print material, and library services to ensure that the information need of user community are met, regardless of their location. It enables libraries to deliver valuable information that already exists within library walls electronically to patrons outside those walls. To create a new digital resources locally and to integrate local digital resources with remote ones.

The number of people accessing digital collection though the WWW also show explosive rates of growth. Finally international organization is making a global information environment of reality. The purpose is to provide digital library development.

PLANNING OF DIGITAL LIBRARY

An essential of digital library is to provide increased interaction to the user and continuing improvement in computing, networking and storage capabilities. Technology will continue to affect library patrons' needs. Digital library integration work touches most areas of library operations. Leaders have often addressed it by creating cross-functional teams that create together to design system and solve problems. Yadav and Chidambaram have a development planning process that should be taken care while the digital library is established.

1. The institute and the library goals should derive digital library initiatives.
2. Based on the goals of the organization explains and new possibilities that data are created by digital technology can solved.
3. Long term planning based on the continuously involving nature.

DIGITAL LIBRARY INITIATIVES IN INDIA

India has seen several digital library initiatives at the institutional, organizational and national level. Some of them are quite successful while other are making significant progress. Some of the nature initiatives of digital libraries in India are furnished below:

1. Archives if Indian labour and the V.V. Giri institute of the labour. (*http://www.* Indialabourararchives.org/ sources/ jnu.htm)

2. Indian institute of science NCSI (*http://vidya-mapak.ncsi.iise. ernet.in/ cgi-bin/library*)
3. Indian Institute of Management Kozhikode (*http://intranet.iimk.ac.in/cgi-bin/library*)
4. Search Digital Library SDL at DRTC Bangalore (*http://drtc.isibang.ac.in/ index.jsp*)
5. Nalanda Digital Library, National Institute of Technology (NIT) Calicut (http://www.nalanda.nitc.ac.in)
6. Vidyanidhi Project (*http://www.vidyanidhi.org.in*)
7. Million Book Universal Digital Library Project-Carnegie Mellon-IISc-ERNET (*http://www.dli.ernet.in*)
8. Indira Gandhi Centre for the ARTS (IGNCA Digital Library)-(*http://ignca.nic,in*)
9. INDEST, Ministry of HRD, GOI (*http://paniit.iitd.ac.in/indest*)
10. National Tuberculoses Institute (NTI), Bangalore (*http://ntiindia.kar.nic.in/*)
11. Indian Institute of Technology. Delhi Library (*www.iitd.ernet.in/*)
12. INSDOC (*www.insdoc.org/*)
13. J-Gate (j-gate.information.co.in/)
14. INFLIBNET (*www.inflibnet.ac.in*)

CHALLENGES IN DIGITAL DEVELOPMENT

With the increasing applications of web technology for library work, several libraries in the country are involved in development efforts on the disseminating information through local internet as well as intranet. But significant efforts on digital library development where meagre in the country due to server constraints.

(a) Infrastructure Constraints : Not only the weak computer infrastructure in the library and affiliating institutions is creating major hurdle, but also the lack of high capacity bandwidth for network and internet access. Hope that situations will soon improve due to the concerted efforts on the various fronts as VSNL and BSNL are engaged in a massive action plan to enhance the communication infrastructure in the country.

(b) Lack of Professional Expertise : Expertise can be generated through either retraining the existing staff members with the help of continuing education programmes or by including digital library components in the professional courses to give the desired exposure to budding professionals. In a professional service stream like information science, strong compartmentalize would not yield any satisfactory results, and it is high time that we should involve computer and communication professionals to assist use in access provision of whatever contents we are so good collecting, ordering and servicing.

(c) Absence of High quality Contents : The overall impact of India research output on the growth of disciplines like science and technology is a matter of introspection. In these disciplines, where considerable progress has been made on digital access provision, most of the publishers, authors, and information providers are based in developing world. Most of the best research papers from the country are getting disseminated through foreign publications due to various reasons. In such a premise, even contents, where our country has a strong hold like arts, folklore, spirituality, traditional knowledge etc. are getting side lined. As we uses and reach of contents in digital form are far more wide reaching than the printed text, and the process of digitization involves cost in terms of contents, systems, experts manpower, care should be exercised on what sort of contents need to be digitized.

(d) Management Support : For the provision of world class information systems, resources and services the libraries need the wholehearted support from the respective management. Institutional supports in term of proper funding, human resources and IT skills enrichment are prerequisites for the development and maintenance of state-of-art digital library system and services. There are many more processing problems being faced by the libraries in India in its pursuit of the building digital libraries.

(e) Lack of ICT Strategies and Policies : A vast majority of the libraries in India do not have laid down policies own ICT panning and strategies to meet the challenges post by technology push, the information overload, as well as the demand-pull from the users.

(f) Rigidity in the publishers' policies and data formats : Having successfully installed and configured a digital library does not qualify a library to automatically populate all its digital collection into the digital library. One has to obtain publishers' consents and copyright permissions for the same. Digital library software's usually accept and process all popular and standard digital formats such as HTML, Word, RTF, PPT, or PDF. Most of the publishers' put their materials in their own proprietary e-book reader format, from which the text extraction becomes almost impossible. A vast majority of the scholarly contents rests in journal literature and due to copyright issues they cannot be easily (almost impossible) find its way into the local repositories of the digital library.

(g) Copyright/IPR Issues : Issue of copyright, intellectual property, and fair use concerns are posing unprecedented array of the problem to the libraries and librarians are struggling to cope with all this related issues in the new digital information environment.

(h) Lack of the proper planning and integration for information resources : Presently the library acquisitions in India are either paper based and electronic. In most of the libraries, paper based document outnumber the electronic subscriptions and acquisitions. Some of the libraries need retro-conversation and digitization of the library holdings too. Literature on the related study show that there is a sever lapse on the libraries with the regard to proper planning of their information resources which are conducive for the developing digital libraries. Also the electronic resources penetrate to the libraries in a multiplicity of complex format and with different access terms and conditions.

These information resources are scattered and distributed across a wide variety of publication types as a vast number of publishers. There is a dire need for proper planning and meticulously framed content integrations model which is achieved and implemented through world standard digital library technology.

THE ROLE OF LIBRARIAN IN DIGITAL LIBRARY DEVELOPMENT

Digital information system management referred to the overall competencies (acknowledge, now –how, skills and attitudes) necessary to create, store, analyze, organize, retrieve and disseminate digital information (text, images, sounds) in digital libraries or any type of information. To disable the roles of the digital librarian, the following concepts are introduced to understand further.

(a) Guardian of the Information Super Highway : The information superhighway is a vision or a metaphor. It envisions fusions of the two-way wired and wireless capabilities of telephones and networked computers with a cable TVs capacity of transmit hundreds of programmes. Service would be delivered by telecommunications networks, cable TV networks, and the internet and mobile communication (William et. al., 1995). Infrastructure that provides bandwidth-on demand and information-on-demand service are called information superhighway. There will be two types of information service such as a public (free) service and commercial service. The use of existing telephone, fax, and analogue TV broadcast service will be supported in the initial information superhighway. The addition, new service such as a video phone, multimedia electronic messaging, digital TV/HDTV broadcast and movie and video on-demand service, will be provided (LU, 1996).

(b) Guardian of the global digital library/the universal digital library : The digital library is a really a transitory phase toward the universal digital library, vast distributed information and active repository accessible from anywhere with increasing improved indexing, extraction and summarization techniques. It will be library without walls or national boundaries.

(c) Digital librarian acts as symbiotic human-machine Guru: The digital librarian act as a intermediately in the task of the massive digitization of the information, its storage, dissemination, managing the achieve and making available digitizing network information to the end user. Digital librarian and computer depend on the each other of processing and dissemination of the digital information and both are interrelated.

(d) Navigation, Browsing and filtering : The navigation of the future would tend to integrate with the human assigned information retrieval from the network universe and would support rapid information navigation and precision retrieval. The digital librarians are an expert navigation, browsing and filtering, digital reference service and electronic information service from the digital information sources.

(e) Multimedia Search and Indexing : In multimedia digital library requires not just standard indexing and retrieval, but also sub-document indexing and summarization techniques more than that of the paper document.

(f) Knowledge and data mining : The digital librarian will require limit knowledge of a data mining and discovery of knowledge form a digital libraries to extracts unmeant information needs of users. For this purpose, unrevised learning techniques such as clustering, and composite terms discovery techniques etc. are useful.

(g) Search and retrieval co-ordination : It require comprehensive acknowledge of retrieval engines and indexing searcher so that the digital library can achieve the global of the creating information queries with respect to the search system.

(h) Digital librarians interface function : Fundamental role of digital librarians in digital libraries is to act as an intermeditory how brings together users and information. Digital library access tools are the right of set of tools using involve way to tackle a plephora of challenges and opportunities for information access technology and faster access (Kikuchi et al., 1996).

(i) The role of a librarian transforms into that of a digital librarian : What will be the role of a librarian in the future? It seems to fit in with the notion that the library will disappear as a institution. the information world. If work become decentralized and telworking becomes the norm, we are going to have "Virtual libraries", with a vast increase in the range and variety of digital information resources. The "electronic cottage" worker becomes the norm, working on a contractual basis for different kinds of organizations, connected to corporate databases and information files online (Wilson, 1995). The logical sequence of this is that the librarian, too, becomes a predominantly online worker, supporting the citizen/worker be selling services. Finding relevant information faster than the competitors, faster than a non-information-worker can find it, and surviving on the basis of superior knowledge of the networks and digital information resources available through them. We already have the words to describe these roles: digital librarian, digital information professional, cybrarian and information broker. A different view of the future might be one where a "digital library" is more like a "knowledge-warehouse", where a complex system of professionals whose expertise supports access ti information acts as an intermediary to a variety of digital and other sources (Kuny and Cleveland, 1998). Although, at this stage, it is difficult to define what the role of the digital librarian will be, in the long term, a few things already are clear. It is especially important to understand that the ultimate goal is not just to facilitate access to digital information just-in-time to the critical want of end-users and additionally electronic publishing, but to create and develop digital knowledge channels, digital knowledge sources which allow synergy between partners leading to mutual exchange and enrichment of digital knowledge domain.

(j) Digital information access : There are a variety of information retrieval techniques, including metadata searching, full-text document searching,. In knowing what can or cannot be retrieved from the digital library information sources, the digital librarian acts as an expert in the acquisition of digital information.

Accessing and retrieval of digital information through digital library access tools: The method used to store, find and retrieve digital information from DIS is called the access method. The technology used to access information digitally provides "navigation paths or digital library access tools" through the digital information.

Mobile information access: a vision of tomorrow: The ability to access information on demand at any location confers competitive advantage on individuals in an increasingly mobile world. The data from shared file systems; relational databases, object-oriented databases, and other repositories must be accessible to programs running on mobile computers.

(k) Tools, Pools and Sources for the digital librarian : There are various tools available to use in digital information systems and they facilitate in accessing, searching, browsing, navigating, retrieving, indexing, storing, organizing and dissemination of digitized information. The list given below is the digital information sources and pools, and these are used as digital access tools which ultimately aim to facilitate universal access to all:

- ***Online public access catalogues (OPACs):*** meta-databases (describe, provide link to other databases/digital information sources; online databases (Knight-Rider, OCLC, MEDLINE).
- ***Internet-based tools*** : e-mail networks, mailing lists, electronic conferences, World Wide Web, Website home pages, Wide Area Information Services (WAIS), Web browsers, Gopher systems, and Veronica Archie, FTP, Telnet, Usenet, Newsgroups, BBS, List servers, discussion groups.
- ***Digital networks/networking:*** BLASE, MEDLINE, NICNET, DELNET AGRIS, INIS, all sorts of networks.
- Hypertext/Hypermedia
- Multimedia (high bandwidth computer networks)

- Multimedia networking protocols
- Cellular and pager networks
- Electronic publishing tools
- Net-dwelling software agents
- Electronically fax/commercial vendors
- Telephone/TV

(I) Competencies and skills of a digital librarian in the management : The competency of a digital librarian is represented by different sets of a skills, attitudes and values that enable a digital librarian to work as digital information professional or digital knowledge worker and digital knowledge communicator. There are skills and competencies which the digital librarian should develop and ability to manage the digital libraries and digital knowledge in terms of digital knowledge management. The following are the skills and competencies required for a digital librarian in the management of digital information systems and digital libraries.

- Internet, WWW
  - Navigation, browsing, filtering;
  - Retrieving, accessing, digital document analysis;
  - Digital reference services, electronic information services;
  - Searching network databases in a number of digital sources and websites;
  - Creating home pages, content conversion, downloading techniques;
  - Web publishing, electronic publishing;
  - Archiving digital documents, locating digital sources;
  - Digital preservation and storage;
  - Electronic messaging, connectivity skills;
  - Web authoring.

- Multimedia, digital technology, digital media processing
  - Multimedia indexing, image processing, object-oriented processing;
  - Interactive digital communications and visualization;
  - Cataloguing and classification of digital documents, digital content;
  - Searching and retrieval of text, images and other multimedia objects;
  - Speech recognition, image visualization;
  - Advanced processing capabilities exploiting digital medium;
  - Conferencing techniques including teleconferencing, video conferencing.
- Digital Information System, online, optical information
  - Interfacing online and off-ramps, twists and turns of digital knowledge;
  - Development of digital information sources;
  - Digitization of print collections;
  - Competency to manage CD-ROM network station;
  - Development of machine readable catalogue records;
  - Design and development of databases;
  - Design and development of software for digital libraries;
  - Conversion of print media into digital media;
  - Knowledge in digital knowledge structures.

Here are additional skills that the digital librarian should develop. One is the ability to think in terms of knowledge networks.

- Internal networks
  - Personal networks;
  - Project terms, competency groups, GroupWare;
  - Internal digital knowledge resource;

- Intranets.

- External networks
    - External knowledge resources;
    - External personal networks
    - Customers, suppliers, partners;
    - Extranets.

(m) Training for the digital librarian : For more than 25 years, schools of information studies have been adapting their curriculam and teaching activities to the new information technologies. All of those changes have occurred within the broad umbrella of information studies. The new digital information system (DIS) creates a major shift in the paradigm of the information transfer process (Deschatelets, 1997). Included as a supplement here is a syllabus for a course on digital information systems, prepared by Prof. M.A Gopinath, Documentation Research and Training Centre, Bangalore (Gopinath, 1996). In this course, each component is considered as a separate paper. The components of each course paper are outlined. The syllabus meets to a large extent the educational requirements of the digital librarian. In addition to that, digital information system management will require co-operation between different academic units. To accomplish that, both creativity and certain entrepreneurial spirit will be required.

Digital information system: International dimensions of digital information; Technological and behavioral dimensions of digital information system; Components of digital information system; information system activities; Input of data resources; Processing of data into information; Output of information products; storage of data resources; control of system performance.

Digital Information management: (Deschatelets, 1997): Computerized text analysis; Database creation:; Database distribution; Design of interfaces; Design of retrieval language document structuring; Language-related industry (e.g. translation, terminology, software); Network-related activities (e.g. translation, terminology, software); Network-related activities (e.g. Internet, intranet, extranet, LAN, WANs); Optical based information products (CD-ROMs, CDI, DVD); Telecommunications; Virtual reality; Communication formats; Competitive intelligence; Data mining; Knowledge mining; technology watch.

Digital technology: Computer system components; central processing unit primary and secondary storage capacities; Types and trends in computers, computer peripherals; Computer software, Application software, Data resources management.

Digital technology media processing: Online tutorial; filter enhancements; frame viewer for digital document distribution internet/WWW publishing support through distribution; Common interfaces; searches within hierarchical classification or domain; searches against keywords or expressions containing Boolean logic; give users easy access to information, service irrespective of their physical location; building more intelligence to applications and services; manage-wise systems; desktop management; network analysis; virus protection; Windows and multimedia presentation; CD-ROMs; simulation; visualizations.

Knowledge base through digital libraries: Interface features; multimedia system and multimedia stream playback; multimodal and hypermedia; information retrieval/access system; training support; surrogation and storage; intellectual property systems; digital preservation systems,; network system; World Wide Web. Apart from the above outlined curriculum, this project report also aimed at training the digital librarian with innovative vigor and approach.

- Online Information access and retrieval
- Information networks and networking
- Advanced Information technology.

Advantages

- Digital libraries are essential to enable more people to create and use vast amounts of distributed information and to contribute to the quality available via the web and future access frameworks.

- Digital libraries remain closely linked advanced in high performance computing and networking and both contribute to and validate these technologies.
- Digital libraries are inertly international knowledge is recorded and store in many forms, often using different languages and symbol systems. To support the creation, maintenance, management, access to and preservation of digital contents. Web is a magic information retrieval rode.

CONCLUSION

Modern Technology has changed the nature of our society and style of working of the people. Library and Information services cannot lag behind and require progress of the civilization. Keeping in view the requirement of time, technological development and global change, librarians are changing their nature, traditional to digital. The target of librarian is not only to provide excellent information services to users but technology has added many new dimensions to this task. All the librarians have to believe in power of Information and take the responsibility to provide effective, efficient, relevant and up to date information to their users. The competencies and skills form the basis for the continual survival and growth of librarianship in this information age. Librarians must recognize the expanding nature of the challenges that confront them and the range of competencies that area required to ensure that the librarians have a viable tomorrow. Charles Darwing theory-Survival of the Fittest applicable here. In this age of shifting paradigms, librarians have to evolve and transform accordingly for better future.

REFERENCES

- Aditya Dev Sood, Uma Chandrasekharan, Digital Library in India: A Baseline Study. Educational Development Center. 2004
- Christine L. Borgman, What are digital libraries? Competing visions.

Information Processing and Management 35 (1999) 227-243

- *http://en.wikipedia.org/wiki/Digital_library*
- M.G. Sreekumar and P.Sreejaya. Digital Library Initiatives and Issues in India: Efforts on Scholarly Knowledge Management. *http://dpspace.iimk.ac.in/bitsream/2259/252/1.05-mgs-ps-paper.pdf*
- N. Balakrishnan, Raj Reddy, Madhavi Ganapathiraju and Vamshi Ambati, Digital Library of India; A Testbed for Indian Language Research. TCDL Current Bulletin. 2006. Volume 3. Issue 1
- N. Balakrishnan. Digital Library of India A Testbed for TCDL Bulleting, Current 2006, Volume 3, Issue 1
- Peter Ingwersen. The role of Libraries and Librarians in Organizing Digital Information. Libri, 1999, vol. 49, pp.11-15
- Sreenivasulu, V. The role of a digital librarian in the management of digital information systems (DIS). The electronic Library. (2000) 18(1):pp. 12-20.
- Tiwari,R.K. Library Services in Electronic Environment. J.K. Business School,2010, Gurgaon.
- Yadav, D.S. Foundation of Information Technology. New Age International Publisher, 2007, New Delhi. Pp2-4

16

Creation of a Digital Library

Pankaj K. Bhardwaj

INTRODUCTION

Digital library is not equal to conventional library. A group of networks of various multimedia systems is called digital library. These are collected at a server to combine various workstations. All information's were in digital format whereas sound, graphic, readable material etc. Collection of personal library and many other libraries can be collected under the networking. Many digital libraries project starting in the world. Indian Technology Institute, Indira Gandhi National Kala Kendra has started their projects at national level in India. User use easily all the material through networking.

Digital libraries are organizations that employ and display a variety of resources, especially the intellectual resources embodies in specialized staff, but they need not be organized on the model of conventional libraries. Though the resources that digital library require serve functions similar to those within conventional libraries, they are in many ways, different in kind. For example, computer and electronic network system and system engineering skills, rather than skills of traditional cataloguers and reference librarians, rank high among the essential staff resources.

The meaning of the term "digital library" is less transparent than one might expect. The word conjures up images of cutting-edge computer and information science research. They are invoked to describe what some assert to be radically new kinds of practices for the management and use of information. And they are used to replace earlier references to "electronic and virtual libraries". The partner institutions in the Digital Library Federation realized in the course of developing their program that they needed a common understanding of what digital libraries are if they were to achieve the goal of effectively federating them.

Digital libraries are organizations that provide the resources, including the specialized staff, to select, structure, offer intellectual access to, interpret, distribute, preserve the integrity of and ensure the persistence over time of collection of digital works so that they are readily and economically available for use by a defined community or set of communities. This is a full of definition by any measure, and a good working definition because it is board enough to comprehend other uses of the term.

TOOLS FOR BUILDING THE DIGITAL LIBRARY

Input Devices

Digital Cameras : Information on digital cameras, including feature comparison charts, from the Berkeley Multimedia Research Centre

Tools for Clients

Adobe Acrobat Reader : Adobe Acrobat Reader allows documents producers to distribute exact facsimiles of their documents to a wide network audience. Adobe makes the software to read these documents freely available for various platforms.

Ariel Document Delivery Software: Information on how to deliver documents over the Internet using the Ariel software from the Research Libraries Group.

CALIPR-Preservation Planning Software: An MS-Windows program to assess the preservation needs of book and document collections for institutional or statewide planning.

CU-See Me: The name says it all - desktop videoconferencing software for the Internet.

Internet Scout Toolkit : Breaking trail in the Internet information wilderness? Better go well-armed.

PKUnzip: To decompress PC files compressed in the "zip" format.

Quick Time Virtual Reality: Download your free MS Windows or Macintosh viewer from Apple Computer.

Real Audio: Delivers sound over the Internet. Get your free player here and hook it up to your Web browser. Those who want to serve sound can look into their Real Audio server.

SGML Tools from Open Text: Including near & Far (a tool for creating and graphically modifying document models (DTDs in SGML), Near & Far Lite, and Near & Far Author.

Stuffit Expander: For decompressing Mac files compressed with Stuffit.

World Wide Web Browsers: From the Internet Scout Toolkit.

Tools for Servers

Dienst: A protocol/server for providing centralized searching of a physically distributed collection. Dienst supports the Networked Computer Science Technical Report Library.

ISite: "An integrated software package including a taxi indexer, search engine and Z 39.50 communication tools to access databases"

Mailing List to Web Converters: These programes will take incoming email messages and archive/convert them into a web-browseable form. We use Hypermail here for this purpose for several electronic discussions, including Web4Lib, [Hypermail|MHonArc|Procmail].

mSQL: Mini SQL: A small but free or low-cost (see licensing information) Structure Query Language (SQL) database program.

Real Audio: Delivers sound over the Internet to Real Audio clients.

Site Search: A set of software tools for "building, integrating and accessing Z 39.50 - based information resources in a Web environment".

SWISH-Enhanced: Fast, free and flexible search software optimized for Web servers. The Digital Library SunSITE uses SWISH-E extensively.

Tei2marc: Tei2marc is written in perl, and based on the University of Virginia Library Electronic Text Center's most current document type definition (DTD), TEILITE.DTD. It handles English language and reads in a header element by element, stores its readings in USMARC format, and creates an output file (in ASCII) following the MARC Computer file format field by field (excluding the leader).

COLLECTION DEVELOPMENT CHALLENGES

In a networked space, libraries continue to extend the breadth and scale of the scholarly and cultural evidence they make accessible to their users. Paper based and analog materials remain important even as libraries become increasingly accustomed to their digital manifestations, such as electronic journals and reference databases. Yet we do not fully understand how to exploit the educational and cultural potential of other information sources. Libraries have focused much attention on digitizing selected special collections and interesting collections have resulted. They tend however to be narrow in scope, shallow in depth, passive in appearance and unsustainable financially and technically. The data that are produced in the context of business, government, research and teaching have potentially vast educational and scholarly value. Yet we have only just begun to consider how such data can be included to effect in our evolving digital library service environment despite the fact that the data are unlikely to cost much to subscribe to or purchase. We need to think creatively about collection development strategies appropriate to the evolving digital library service environment. World Cat Selection and ordering process for new library materials and delivering the corresponding World Cat records.

Not all the information/documents are needed to be digitized or can be digitized which are available in the library. Selection regarding the right content for right user at the right time is must (Lynch 1994). Librarians and archives have to choose which books, articles, photographs, films and other materials are to be converted from paper or film into digital form.

Digital Storage and Preservation: Digital preservation essentially aims at taking steps to ensure the longevity of electronic document. It applies to documents that are either 'born digital' and stored on line or to the products of analog to digital conversional long-terms access is intended. There is a wide range of digital formats available and to make smaller more complicated, different digital object have different preservation requirements. These can be depend on the reason the record is being preserved, how long it needs to be preserved, the context and history of the record and its original format. Digital preservation does not mean the same thing for each digital object. In all cases the record must be preserved so that retains its integrity and is authentic and usable.

Digital Library Services: While wide-area file systems score high marks for providing ubiquitous file Services, a focus on storage issues ignores the collaborative activities that take place in this environment. To overcome the challenges to collaboration listed in the previous section, it is helpful to view the wide-area file system as a large repository of digital objects that requires both storage and content management.

The file system already provides some of the basic building blocks from which digital libraries are constructed. A file is a digital object that manages some simple digital material (the contents of the file) and metadata (e.g., the owner and size of the file). Associated with the file are access controls that provide crude limits on how an object is used. The name of the file is universal handle for the object that identifies the file server where the object resides and the file's location within the server. Although these basic building blocks provide some of the necessary services, several enhancements are required for managing a large digital library. Our experience building systems that integrate file services with digital library technology suggests that the following list of enhancements is necessary.

First, the file system must accommodate extensible, user-level metadata to represent properties of a file such as its history and relationship to other files. However, more expressive representations might be necessary to represent more sophisticated properties of files. Secondly, the file system must explicitly type each object. The primary purpose for associating a type with an object is to constrain the metadata stored with the object. That is, the type defines a schema for metadata attributes. The type also provides information about the operations that can be performed on an object. For example, the data file for a calendar application support operations such as "Add Appointment". In this way, the type system makes file self-describing. Through the use of relationships between types, the type system can accommodate the diversity of format that accompanies federated systems with minimal loss of interoperability. In particular, our experience suggests that the use of inheritance to relate types is a powerful tool for providing best-effort interoperability within federated system inheritance enables the specification of a common role for files with different format. The role of the file determines the schema in a base type. Each format is managed by a subtype of the role where the implementation of the operations depends on the format of the file. In addition, inheritance represents specializations among type. A specialization is a type that customizes the basic structure of another type. Within the file system, this regions of a file considered unstructured by another application that operates on the file. For example, a complier throws out any comments that are contained in a file. The application that manages the development environment, however, assumes a structure for the initial comments in the file and extracts function references, author names, and modification history.

Meta-objects constitute the third enhancement of the file system interface. Kahn and Wilensky use the term meta-object to refer to an object whose primary purpose is to store and manage references to other objects. There are many uses for meta-objects in the file system. A meta-object contains references to all of the files that are part of a software package. Dependencies between packages are represented by dependencies between meta-objects. A meta-object contains references to the files that belong to a software development configuration. Another meta-object might refer to the set of changes that are required to translate one configuration to equivalent representations of a file.

Identification and retrieval of objects through queries on the digital material and metadata dramatically simplifies file location and is the final enhancement to the file system interface. One use of the service is to integrate file location with file system browsers and shells. For example, the semantic file system embeds queries within the name of directory. Any application can easily find files within a directory tree by creating a directory whose name is the query. Search embedded within applications is another use of this service. Consider an alternative to mailbox folders where meta-objects with an associated query represent dynamic views on collections of messages. Rather than copy a massage into each relevant folder, the meta-object contains a reference to a single copy of the message. This approach supports multiple classifications of messages without adding the administrative overhead of managing multiple copies of each message.

Information Retrieval: A digital library is a metaphor for access to collections of electronic documents through a network. The classic research area dealing with the electronic search for documents is Information Retrieval. The study of information retrieval has produced a number of methods over the last several decades for accessing information stored within digital libraries. Information retrieval systems provide user centric, retrieval methods. The user through the formulation of complex queries and relevance feedback imposes his/ her structure on the collection. Information retrieval systems are capable of extracting the underlying concepts representing documents and using them to represent the documents in the search space. They are capable of suggesting to the user alternative terms of search for when the user query terms do not match those used to index a collection. Information retrieval systems can also be used to analyze unfamiliar collection to reveal hidden structure existing within them.

Information retrieval by itself is highly effective. If the user has come for knowledge of the domain of discourse. It is less helpful if the user is unfamiliar with the terminology, multiple domains are represented, or the collection is highly dynamic. Problems have arisen in the design of on-line catalogs which utilize information retrieval methods to match customer requests with large collections of stored product information. The catalog systems fail when customers ask for products using terminology not found in the product descriptions.

The diversity of the file types and metadata complicates the integration of services for content- based retrieval with the system interface. Specifically, vast differences in the type and use of metadata imply that no single, standard interface for content-based access to files will be sufficient for all types. For example, metadata typically associated with an HDF file that contains satellite telemetry data is numeric, highly structured, and will be used to generate specialized browse structures. In contrast, metadata associated with an HTML file is textual and is used primarily for full – text retrieval.

CONCLUSION

Creating such a digital library will not be easy or inexpensive, but it is possible. To do so, we must consider not only the obvious challenges, such as copyright restrictions and finding, but also some less obvious challenges, such as deciding how to organize the effort and establishing partnerships outside the library. Fundamentally, building a digital library will require change within the library itself.

REFERENCES

- Singh, Sanker: Internet and Modern Library 2006. pp. 76-84.
- Shaista Muqueen: Preservation of Digital Collection in India. pp. 247-248.
- Jonathan T.Hujsak : Digital Libraries And Corporate Technology Reuse. D-Lib Magazine, January, 1996 ISSN 1082-9873. pp. 3-6.
- Bowman 94: Mic Bowman, ChandaDharap, MrinalBaruah, Bill Camargo and Sunil File System for Information Management. Proceedings of the Conference Intelligent Information Management Systems. Washington, DC. June, 1.
- Bowman 96: Mic Bowman and Ranjit John. The Synopsis file System: From Filestc Objects. Workshops on Distributed Object and Mobile Code. Boston, Massachusetts, June, 1996.
- Bowman 97: Mic Bowman. "Managing Diversity in wide-Area File System". Appe IEEE Metadata '97 Conference. Greenbelt, Maryland. September 1997.
- Daniel 97: Ron Daniel and Carl Lagoze. Extending the Warwick Framework: From Metadata Containers to Active Digital Objects. D-Lib Magazine, November, 1997.
- Kahn 95: Robert Kahn and Robert Wilensky. A Framework for Distributed Digital Services. May 1995.
- DonandJ.Waters : What Are Digital Libraries? pp. 1-6.

Part D
Total Quality Management

17

Total Quality Management in Academic Libraries

Dr. (Mrs.) Nirmal Goyal

INTRODUCTION

The libraries have transformed drastically from storehouses for books and journals to the powerhouses of knowledge and information in the 21st century. Gradually the social and economic changes have prompted the libraries to develop services. The staff has a vital role in the satisfaction of users. The library being a service organization, its prime objective is to provide the right documents, information and services to its users. Only the users' satisfaction survey will facilitate the assessment of their satisfaction with products and services offered. Effectively implementing quality management in libraries requires an understanding of applying appropriate quality management concepts and techniques. Nowadays, electronic resources, networks and the World Wide Web represent a large portion of the library services. In this competitive educational environment, most of institutions in India are thriving to establish reputation by way of imparting quality education. Quality means user satisfaction, competitive cost, timely delivery, etc. According to Ross, "TQM is the integration of all functions and processes within an organization in order to achieve continuous improvement of the quality of goods and services". The goal is user satisfaction. Library users can only describe quality by the characteristics of the service provided to the users. From the perspective of the user, the criteria for judging satisfaction with a service can be reduced to four elements:

- A service is available at the moment it is needed, or
- The information supplied is exactly correct
- The service is of a high quality, and it is delivered by
- Professional well trained staff.

Main meaning of quality is user satisfaction through information/ document or by service. The user in the academic library is the reader/student/ faculty member. Here the user is not an outsider, but part of the academic community. Quality is what one needs and wants, not what you think is needed or what is convenient for you to deliver' Thus TQM is basically a philosophy or concept or approach aiming of satisfying user need on a continuous basis.

IMPORTANCE OF TOTAL QUALITY MANAGEMENT (TQM) FOR LIBRARIES

The importance of TQM for libraries is not only centered around the user's needs but also in anticipating and exceeding the demands of the fast changing environment of service delivery in libraries. Most libraries today operate according to strategic plans containing vision and mission statements, goals and objectives and short, medium and long-term plans. To make this all effective, TQM requires that the management of the library commit itself to the process and actually set the example in displaying a commitment to continuous quality improvement. The primary purpose of an academic library is to support the teaching, research, and other academic programs of its parent organization. An academic library is part of a service organization which delivers products personally to the customer. The increasing expectations of users have challenged libraries to improve their quality of services. Limited by increasingly due to budgetary restrictions, librarians feel more pressure to fully exploit available resources. Therefore, several libraries and information services have adopted quality management practices in recent years. Quality management is increasingly integrated into library services. Libraries have developed numerous programs to fulfill user requirements and concentrate on administrative activities, building the collection, and serving the users. Therefore, the functions of a library can be broadly categorized as administrative management, technical services and public services. Administrative management defines the objectives of the library, allocates the resources to achieving such objectives, co-ordinates related activities.

FIVE LAWS: FOUNDATION FOR QUALITY SERVICE

S.R. Ranganathan formulated the five Laws of Library Science in 1928 which were later published in 1931. These are:

1. Books are for use.
2. Every reader his/her book.
3. Every Book its reader.
4. Save the time of its Reader.
5. Library is a growing Organism.

Later these laws were slightly modified and the word 'books' was replaced by 'documents' to include the work and services of documentation. Afterwards, there application was made in the context of information Science. These laws are considered foundation for quality service. Law makes us understand the mission or purpose of our existence. It is imperative to have clarity in mission, objectives and strategies to achieve them for providing quality service in a Library & Information center. The first law "Books are for use" is the most important and principle among all the laws and the next are supportive or mere extension or the first law. The first law gives us an insight to understand the mission or purpose of our existence. As in a library, books are available for active use and not for preservation. If books are not for use, what libraries are meant for and what should the library do with these books? Obviously, the answer to these questions may be different for one library to another according to the parent institutions it serves. But the answers to these questions make the reason for existence of every library very clear. The second, third and fourth laws are profound – a fundamental statement of goals that every library should strive for. The fifth law gives a vision to achieve goals through strategies to meet the users need –present and the potential on a sustainable basis. Perhaps, this is the thrust of the 'library is a growing organism', Thus, Ranganathan's approach to clarify mission and/or goals and vision to achieve them are very much in tune with the quality management necessitated in a service set –up.

Focusing on Users: Ranganathan considers library service essentially a service, where the reader (user), document (information) and the librarian (service provider) meet, and the user is the paramount. Information and the service provider are there for service of the user". Therefore, the sole aim of the library staff and information resources is directed at, meeting users need satisfactorily. Thus Ranganathan considers 'user' as supreme in a Library & Information center. User focus approach in library environment demands the library and information centre to procure, process and distribute information from users' perspective. It implies that efforts should be made to meet every information need of the user that he intends to demand. For user focus approach, the following are imperative:

Knowing the user Community: Ranganathan considers the 'First thing every librarian perform is to get firsthand knowledge of the users whom he has to serve. It would be unwise to start with standardized nations about the requirements'. Knowledge about users gives us an insight into whom we are serving but also it is helpful in user segmentation which may be an important to meet users demand promptly.

Identifying Users Need and to Anticipate Them: User surveys and user studies not only assess users' need and to anticipate them, requires continuous programme of user education, enabling users to inform them about resources of the library. This direct contact with the readers brings with it opportunities to observe their tastes and wants, their actions and reactions and their likes and dislikes", so that the service providers can provide information according to their requirements.

User Staff Relationship: Library service is not an activity or one time service. It has a potential to serve users regularly which requires good relations between the users and the staff. 'Both of them should be psychologically close to each other. According to Ranganathan, the user should be given prompt and exact service in a personal way. To make him love to come back to the library quite often, he must be attended by a library staff regularly.

Users Involvement in Service Delivery Process: If users need becomes user center service means quality service. Library staff shall have to regard the user at the starting and ending point and right through. User satisfaction is the key goal of the librarian as a manager. In Ranganathan's approach toward user is central to all activities of acquisition, organization and dissemination and user plays a vital role in these processes and activities. Thus, Ranganathan's idea of knowing users' community; identifying their needs and anticipate them; individual care; cheerful assistance to users; friendly attitude toward user; helpful policies, programmes and techniques according to user requirements called Quality Services.

FACILITIES IN A QUALITY BASED LIBRARY

A) Physical Facilities

1. Good library is easily accessible.
2. Good layout for a good library.
3. Sufficient Space, lighting and ventilation.
4. Clean, tidy and hygienic.
5. Cozy and comfortable furniture.

B) Library Collection

6. Good collection of textbooks, journals, reference books, online journals, e-books, etc. is needed in a good library.
7. Good library displays new arrival of books in separate shelves.
8. Good library offers open access to the collection.

C) Library Staff

9. Staff in a good library should be experienced with knowledge of modern technology.
10. Staff should help the users to locate the documents needed and do their works in time.
11. Sufficient staff to run the library.

D) Technical Processing

12. Good library acquire new documents in time.
13. Shelf arrangement and rectification is a never ending process in a good library.
14. Good library has proper catalogue or database for collection (OPAC etc.)
15. Good library has prompt processing, charging and discharging system

ICT BASED LIBRARY ACTIVITIES REQUIRED IN QUALITY BASED ACADEMIC LIBRARIES

Data Processing: Data processing is a process that uses a computer program to summaries, analyze or otherwise convert data into usable information. The process may be automated and run on a computer. In the data processing we can do Data Entry, Data Coding, Data Transformation, Data Summarization, etc.

Circulation: A Circulation Department is one of the key departments of a library. It provides lending services and facilities for return of loaned items. Renewal of materials and payment of fines are also handled at the circulation desk. Circulation staff may provide basic search and reference services, to library users.

Cataloguing: Online Cataloguing has greatly enhanced the usability of catalogs, OPACs have enhanced usability over traditional card formats. The online catalogs do not need to sort statically; the user can choose author, title, keyword or systematic order dynamically. Most online catalogs offer a search facility for any word of the title is reached even better.

Prepared in house database: A library is a collection of sources, resources, and services, and the structure in which it is housed it is organized by the library for the use of library members. Modern Libraries are increasingly being redefined as places to get unrestricted access to information in many formats and from many sources.

CD Rom searching: The CD- ROMs coming along with books are assigned accession numbers and are kept at the computer section to be issued to the users to get information whenever needed. Library has also subscribed to CD ROM database provides for online access.

On-line Networking: Networking is one of the most effective ways of serving users needs comprehensively. Networked access to databases would help to get newly- published information to library users. Online information services are anticipatory or responsive. Both these services promote the use of library materials, make available library materials to users and thus meet user requirements.

Photocopying: The technology of reprography made a big

impact on the document delivery system. Most of the academic libraries have reprographic machines and provide photocopy of any document on demand.

News Clipping Scanning Service: Newspaper constitute an important source of information as they contain the latest information in the form of news with, often daily, updating. Print media is useful for research needs but many organization and individuals are turning to online newspaper clipping services and some organization are doing this by their library.

Online Reservation Service: The Online Reservation Service allows you to reserve books and journals which are on order, being processed by the library or on loan to another reader. User can place a reservation at the Issue or Information Support Desk using the request option on the on-line catalogue.

Database Searching Service: Through this service, we regularly provide the users with the exact information they need, depending on their interest profile, from our collection of major national and international database (retrospective and current) on our subject. The databases are in CD ROM or computerized form which saves their valuable time and energy, as the information available here is pinpointed and readily accessible.

Internet Access: The use of the internet around the world has been growing rapidly over the last decade. Libraries provide free or controlled access to internet and email. Depending upon the availability users can be given time slots for use of internet facility. Usually internet enabled terminals are provided in the library that can be used for internet access and email etc.

E-Query Services: E-Query Service is a Web-enabled contemporary reference service offered to the registered members of the Library together handle queries received in person or by e-mail. E-Queries may sometimes need to be followed-up with telephone, fax, regular e-mail, or personal interactions. Library, appropriate and brief information gathered in response will be sent to the enquirer through e-mail within three consecutive working days from the date of receipt of the query.

CONCLUSION

In hub of Information and technology Libraries should cope with the pace in modern era. Present circumstances in the library environment of change and uncertainty, growing demands, the influence of information technology and reconstruction and development, makes it essential that this process be arranged on a rational basis. The application of the philosophy of TQM offers a formal and systematic approach to these problems and could result in a process where continuous improvement of services is the final result. Although there is evidence that this is true, TQM is not a quick solution: it could take up to three years to reap the benefits of a properly implemented TQM program. TQM could, however, lead to an alternative way of doing things and enable libraries to be more flexible and responsive manner.

REFERENCES

- B U Kannappanavar and H M Chidananda Swamy, Total Quality Management in Engineering College Libraries: A Study In: Chandra R.,ed. Libraries, Information-Literacy and Lifelong Learning. Seminar papers of the 51st All India Library Conference, 16-18 December, 2005. Delhi : Indian Library Association held at Kurukshetra University, Kurukshetra
- Maharan, Balu, Koe Parda "Revitalizing Academic Libraries." University News, Nov. 2000.
- Ranganathan S.R. Five Laws of Library Science, Bombay : Asia Pub.,1963
- Ranganathan S.R. Library Administration, Bombay : Asia Pub.,1959
- Ranganathan S.R. Library Manual, Bombay : Asia Pub.,1960
- Singh, Sewa. "Library and Information Science: Growth and Trends." University News. Feb 7, 2000.

18

Application of Total Quality Management in Engineering College Libraries of Kurukshetra: A Study

Ravinder Kumar

ABSTRACT

This paper describes the current status of Total Quality Management in engineering college libraries of Kurukshetra. The population in this study was selected faculty members, PG and UG students. **Questionnaire method was the central instrument for the data collection. Observation and interview tools were also used in this study. The paper talks about the** success of TQM. It depends on many types of variables, majority of which have a direct relationship to the institution's culture, customers, capability and infrastructure. Therefore, each institution/library should frame its own approach to develop its distinctive strengths and focus on the specific weaknesses.

INTRODUCTION

Quality is a common term that has been used in day to day conversion and it is delighting the customers by fully meeting their needs and expectations. Quality is determined by the customer and the market place and includes all products and service attributes. Broadly the concept of quality is the aim of TQM. The aim of TQM is to deliver the highest value for the customer at the lowest cost, while achieving sustained profit and economic stability for the organization. Total Quality Management is a process the output of which depends upon customer satisfaction and continuous improvement. It provides a way to improve quality by examining the work in a systematic, oriented, consistent and organization wide perspective. TQM is a customer's need driven management programme. It is prevention oriented and believes in delighting customers first time, every time and all the time.

"TQM is defined as managing the entire organization so that it excels in all dimensions of products and services which are important to the customers" (Chase, 1992). "A system of continuous improvement, employing participative management and centered on the needs of the customers" (Jurow and Barnard, 1993).

REVIEW OF LITERATURE

A number of studies have been applied on Total Quality Management in different University libraries and college libraries. Syamalamba Rani (2006) emphasized the implementation of Total Quality Management (TQM) practices in academic libraries, particularly in Maris Stella college library, Vijayawada, India. The highlights of the implementation of TQM program, including the implementation of barcode technology and the procedure adapted in bar- coding books have been discussed. Valls and Verguerio (2006) discussed the use of ISO 9000 standards for the introduction of quality management in information services with a special emphasis on the Brazilian experience. The research supported the idea that ISO 9000 standards are a guideline for the implementation of quality management in organizations of different types and sizes. Wang (2006) provided a retrospective overview of total quality management (TQM) in the context of library services: Studies of both theoretical principles and experimental implementations demonstrated that it is worthwhile to introduce TQM in the academic libraries. Moghaddam et al. (2007) discussed the implementation of Total Quality Management and its application to libraries. Implementation of TQM is not a guarantee of the highest quality but it is a step in the right direction. Successful TQM implementation requires a thorough understanding of critical success factors, barriers to achieve these factors, and managerial tools and techniques to overcome these barriers. Kaur (2010) revealed that academic staff perceives the quality of library services to be just above average. Academic staff also believes that the library has a positive impact on their teaching, learning and research. The overall satisfaction with the library services received a satisfactory rating. Mehralizadeh and Safaeemoghaddam (2010) revealed the applicability of quality management systems and models to higher education that in many cases the current evidence of application of TQM is not compatible with the assumed criteria of the Røvik model. Nattar, S. (2010) explained the concept of Total Quality Management as applied to Library and Information Centres and how it is effective in Library Objectives in this digital era. It also highlights the LIS standardization of work, Quality Measurement procedures and improvement of its internal functional system.

OBJECTIVES & SCOPE OF THE STUDY

The following were the main objectives of the study:

- To have a comparative analysis of services and facilities provided by in different engineering college libraries of Kurukshetra.

- To know the current status of quality management approaches.
- To know the quality awareness level among the library information science professionals.
- To suggest improvement for TQM application.
- The data was collected from the faculty members, Post Graduate students and Under Graduate students of engineering colleges of Kurukshetra.

RESEARCH METHODOLOGY

This study was based on survey research. Questionnaire method was the central instrument for the data collection. The questions of the questionnaire were designed according to the objectives of the study. Observation and interview tools were also used to collect the data. The collected data was analyzed through percentage.

DATA ANALYSIS

Table-1 General Information about Institutions

Name of Institutes	*Year of Establish-ment*	*Faculty Strength*	*Students Strength*	*Library Building Separate/ within College*
SKIET	1997	55	692	Separate Building
KITM	2007	60	650	Part of college Building
GIMT	2007	55	750	Part of college Building
TERI	2007	55	692	Part of college Building
UIET	2004	52	1000	Part of college Building

The above table shows that SKIET institute is the oldest institute. Strength of faculty members are maximum in KITM and the strength of students are maximum in UIET as compared to other institutes included in the study.

Table-2 Missions, objectives and standards for performance

Name of Institutes	*Mission Statement* Yes	No	*Objectives* Yes	No	*Standards For Performance* Yes	No
SKIET	✓		✓		✓	
KITM	✓		✓		✓	
GIMT	✓		✓		✓	
TERI	✓		✓		✓	
UIET	✓		✓		✓	

Table-2 reveals that all the institutes have mission statements, set objectives and standards for performance.

Table-3 Collections

Name of Institutes	*Text Book*	*Reference Book*	*Periodicals*	*Book Bank*	*Audio Visual materials*
SKIET	25000	2000	68	10000	1500
KITM	12102	1000	46	4000	1000
GIMT	14950	3650	75	4090	750
TERI	14000	1783	61	4643	1100
UIET	15000	1500	40	1500	100

Table-3 reveals that out of five college libraries, the library of SKIET is having maximum collection as compared to other libraries.

Table-4 Book selection procedures

Name of Institutes	*Revision* Yes	No	*Faculty Participation* Yes	No	*Student Participation* Yes	No
SKIET		✓	✓		✓	
KITM	✓		✓		✓	
GIMT	✓		✓		✓	
TERI	✓		✓		✓	
UIET	✓		✓			✓

Table-4 shows that the libraries of KITM, GIMT, TERI and UIET revise their book selection procedure as and when required and suggestions are taken from faculty as well as the students. Only the library of SKIET does not revise book selection procedure but take suggestions from faculty as well as students while selecting books. Further, the libraries of four institutes i.e. SKIET, KITM, GIMT and TERI have expressed that the suggestions of students are helpful in selecting books.

Table-5 Technical processing

Name of Institutes	*Classification and Cataloging*		*Card catalogue should continue even after computerization*		*Average time to process a new book to provide to a user*		
	Yes	*No*	*Yes*	*No*	*1 day*	*2-3 days*	*week*
SKIET	✓		✓			✓	
KITM	✓			✓	✓		
GIMT	✓			✓	✓		
TERI	✓		✓		✓		
UIET		✓		✓			✓

From the table-5 it is clear that except UIET library, books have been classified and catalogued in all the other ~~four~~ libraries. Further, the librarian of SKIET and TERI feel that even after the complete automation, the manual system should also prevail simultaneously. Three of the libraries i.e. KITM, GIMT and TERI take only one day for technical processing. The library of SKIET takes 2 to 3 days whereas library of UIET takes one week for the purpose.

Table-6 Services provided by libraries

Name of Institutes	*OPAC*	*Circulation*	*Reservation*	*ILL*	*Reference Service*	*CAS*	*Photocopy*	*E-mail*
SKIET		✓	✓		✓		✓	✓
KITM	✓	✓	✓	✓	✓	✓	✓	✓
GIMT		✓	✓		✓		✓	✓
TERI		✓	✓		✓			✓
UIET		✓			✓			

Table-6 shows that only the library of KITM is providing all the services.

Table-7 Purpose of using the library

Name of institutes	*Borrow & Return the Document*	*For use of Electronic source*	*For Information needs*	*For News-papers & Magazines Reading*	*For Research Purpose*	*For Internet Facility*
SKIET N=27	23 (85.18%)	4 (14.81%)	10 (37.03%)	22 (81.48%)	13 (48.14%)	7 (25.92%)
KITMN=32	25 (78.12%)	10 (31.25%)	14 (43.75%)	25 (78.12%)	19 (59.37%)	12 (37.05%)
GIMTN=30	21 (70%)	5 (16.66%)	17 (56.66%)	23 (76.66%)	18 (60%)	5 (16.66%)
TERIN=27	18 (66.66%)	3 (11.11%)	21 (77.77%)	25 (92.59%)	14 (51.85%)	2 (7.40%)
UIETN=24	23 (95.83%)	2 (8.33%)	20 (83.33%)	14 (58.33%)	9 (37.05%)	2 (8.33%)
Total = 140	110 (78.57%)	24 (17.14%)	82 (58.57%)	109 (77.85%)	73 (52.14%)	28 (20%)

From the table-7 it has been found that most of the respondents i.e. 78.57 percent are using the library for issue and return of books while 77.85 percent users are using the library for reading Newspapers & Magazines. Only 17.14 percent respondents use the library for electronic resources, for getting information.

Table-8 Total Quality Management in libraries

Name of Institutes	*Adoption of TQM*		*ISO certified*		*TQM brings positive effect*	
	Yes	*No*	*Yes*	*No*	*Yes*	*No*
SKIET	✓		✓		✓	
KITM	✓		✓		✓	
GIMT	✓		✓		✓	
TERI	✓		✓		✓	
UIET	✓		✓		✓	

Table-8 shows that all the college libraries are adopting TQM techniques and agree that TQM helps in bringing positive effects in providing library services. All the institutes are ISO certified.

Table-9 Response of reference queries

Name of Institutes	*Personal*	*Telephonic*	*E-mail*
SKIET	✓		
KITM	✓	✓	✓
GIMT	✓	✓	
TERI	✓	✓	
UIET	✓		

Table-9 reveals that all the libraries are providing reference service and only three libraries i.e. of KITM, GIMT and TERI are answering the queries through telephone. Further, it is pertinent to mention that only the library of KITM is providing reference service through E-mail.

Table-10 Subscription of electronic journals

Name of Institutes	*Subscription*		*Economic to use*	*Easy to Maintain*	*Quick Retrieval*	*Solve the Problem of theft Mutilation*
	Yes	**No**				
SKIET		✓				
KITM	✓		✓	✓	✓	✓
GIMT	✓		✓	✓	✓	✓
TERI	✓		✓	✓	✓	✓
UIET		✓				

Table-10 reveals that only the three college libraries i.e. KITM, GIMT and TERI subscribe the electronic journals. The reason for subscribing electronic journals as given by all the 3 college librarians are that electronic journals are economic to use, easy to maintain, quickly retrieved and the problem of theft is solved.

Table-11 Library automation

Name of Institutes	*Automation*		*LAN Facility*		*Barcode Technology*	
	Yes	*No*	*Yes*	*No*	*Yes*	*No*
SKIET	✓		✓			✓
KITM	✓		✓		✓	
GIMT		✓		✓		✓
TERI	✓		✓			✓
UIET		✓		✓		✓

Table-11 reveals that SKIET, KITM, and TERI have automated their libraries and have LAN facility. Only the library of KITM has barcode technology being used.

Table – 12 Availability of latest publications

Name of Institutes	*Very often*	*Often*	*Not Very often*	*Not at all*
SKIET n=27	4(14.81%)	14(51.85%)	5(18.51%)	4(14.81%)
KITM n=32	8(25%)	16(50%)	6(18.75%)	2(6.25%)
GIMT n=30	6(20%)	16(53.33%)	5(16.66%)	3(10%)
TERI n=27	7(25.92%)	14(51.85%)	4(14.81%)	2(7.40%)
UIET n=24	5(20.83%)	11(45.83%)	5(20.83%)	3(12.05%)
Total = 140	30(21.42%)	71(50.71%)	25(17.85%)	14(10%)

The table-12 shows that the majority of respondents i.e. 51.85 percent of SKIET, 50 percent of KITM, 53.33 percent of GIMT, 51.85 percent of TERI and 45.83 percent of UIET are getting latest publication of books often.

From the table-13 it is revealed that maximum respondents i.e. 93.75 percent of KITM, 91.66 percent of UIET and 92.59 percent of TERI are using the library due to better library collection. 59.28 percent users in all the institutions are using the library due to better location of the library. 47.85 percent of respondents say that the convenient library opening hours encourage them to use the library more.

Table-13 Factors that encourage the use of Library services

Name of institutes	*More convenient opening hours*	*Better location of the library*	*Library Collection*
SKIET N=27	7 (25.92%)	21(77.77%)	19(70.37%)
KITMN=32	12(37.05%)	11(34.37%)	30(93.75%)
GIMTN=30	16(53.33%)	13(43.33%)	26(86.66%)
TERIN=27	18(66.66%)	15 (55.55%)	25(92.59%)
UIETN=24	14(58.33%)	23(95.83%)	22(91.66%)
Total = 140	67(47.85%)	83(59.28%)	122(87.14%)

Table-14 User's satisfaction regarding physical facilities and services

Name of Institutes	*Timing of library*	*Seating Arrangement*	*System of Access*	*Quality of Collection*	*Library Service*
SKIET	a	a	a	a	a
KITM	a	a	a	a	a
GIMT	a	a	a	a	a
TERI	a	a	a	a	a
UIET	a	a	a	a	a

Table-14 shows that the users of all the college libraries are satisfied with the opening hours, seating arrangement, system of access, quality of collection and the services being provided.

Table-15 Personal interest of library staff in providing services

Name of Institutes	*Very Often*	*Often*	*Not Very Often*	*Not at all*
SKIET n=27	8 (32.43%)	11(43.24%)	6(16.21%)	2(8.10%)
KITM n=32	11(35.71%)	15(42.85%)	4(16.66%)	2(4.76%)
GIMT n=30	6 (25%)	12(42.05%)	8(20%)	4(12.05%)
TERI n=27	7 (29.72%)	10(37.83%)	6(18.91%)	4(13.05%)
UIET n=24	6 (29.41%)	10(47.05%)	5(17.64%)	3(5.88%)
Total = 140	38(27.14%)	58(41.42%)	29(20.71%)	15(10.71%)

Table-15 reveals that 40.74 percent respondents of SKIET,

46.87 percent of KITM, 37.03 percent of TERI and 41.66 percent respondents of UIET have replied that the library staff takes personal interest in helping the users.

FINDINGS OF THE STUDY

The findings of the present study have provided a good insight into the current status of TQM practicing in engineering college libraries.

The findings are as follows:-

1. All the colleges were established during the last decade. This shows that Engineering education has got a boost in Kurukshetra during the last decade.
2. 80 percent colleges do not have independent library building. This fact shows that the colleges are not giving much attention to libraries.
3. All the libraries have good collection of text books, 60 percent libraries have the reference books, 80 percent libraries have Book Bank facility, 80 percent libraries have periodicals and only 20 percent libraries have audio-visual materials. This shows that most of the college libraries have sufficient reading materials.
4. All the libraries have adopted total quality management and their organizations are ISO certified. All the libraries believe that TQM brings positive effect to their library.
5. All the libraries are providing personal reference services and 60 percent libraries are providing reference services through telephone but only one library is providing reference service through E-mail. All the libraries are providing reference service to the users quite sufficiently.
6. 80 percent libraries are revising their book selection policy regularly and the same percentage of libraries take suggestions from user for book selection. And 80 percent libraries feel that student's participation is helpful in book selection policy.

7. Most of the libraries subscribe the electronic journals.
8. Four libraries out of 5 are using the classification and cataloguing scheme to classify and catalogue the documents.
9. Most of the respondents i.e. 71.57 percent are using the library for issue and return of books. But only a few respondents use the library for electronic resources.
10. All the libraries have good library collection.
11. All the libraries are getting latest publication of books oftenly.
12. Most respondents found that library staff is efficient in providing the library materials to the users.

SUGGESTIONS

There is a need to develop standards/ norms for assessing quality of information services with particular reference to Engineering college libraries. There is a need to evolve methodologies and mechanisms for improvement of quality information services. More funds to be allocated for studying the quality of information services on project basis Training of staff members in providing quality information services. All the libraries should have good collection of textbooks, journals, reference books and online journals for the implementation of TQM.

REFERENCES

- Chase, R.B., and N J Aquilino. 1992. Production and Operation management: A life cycle approach. irin: Homewood.
- Jurow, S., and Barnard S.B. 1993. Introduction: TQM fundamentals and overview of contents. Journal of Library Administration 18 (1/2): 1-13.
- Kaur, Kiran. 2010. Service quality and customer satisfaction in academic libraries: Perspectives from a Malaysian university. Library Review 59(4): 261 – 73.
- Moghaddam, Golnessa Galyani, and Mostafa Moballeghi. 2007. Total quality management in library and information sectors. The Electronic library 26(6): 912-22.

- Nattar, S. (2010). Total quality management in library and information centres. Pearl: A Journal of Library and Information Science 4(1): 28-31.
- Syamalamba Rani. 2006. Need for TQM in academic libraries: A case study of Mansstella College. Journal of Library and Information Science 31(2): 113-18
- Valls, Valeria martin, Waldomiro De castro, and Santos vergueiro. 2006. Quality management on information services according to ISO 9000. New Library World 107 (11/12): 523-37.
- Wang, Hong. 2006. From "User" to "Customer": TQM in academic libraries. Library Management 27 (9). 606-20.
- Yadollah, Mehralizadeh and Massoud Safaeemoghaddam. 2010. The applicability of quality management systems and models to higher education: A new perspective. The TQM Journal 22(2): 175 – 87.

19

Total Quality Management in College Libraries: An Overview

Suresh Kumar

INTRODUCTION

There is a lot of change in libraries in few years. Now days the functioning of the library change through electronic sources, network services in this competitive educational environment. Most of the education institutions are establish their reputation through quality management for providing good education.

The library has a store house of books and journals similarly, the store house of knowledge and information. There is a lot of change in library services; library staff provides maximum information with the help of books, journals and electronic services. It's the aim of quality management in college library. The quality management techniques in college library services and public library their effectiveness and positive impact on the readers and increasing the library services to maximum satisfaction of the users. The duty of the librarian and information officer to provide the high quality services to the users through adopts the techniques of quality management with a rapidly changing environment in library sources.

The library staff tries to fulfill the aims of the users through quality management. The library attract to more users for quality information. It is the evident management skill must match these more demands on the library and information services. The application of total quality management could assist librarian and information officers very well total quality management discussing approach and improve same modifications importance of libraries to improve the suitability of library and information service environment.

There are various methods, tools and techniques to measure, control and improve the quality of library services. Quality management provides get the importance and achieve the goal and provide the maximum services to the readers with the help of modern libraries for the benefits of the library as well as user community.

QUALITY MANAGEMENT

The origin of word 'quality' has several definitions. The strategic definition is to fulfill the user's requirements in good manner.

(1) According to Journal "the quality is fitness for purpose"

(2) According to Robinson, "quality is meeting the requirements of user now and in the future"

(3) According to Sarkar, "quality of a library service is the ability of the library service to meet the user's requirement".

TOTAL QUALITY MANAGEMENT

The setting of standards and their use in managing the quality of library services is not a new concept. In the modern would how the quality of library services could improve and for the improvement to be maintained for a long time. People thought that the only way to achieve quality was through a proper system of inspection and achievements of their standards and better equipment methods. The use of library recourses serve the benefit of the user in a very few time provide the maximum information what they are required.

Kruger(1995-96) stated that TQM can be described as a management approach to long –term success through customer satisfaction. It is however, true that most management consultants agree about a number of essential components in describing the concept of total quality management. For examples there should be a

- strong focus on the users
- through commitment to quality and continuous improvement, for example in service delivery
- reliable system of information supply for decision making
- proper training system for staff
- long term thinking
- knowledge about user needs and commitment to meet those needs and ultimately to exceed users expectations
- the library staff can create a vision based on the needs of users
- confidence in staff that they can deliver quality service to users

The two people associated with the birth of the TQM movement are W. Edwards and J. M. Juan. Some forty years ago Deming, father of the quality revolution, associated the Japanese to become the world manufacturing leaders they are today the library services adopted the Deming thinking. User's expectations of the ability of a library or information service to deliver high quality service are growing. The importance of information as a recourse is being more broadly recognized by government, organizations and other social structures.

The user demand for services is the influence of information technology, students for example are becoming more computer literate and the academic library environment has changed substantially in the increased range of technology which can be used as channels for its service delivery. The librarian or information officer has become more useful to provide the library services to the users in library.

If the users want to more information itself training in the use information systems is very important. By training users and staff, both can be empowered to do more and in the process achieve better results for the organizations as a whole and for the satisfaction of their own aims. Libraries and information services are intrinsically compact to manage. Demands are increasing and recourses are limited. Libraries are striving to give the best to their users; quality service must be the departure point. If this is true then libraries are a natural entity for the applications of TQM. Most libraries are providing excellence services to the users. Library users can only describe quality by the characteristics of the service

(1) Service is available at moment it is needed

(2) Provide correct information

(3) The services of a high quality provide by professional well trained staff.

(4) Quality is what one needs and wants, not what you think is needed or what is convenient for you to deliver.

The TQM for libraries is not only centered around the user's needs but also exceeding the demands of the fast changing environment of service delivery in libraries. The library management commits itself to continuous quality improvement. TQM as part of the future plans of a library consists is not only changing certain procedures, but a total rethink of all its operations where the culture oriented by framework quality service to the users

PRINCIPLES OF LIBRARY ORGANIZATION BY TOTAL QUALITY MANAGEMENT

Some principles of TQM use for provide the good library services are:

- Create service broachers and information kits.
- Record of users in library services.
- Developing library services.
- Open access system in library.
- Division of work among the library staff.
- Maintain discipline is to provide good leadership to staff.
- Unity of Command: an organizational structure should be such that each employee is supervised by only one supervisor.
- Unity of direction: unity of direction is provided by means of properly arranging the organization.
- Appointment of qualified staff.
- Library hours according to the need of the users.
- Co-ordination among the inter departmental library.
- Improve user and staff training materials.
- Create a library advisory committee.
- New techniques in library to attract the more users.
- Improve the physical layout of library.
- Give the proper direction of library sources.

FACILITIES IN A GOOD LIBRARY

- Good library is easily approachable to use library materials.
- Good layout for a good library.
- Sufficient space, lighting and ventilation.

- Good furniture chairs and reading tables.
- Audio-visual system in library.
- Cleanness in library.
- Good collection of text books, journals, reference books, online journals, and e-books etc is needed in a library.
- Display of new arrival of books.
- Library staff be appointed with knowledge of modern technology.
- Library staff should help user to locate books; journals needed do their work time.
- All books journals and other library materials should be proper classified.
- Update of library catalogue.
- Arrangement of new reading materials in time.

PATTERNS OF ORGANIZATION

- Functional arrangement.
- Subject arrangement.
- Arrangement by area.
- Arrangement by person served.
- Arrangement by materials.

(1) Functional Arrangement : Functional arrangement usually provides for following section or departments.

Acquisition, classifications and cataloguing, reference services, circulation and maintenance sections. There may be periodical section; accounts section administration section, departmental libraries, special reading rooms and collections. In case these sections based on functional approach work autonomously, then this is not desirable. It is essential to combine these into larger units on the basis of related activities. We may have technical services division would include acquisition section, cataloguing section (classification & cataloguing) maintenance section, etc.

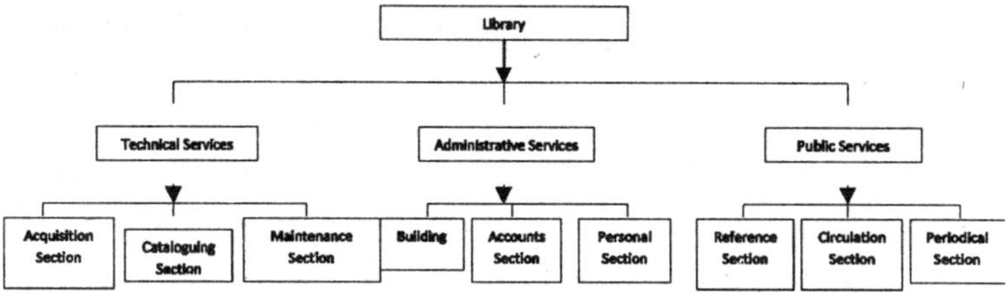

Chart 1 (For a Large Library)

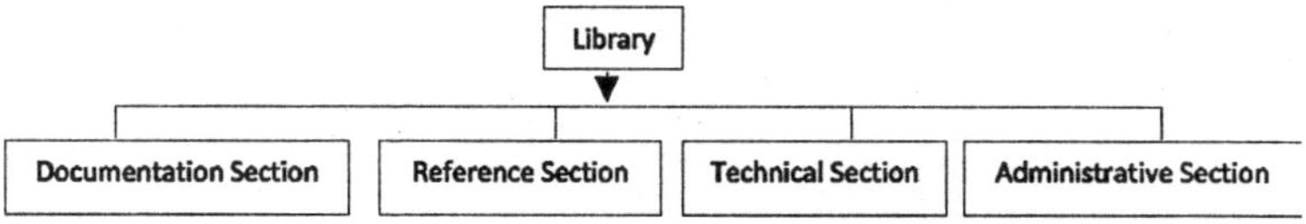

Chart-2 (For a medium special library)

(2) Subject Arrangement : Subject arrangement can be used as a basis for organizations of a library. Subject departments are generally open-shelf study areas with stacks adjacent to study areas. Subject department serve as 'Special Libraries' for the users. In practice, in public libraries major fields of knowledge are divided into four to six large groups .Within each such group, documents have close subject relationship. In public libraries in USA, there most common subject departments are art and music, business and industry, local history and genealogy. In academic libraries subject departments are usually broad in scope. Many academic libraries adopt divisional pattern, where major groupings are the humanities, social sciences and sciences. A senior staff member is made in-charge of each of the subject department/ division, he should be subject specialization.

(3) Arrangement by Area : Libraries has used arrangement by area or territory in their organization structure. Public libraries take into consideration the area to be served for setting up their branch libraries, deposit centers and mobile library service, library law etc.

(4) Arrangement by Person Served : Some libraries have set up children's rooms and organized services to serve teenagers, blinds, physically handicapped, economically and culturally disadvantaged groups to take care of the different categories of groups.

(5) Arrangement by materials : Arrangement by materials leads to following sections for department books section, maps section, periodicals section, films section, government section etc. Arrangement by materials is considered useful for national and depository libraries, large university and public libraries separate certain material by from. But libraries put various forms along with broader departments.

TQM IN THE ACADEMIC LIBRARY

The user in the academic library is the user reader/student/ staff. Here the customer is not an outsider, but part of the academic community. India's University Grants Commission has set up NAAC. NAAC conducts audits and inspection on the quality of service provide by educational institution including library service. In light of this academic libraries must develop systems philosophies and strategies for managing quality. Academic library is to support the teaching research and other academic environment of its parent organization.

MANAGING QUALITY IN AN ACADEMIC LIBRARY

An academic library fulfilling the user's satisfaction expectation. Librarian must find out what readers want.

(1) Who are the users?

(2) What do they want?

(3) Availability of sources of reading materials of library

The users are to gain maximum benefit from a service. They must know how to use it. So, properly planned user education is a must for an academic library. Getting feedback from the users about the quality of service, through given a questionnaire to improving service. Proper arrangement of desk staff are the front line staff that play a critical role is an academic library. All academic library staff must receive training, including skill training, on the job guidance, retraining will trained staff pillars for quality service in academic library. They play important role to provide better quality services, develop a culture to work and commitment toward quality service in an academic library.

REFERENCES

- Elizabeth store, Training for the improvement of Library administration Urbana, University of Illinois graduate –school of Library Science, c 1967.
- *JosepHC ' Wheeler and Herbert Goldhar , Practical administration of public libraries , New work ,Harper and Row , 1962 chep 10 and 19.*
- *Littleton*, Colo.: *Libraries Unlimited, 1977*
- *Louis Round Wilson and maurice F. Tauber , The University Library , 2nd Ed. New York , Columbia*
- *Robert D.* Stueart and *John Taylor East- lick Library Management*
- University press 1964.

20

Electronic age Information: An Evaluation Perspective

Kulveen Kaur

ABSTRACT

The application of technology has not only made the libraries smart but also requires the users to be smart enough for accessing the required information accurately and the librarians to be smartest for facilitating between the user and the electronic media so that the highly authentic information is transferred efficiently and effectively. The information available in electronic form has grown by heaps and bounds within this decade. But the explosive growth of electronic information poses threats to the quality of information. The paper emphasizes upon the check points for evaluating the information in an electronic age. It also discusses the role of librarians as information professionals in facilitating and guiding the users about the various checkpoints for quality information.

INTRODUCTION

In this globalised world, constant change can be experienced every day. The electronic era has brought a revolution in the way people socialize, govern, interact, do work and has been integrated in every walk of life. To adapt successfully to the change one should have open mind and vision. Thompson, 1982 concluded in his book that "the librarians and libraries that do not accept the change will inevitably be victims of the evolution. For the dinosaurs it will indeed be the end." Electronic medium has revitalized the information access process and technological innovation has given rise to electronic form of knowledge. E-resources are the wave of the future. These can be accessed through electronic means like computers, tablets, smart phones, e-book readers, etc. and has many advantages over traditional form of print resources. The easy handling, small size, customization, and anywhere anytime accesses of e-resources are some of the features that users love to exercise and explore. E-resources forms the integral component of the collection in the libraries giving rise to a shift from print to non-print, books to e-books, journals to e-journals, e-consortiums, web-portals, e-databases, etc.

E-resources in alliance with internet is the sign of modern age and is an invaluable tool of teaching and learning. The demand for the Information Communication Technologies (ICT) enabled services and e-resources among the researcher's community has increased manifold over the years. This has greatly affected the information retrieval habits of the users. Users just go for googling the information without knowing the efficacy and credibility of the documents. The use of web 2.0 tools has made the task of on-line publishing very simple. Everyone is adding anything on the web. Though the invention of technology in general and e-documents particularly is truly a blessing but electronic resources present a number of hurdles that are not encountered with traditional library resources. This has complicated the information retrieval process and has put a strain on the information professionals to keep check on the authenticity of the electronic information. It is seen that most of the electronic information is not peer reviewed and information professionals have to be very careful in judging between information and misinformation. In today's times where information is multiplying rapidly in electronic formats it is vital to discuss the issues relating to the authenticity and reliability of information. Several check points have been discussed here to measure the credibility and quality of information.

CHECK POINTS FOR QUALITY INFORMATION

Ojala (2004) describes that "quality in an online information context is to recognize it as a combination of authoritative, timely sources and searcher knowledge." The rise in the number of electronic resources has brought along, the threats of misinformation and dubious information. This has put the questions on the quality of the information resources. It is essential that for finding right and qualitative information the user is information literate and evaluates the needed information critically. The information literacy standard i.e. "The student who is information literate evaluates information critically and competently" also emphasizes upon the skills of evaluation. D'Angelo (1971) and Yinger (1980) relate "evaluation" with "critical thinking". Bull et.al. (2001) describes Authority, Domain and Internal and External Consistency as the three quality check points for evaluating electronic information. Jim Kapoun also presents five point checklist criteria for evaluating Web pages based on which a librarian would use when evaluating print items for inclusion in a library collection. These are accuracy, authority, objectivity, currency, and coverage. Scheeder in 2005 also emphasizes upon some check points which are described as follows:

Authoritative: It relates to the reliability, authenticity, peer reviewed and official information. While evaluating the information following are the points one must go through while gathering information:

- User must check who is behind the information.
- User must check that does the website claims to be official.
- User must check for its liability.
- User must check who is the author.
- User must check the type of information (primary or secondary).
- User must check the footnotes and references.

Timely: This relates to the up to date of information. User must check that how frequently the e-information is updated whether fortnightly, monthly or so.

Accurate: it relates to checking the information with facts

- User must check that the information is free from errors.
- User must check that the information is peer reviewed.
- User must check that the piece of work is verified from the facts.

Objectives

- User must check the biasness of information.
- User must be careful to present all sides of the issue.

Tailored to the needs of the client

- User must check its relevancy
- User must check the specificity of information e.g. in a website, links are provided that decides the relevancy of the information. It saves time and this criterion speaks directly to the needs of the member who is busy and stressed.

LIBRARIANS AS FACILITATORS

Technological advances have changed the age old image of libraries. However the availability of electronic documents on the web offers immense value to the users but at the same time the lack of proper knowledge of evaluating the information causes havoc as the World Wide Web has no policy statements in publishing information. Anyone can publish anything on the Web. There is a whole heap of bogus websites and bogus information available. In fact users consider that everything available on the internet is accurate and are not able to judge the dubious nature of information. Librarians being the information professional play a significant role in guiding and teaching the users in finding right information by organizing seminars, workshops, talks , etc. Besides this librarians also assist the users in the skills of comparing and art of corroborating the information.

CONCLUSION

The adoption of different technologies in the libraries and the use of electronic media facilitate knowledge transfer, sharing of resources and provide universal access to global information. Timely access, accurate and relevant information in any format is the key issues for the effectiveness of any organization. Various curriculum-based information literacy initiatives and talks on vitality of evaluation of information must be taught in the syllabi. The situation today demands the technological up-gradation of information professionals so that the information can be steered effectively to the right user at the right time. Also, the librarians and other professionals working with electronic information resources must explicit the protocols and the check points for evaluation on the library websites. Cooperative ventures among librarians should be initiated for safe and reliable search so that the relevance of the library profession can be ensured.

REFERENCES

- Bull et.al. (2001). Evaluating and using web-based resources In *Learning & Leading with Technology. 28(7)*
- D'Angelo, E. (1971). *The teaching of critical thinking*. Amsterdam: B.R. Gruner In Fitzgerald, M. A. (n.d.). *Evaluating information: An information literacy challenge*. Retrieved from http://www.ala.org/aasl/aaslpubsandjournals/slmrb/slmrcontents/volume21999/vol2fitzgerald
- Jim Kapoun, J. (1998). Teaching Undergrads Web Evaluation In Meola, M. (2004). Chucking the Checklist: A Contextual Approach to Teaching

Undergraduates Web-Site Evaluation In *Portal: Libraries and the Academy, 4(3).*

- Ojala, M. (2004). *Why information quality matters and how to convince users of the value of quality.* Presented at INFORUM Conference on Professional Information Resources. Retrieved from http://www.inforum.cz/pdf/2004/Ojala_Marydee2.pdf
- Scheeder, D. (2005). *Information quality standards: Navigating the seas of misinformation*. Paper presented at71th IFLA General Conference and Council Libraries - a voyage of discovery, Oslo, Norway. Retrieved from archive.ifla.org/IV/ifla71/papers/192e-Scheeder.pdf
- Thompson, J. (1982). The End of Libraries London, Bingley. In Law, Derek (2007) Beyond the hybrid library: Libraries in a Web 2.0 world. In: Digital convergence - the future of libraries. Springer, Berlin.
- Yinger, R.J. (1980). Can we really teach them to think? In *Fostering critical thinking,* Ed. R.E. Young, 11–31. San Francisco: Jossey-Bass. In Fitzgerald, M. A. (n.d.). *Evaluating information: An information literacy challenge*. Retrieved from http://www.ala.org/aasl/aaslpubsandjournals/slmrb/slmrcontents/volume21999/vol2fitzgerald.

Part E
Miscellaneous

21

Usability of Online Public Access Catalogue in Kurukshetra University and Panjab University Libraries: A Comparative Study

Rajinder Kumar

ABSTRACT

This paper examines the use of Online Public Access Catalogue in Kurukshetra University and Panjab University libraries: a comparative study. OPAC is an information retrieval tools for searching their desired documents in the libraries. A questionnaire-based survey approach on use of OPAC was conducted for A.C. Joshi Library and Jawaharlal Nehru library on various categories of users such as faculty members, research scholars and postgraduate students, in which covered different disciplines such as Pure Sciences, Social Sciences, and Humanities. In this study covered the various aspects of OPAC searching like frequency of use, purpose, ease of use, satisfaction level, etc. The study showed that the level of awareness of OPAC is more in PU in the comparison of KU. Users of both the universities mainly search their documents in OPAC by title, author, keyword and subject. The study described that a maximum number of users access their required library material through OPAC despite encountering problems slow query processing speed, less awareness of advanced features, unavailability of staff assistance, insufficient number of terminals and lack of power backup. The study is suggested that both the libraries should provide orientation progrramme and always provide assistance facility near the OPAC system.

Keywords: Library catalogue, information retrieval, OPAC, libraries, university library, KU, PU

INTRODUCTION

Information plays an important and significant role in the life of every human being. Information is most important for the improvement of social, educational and technological advancement, Information handling traditionally comes within the domain of library. Library tries to fulfill all information requirements of users through proper information processing, retrieval and dissemination systems. A library collects many documents like books, thesis, manuscripts, maps, periodicals, pamphlets, motion pictures, tapes and other printed and non printed reading materials. We can well imagine as to what will happen if these reading materials are not organized properly manners. Even if they are organized on shelves properly, no person whether user or staff will be able to know and remember what documents are available in the library if the person does not know the subject of the required documents. So we need an information retrieval system that is able to access what documents are in library and whether a particular document is available in the library. This information retrieval system should fulfill all the search approaches about the documents like author, title, publisher, call number etc. This type of retrieval system in the context of a library is called library catalogue. The different types of library catalogue are used to search the required information of user group in the library. Traditionally book catalogue, sheaf catalogue and card catalogue had been used in the libraries but now in digital era computerized catalogue has been adopted in the libraries. Online Public Access Catalogue (OPAC) is totally based on computers and allows users to access documents available in the libraries. OPAC can be accessed very easy and quickly from any part of the world with the help of computers. According to Online Dictionary of Library & Information Science (ODLIS) (2007) "OPAC is an acronym for Online Public Access Catalogue, a database composed of bibliographic records describing the books and other materials owned by a library or library system, accessible via public terminals or workstations usually concentrated near the reference desk to make it easy for users to request the assistance of a trained reference librarian. Most online catalogs are searchable by author, title, subject and keywords and allow users to print, download or export records to an E-mail account."

"An OPAC (Online Public Access Catalogue) is a database of bibliographic records describing the holdings usually of one particular library. It allows searching by name, title, and subject, and offers online access through public terminals." (O'Brien 2003, 466)

Now days, a number of libraries are providing OPAC searching facility to their users to find out their documents. In such a situation, the libraries should observed periodically how much comfort the users feel with this service so that some initiatives could be taken timely to improve this facility. Therefore, a study has been undertaken on the use of OPAC by the users in Kurukshetra university, Kurukshetra and Panjab university, Chandigarh

ABOUT JAWHAR LAL NEHRU LIBRARY AND A.C JOSHI LIBRARY:

Kurukshetra University was established in 1956 as a unitary residential university. Its campus is situated on the western bank of Brahm Sarover (the holy tank). (*www.kukinfo.com*) The Kurukshetra University Library named officially as Jawaharlal Nehru Library was shifted to its present premises in 1967. At present Sh. R.D. Mehla is the Librarian in the university library. The library provides following services to the users: circulation, inter library loan, document delivery, OPAC, reference, periodicals consultation, reading room, Internet, E-journals access, book bank, training programme for searching OPAC system, and assistance in using OPAC. Since 2003 the library uses Libsys software package which is an integrated multi-user library management system that supports all in-house operations of the library. Ten terminals are installed.

The Panjab University Library is officially named as A.C. Joshi Library. At present Sh. Raj Kumar is the Librarian in the university library. The library provides following services to the users: circulation, inter library loan, document delivery, library OPAC/ Web-OPAC, CAS, reference, referral, periodicals consultation, reading room, Internet, e-journals, book bank, training programme and regular assistance for searching OPAC system. The library uses Techlib Plus software package from 1997, which is an integrated multi-user library management system that supports all in-house operations of the library. Five terminals have been installed adjacent to the Reference Section from 1998 for OPAC search.

REVIEW OF RELATED LITERATURE

Many studies have been published on the use of OPAC. In this study a few number of studies on the use of OPAC in libraries have been carried out some studies are national and some are international level. Shiv Kumar (2011) studied the effect of web searching on the OPAC: a comparison of selected university libraries of the Punjab region viz PUC, PUP and GNDU. He found that maximum of frequency i.e. 10.6% of PUP searched the OPAC very frequently. The study revealed that the majority of the users' i.e 82.9 % in PUP used the simple search very frequently. The data revealed that the majority of users i.e. 50.3% in PUC were not aware about on-screen help which was available on the search screen of the OPACs. Velmurugan and Amudha (2011) examined the use of OPAC by the VHSN college users. The study revealed that the majority of the users who were coming to the library more than half (i.e. 58.75%) used OPAC only. Most of the users (i.e. 79.14%) were accessed OPAC through author and title approaches and consulted it for found the documents in the library. The majority of the users (i.e. 60.42%) were very satisfied in accessed OPAC and a small percentage of the users were not satisfied. Mulla and Chandershekhra (2009) studied the effective use of online public access catalogue (OPAC) at the libraries of engineering colleges in Karnataka. The study revealed that 58.67 % users were male while 41.33% female. The majority of the users i.e. 90.29% consult the OPAC to know the location of books in the Villen-Ruedo, Senso and Moya-Anegan (2007) examined the use of OPAC in university of Granada, Spain. The study revealed that the experimental science respondents mainly used OPAC by author approach (i.e 52.06 %) while 65 % health science users used it by title approach. Ortiz-Repiso et.al (2006) described the use of OPAC of the Spanish Council for the Scientific Research Library Network by researchers. The findings showed that the majority of the respondents accessed the OPAC mainly for journals (i.e. 54.44 %). 85 % users were satisfied with the use of it by author or title approach (i.e. 88.87 %). Amar Nath and Sharma (2006) studied the use of OPAC by the research scholars in Panjab University Library Chandigarh. The study examined that 68.33 % users used OPAC while 10 % users searched manual information retrieval system. Most of the users searched it by author approach 32.50 % followed by title approach 23.33 %. The maximum number of respondents consulted it to check whether the required documents were available in the library or not. The majority of the respondents were satisfied with the help given by library staff in the use of it.

Ariyapala and Edzan (2002) investigated the OPAC use behavior of foreign PG students at University of Malaya (Malaysia) Library. Most of the foreign PG students indicated that there was no OPAC facility provided in their home countries and if provided it was limited to university libraries. The study found that the respondents used OPAC by title and users felt that OPAC was easy to use.

OBJECTIVES OF THE STUDY

This study focuses on the effective use of OPAC at Kurukshetra university and Panjab university libraries: a comparative study. The study was carried out to know the views regarding the use of OPAC. The present studies aimed to achieve the following objectives were:

- To know the user awareness of use of OPAC and its various facilities
- Find out the frequency of use of OPAC
- To determine the satisfaction level of use of OPAC
- To identify the purpose and utilization of the use of OPAC
- To understand the difficulties faced by the users while they were using OPAC
- To suggest, suitable measures to improve the OPAC services for the benefit of the users.

SCOPE OF THE STUDY

The present study was included Teachers, Research scholars and Postgraduate students of Kurukshetra university, Kurukshetra and Panjab university, Chandigarh. The main objectives of the study was to know the purpose, knowledge, satisfaction, frequency of using OPAC and problems faced by the users when they were using OPAC system. In this study was covers various disciplines such as pure Science, Social Science and Humanities.

RESEARCH METHODOLOGY

The sampling method had been adopted in this study.

Keeping in view the objectives of the study the researcher used questionnaire based survey method to collect the data. The data was collected in the year of 2008-09. A stratified random sample of 301 was selected for the purpose of the study 150 users of KU while 151 of PU. Besides questionnaire method observation and interview techniques was also used. The questionnaire was totally based on objectives of this study such as: awareness of OPAC; purpose of use; frequency; satisfaction; and problem faced while they were using OPAC. The collected data was analyzed through SPSS statistical packages.

DATA ANALYSIS

Table – 1 Gender of the Respondents

Gender	*KU*	*PU*	*Total*
Male	89 (59.33%)	81(53.64%)	170 (56.47%)
Female	61 (40.66%)	70 (46.35%)	131 (43.52%)
Total	150 (100%)	151 (100%)	301(100%)

Table–1 presents the users' profile through their gender wise. Majority of the users in both universities were male (56.47 per cent) while 43.52 per cent users were female. In PU, male users (53.64 per cent) were proportionately less than they were in KU (59.33 per cent). Thus proportionately more female users (46.35 per cent) responded in PU than in the KU (40.66 per cent).

Table – 1.2 Academic of the Respondents

Status	*KU*	*PU*	*Total*
PG Students	65 (43.33%)	69 (45.69%)	134 (44.51%)
Research Scholars	55 (36.66%)	54 (35.76%)	109 (36.21%)
Faculty Members	30 (20%)	28(18.54%)	58 (19.26%)
Total	150 (100%)	151 (100%)	301(100%)

Table-1.2 presents the status wise distribution. The PG students (44.51 per cent) formed the largest number of users, followed by research scholars (36.21 per cent) and faculty (19.26

per cent). In KU, 43.33 per cent users were PG students, 36.66 per cent were research scholars and 20 per cent were faculty while in PU, 45.69 per cent users were PG students, followed by 35.76 per cent research scholars and 18.54 per cent faculty.

Table - 1.3 Disciplines of the Respondents

Discipline	*KU*	*PU*	*Total*
Social Sciences	65 (43.33%)	45 (29.80%)	110 (36.54%)
Sciences	48 (32%)	50 (33.11%)	98 (32.55%)
Arts and Languages	37 (24.66%)	56 (37.85%)	93 (30.89%)
Total	150 (100%)	151 (100%)	301(100%)

Table-1.3 presents the discipline wise distribution of users. The Social Science users (36.54 per cent) formed the largest group, followed by Sciences (32.55 per cent) and Arts and Languages (30.89 per cent). In KU relatively more Social scientists (43.33 per cent) responded to the questionnaire while in PU 37.85 per cent users were from Arts and Languages followed by 33.11 per cent from Sciences and 29.80 per cent from Social Sciences.

Table-2 Frequency of library visits

Frequency	*KU*	*PU*	*Total*
Daily	55 (36.66%)	67 (44.37%)	122 (40.53%)
Twice or more in a week	39 (26%)	30 (19.86%)	69 (22.92%)
Weekly	28 (18.66%)	21 (13.90%)	49 (16.27%)
Rarely	28 (18.66%)	33 (21.85%)	61 (20.26%)
Total	150 (100%)	151 (100%)	301(100%)

÷ 2= 3.761, Sign = .288

Table-2 presents the frequency of visits of users to the libraries. The table shows that all the users visited the library. The maximum number of users in both the universities (40.53 per cent) visited the library daily, followed by 22.92 per cent twice or more in a week and 16.27 per cent weekly. In PU, more users visited the library daily (44.37 per cent) than in KU, (36.66 percent) on the other extreme also, more users (21.85 per cent) visited PU library rarely than KU library (18.66 percent). When difference in the library visits of users was subjected to statistical test, it was not found significant. Thus it can be said that users in both the universities visited their respective libraries with more or less same frequency.

Table-3 OPAC Awareness

Response	*KU*	*PU*	*Total*
Yes	80 (53.33%)	124 (82.11%)	204 (67.77)
No	25 (16.66%)	14 (9.27%)	39 (12.95%)
Somewhat	45 (30%)	13(8.60%)	58 (19.26%)
Total	150 (100%)	151 (100%)	301(100%)

÷ 2= 30.245, Sign. = .000*

Table–3 examined the awareness of OPAC. The response on this aspect was quite different in both the universities. In KU, the response was as low as 53.33 percent while 82.11 percent users were aware of OPAC in PU library. In KU, 30 percent users stated that they were somewhat aware of the OPAC, while only 8.60 per cent were of this opinion in PU. The statistical analysis of the response shows that the difference in response of both the universities was statistically significant. Thus it can be said that the level of awareness of OPAC was more in PU than in KU.

Table-4 Source of Learning the Use of OPAC

Source	*KU N =122*		*PU N = 138*		χ^2	*Sign.*
	Yes	*No*	*Yes*	*No*		
Self efforts	60 (48.78%)	63 (51.21%)	65 (47.10%)	73 (52.89%)	.073	.786
Library staff assistance	38 (30.89%)	85 (69.10%)	52 (37.68%)	86 (62.31%)	1.326	.250
Friends, Colleagues etc. assistance	24 (19.51%)	99 (80.48%)	22 (15.94%)	116 (84.04%)	.571	.450
Orientation/ Training progrramme	7 (5.69%)	116 (94.30%)	4 (2.89%)	134 (97.10%)	1.256	.262

Table-4 describes the learning sources used by users for learning OPAC use. In KU, 48.78 percent users learnt use of OPAC by self efforts, 30.89 percent were helped by library staff, and 19.51 percent received help from their friends, colleagues etc. and 5.69 percent attended formal training. While in PU, users 47.10 percent learnt use of OPAC by self efforts, while 37.68 percent were assisted by library staff, 15.94 percent learnt the use of OPAC from their friends, colleagues etc. and only 2.89 percent attended some training programme. When these results were statistically tested, the difference in the response was not found significantly different.

Table-5 Frequency of Use of OPAC

Frequency	*KUN =122*	*PUN =138*	*TotalN = 260*
Almost daily	15 (12.29%)	27 (19.56%)	42 (16.15%)
Weekly	41 (33.60%)	49 (35.50%)	90(34.61%)
Monthly	12 (9.83%)	16 (11.59%)	28 (10.76%)
Rarely	54 (44.26%)	46 (33.33%)	100 (38.46%)
Total	122 (100%)	138 (100 %)	260 (100 %)

χ^2= 4.383, Sign.= .223

Table–5 presents the users frequency of use of OPAC. In KU, only 12.29 percent users used OPAC daily, 33.60 percent weekly, 9.83 percent monthly and 44.26 percent rarely. In PU, more than 55 percent users used OPAC at least once a week, while 11.59 percent used it almost monthly and a sizeable percentage (i.e. 33.33 percent) used rarely.

But on statistical analysis, the difference in the response was not found significant at .05 level. It means, despite difference of numbers, the response was broadly similar in both the universities

Table-6 Purpose of using OPAC

Purpose	KU N = 122		PU N =138		χ^2	Signi.
	Yes	No	Yes	No		
Check number of copies	108 (88.52%)	14 (11.47%)	121 (87.68%)	17 (12.31%)	.834	.044
Finding biblio-graphical details	103 (84.42%)	19 (15.57%)	120 (86.95%)	18 (13.04%)	.340	.560
Check document availability	60 (50%)	62 (50.81%)	87 (63.04%)	51 (36.95%)	5.065	.024*
Locate the Documents	55 (45.08%)	67 (54.91%)	43 (31.15%)	95 (68.84%)	5.345	.021*

Table-6 shows the users purpose of consulting the OPAC. In KU, the highest number of users (88.52 per cent) consulted OPAC to check the number of copies of the required document in the library. 84.42 percent users consulted OPAC to find the bibliographical details; 50 per cent users used it to check whether the required document was available in the library or not and 45.08 per cent consulted to locate the document. 87.68 percent respondents in PU consulted OPAC to check the number of copies of the required document in the stock. It was followed by checking of bibliographical details (86.95 per cent) and then checking the availability of the document in the library (63.04 per cent). Only 31.15 percent consulted OPAC for locating the document in the library. When this response was subjected to statistical analysis, it was found that on two purposes, namely checking number of copies of documents and finding bibliographical details the response in both universities was broadly similar, while for rest two purposes, namely checking document availability and locating the document in the library, the response in both the universities was significantly different. It means, KU users consult OPAC more than PU users for locating the document while PU respondents use OPAC significantly more for checking document availability.

Table-7 OPAC Search Approaches

Approach	*KUN = 122*		*PUN = 138*		*χ^2stat*	*Signi*
	Yes	*No*	*Yes*	*No*		
Title	65 (53.27%)	57 (46.72%)	71 (51.44%)	67 (48.55%)	.087	.768
Author	54 (44.26%)	68 (55.73)	62 (44.92%)	76 (55.07%)	.012	.914
Subject	54 (44.26%)	68 (55.73%)	51 (36.95%)	87 (63.04%)	1.436	.231
Keyword	27 (22.13%)	95 (77.86%)	54 (39.13%)	84 (60.86%)	8.724	.003*
Place	12 (9.83%)	110 (90.16%)	9 (6.52%)	129 (93.47%)	.958	.328
Publisher	10 (8.19%)	112 (91.80%)	8 (5.79%)	130 (94.20%)	1.003	.317
Call number	6 (4.91%)	116 (95.08%)	10 (7.24%)	128 (92.75%)	.608	.436

Table-7 shows the users approaches of searching OPAC. In KU, the most preferred search approach was title approach (53.27 percent), followed by author (44.26 percent), subject (44.26 percent), keyword (22.13 percent), place (9.83 percent), publisher (8.19 percent) and call number (4.91 percent). In PU also, most of the users searched OPAC by title approach (51.44 percent), followed by author approach (44.92 percent), keyword search (39.13 percent), subject (36.95 percent), call number (7.24 percent), place (6.52 percent) and publisher (5.79 percent). The results are broadly similar in both the universities. In both the universities mainly title, author and subject approaches were used. In PU, keyword approach was also used. When response in various approaches was subjected to statistical testing it was found that, except keyword, it was similar on all other approaches. PU users used keyword approach significantly more than KU users.

Table-8 Complex Search Tools

Type	*KUN =122*		*PUN = 138*		χ^2	*Sign.*
	Yes	*No*	*Yes*	*No*		
Boolean logic	31 (25.40%)	91 (74.59%)	19 (13.76%)	119 (86.23%)	5.650	.017*
Phrase searching	29 (23.77%)	93 (76.22%)	28 (20.28%)	110 (79.71%)	.458	.498
Truncation	29 (23.77%)	93 (76.22%)	69 (50%)	69 (50%)	18.969	.000*
Word proximity	22 (18.03%)	100 (81.96%)	25 (18.11%)	113 (81.88%)	.000	.986

Table-8 presents the use of various complex search tools. In KU 25.40 percent users used Boolean logic, followed by truncation (23.77 percent), phrase searching (23.77 percent) and word proximity searching (18.03 percent). In PU also, half the number of responding users used truncation, followed by phrase searching (20.28 percent), word proximity searching (18.11 percent) and Boolean logic (13.76 percent). Interestingly, use of two tools namely truncation and Boolean logic was significantly different in both the universities. PU users used truncation significantly more than KU users while the latter used Boolean logic significantly more.

Table-9 Query Processing Speed

Processing speed	*KUN = 122*	*PUN =138*	*TotalN = 260*
Very fast	14(11.47%)	21 (15.21%)	35 (13.46%)
Fast	34 (27.86%)	37 (26.81%)	71(27.30%)
Moderate	39 (31.96%)	45 (32.60%)	84(32.30%)
Slow	29 (23.77%)	30 (21.73%)	59 (22.69%)
Very slow	6 (4.91%	5 (3.62%)	11 (4.23%)
Total	122 (100%)	138 (100 %)	260 (100 %)

χ^2= 1.083, Sign. = .897

Table-9 shows the query processing speed of OPAC systems in both the universities. In KU, a little less than 40 percent users considered the query processing speed to be fast or very fast; 31.96 percent considered it as moderate and more than 28 percent felt that the speed was slow or very slow. More than 41percent in PU considered the query processing speed of the OPAC system as fast or very fast but 32.60 percent felt that it was moderate, while more than 25 percent considered it slow or very slow. When this response was subjected to statistical testing , it was found that the difference in the response was statistically not significant, which means the views of the users of both the universities were broadly similar on query processing speed of their OPAC system.

Table-10 Satisfaction with the OPAC

Satisfaction	*KUN = 122*	*PUN = 138*	*TotalN = 260*
Fully satisfied	22 (18.03%)	23(16.66%))	45 (17.30%)
Satisfied	38 (31.14%)	50 (36.23%)	88 (33.84%)
Neither satisfied nor dissatisfied	36 (29.50%)	41 (29.71%)	77 (29.61%)
Dissatisfied	15 (12.29%)	17 (12.31%)	32 (12.30%)
Very dissatisfied	11 (9.01%)	7 (5.07%)	18 (6.92%)
Total	122 (100%)	138 (100 %)	260 (100 %)

χ^2= 1.083, Sign. = .897

Table-10 shows users' satisfaction with OPAC facility. In KU, 18.03 percent users were fully satisfied, 31.14 percent satisfied, 29.50 percent neither satisfied nor dissatisfied and more than 21 percent were either very dissatisfied or dissatisfied. A broadly similar response was shown in PU, where about 53 percent users were either satisfied or very satisfied with the OPAC facility. A sizeable number of users (i.e29.71 percent) were neither satisfied nor dissatisfied but more than 17 percent users were dissatisfied with OPAC facility. This response of both the universities was not found statistically different.

Table-11 Problems faced in OPAC Search

Problems	KUN = 123		PUN – 139		Chi squarestat	Sign.
	Yes	No	Yes	No		
Slow query processing speed	53 (43.08%)	70 (56.91%)	64 (46.04%)	75 (53.95%)	.230	.631
Less awareness of advanced features	46 (37.39%)	77 (62.60%)	48 (34.53%)	91 (65.46%)	.233	.629
Unavailability of staff assistance	40 (32.62%)	83 (67.47%)	43 (30.93%)	96 (69.06%)	.076	.783
Insufficient no. of terminals	33 (26.82%)	90 (65.21%)	43 (30.93%)	96 (69.06%)	.534	.465
Lack of power backup	32 (26.01%)	91 (73.98%)	28 (20.14%)	111 (79.85%)	1.275	.259
Inappropriate location of terminals	18 (14.63%)	103 (83.73%)	13 (9.35%)	1258 (9.42%)	1.821	.177

Table-11 presents an analysis of the problems faced by users in OPAC use. In KU, 43.08 percent users faced problem of slow query processing speed, 37.39 percent had less awareness of advanced features of OPAC, 32.62 percent found no staff to assist, 26.01 percent had problem with lack of power backup and 14.63 percent found the terminals to be at inappropriate location. A more or less similar response was given by the users of PU. Almost half the number of users (i.e46.04 percent) felt query processing speed was quite slow. 34.53 percent users were less aware of advanced features of OPAC. Infrastructural problems like unavailability of staff assistance and insufficient number of terminals were faced by 30.93 percent users. 20.14 percent felt lack of power backup and 9.42 percent found terminals at inappropriate place.

Interestingly, despite minor variations similar problems were faced by respondents in both the universities.

FINDINGS OF THE STUDY

- The frequency of library visits of users does not differ significantly both the university.
- The level of awareness of OPAC of PU users is more than those of KU.
- The purpose of using OPAC is mainly similar in both the universities. The users use OPAC for checking the number of copies of documents and for finding bibliographical details.
- More numbers of users of PU consult OPAC for document availability; the KU users use it for locating the documents.
- Users of both the universities mainly search their documents in OPAC by title, author, keyword and subject (in decreasing order of preference).
- The common problems faced by the users of both the universities are as following in the decreasing order of preference: slow query processing speed, less awareness of advanced features, unavailability of staff assistance, insufficient number of terminals and lack of power backup.

RECOMMENDATION OF THE STUDY

The following suggestions are being given below on the basis of the findings of the study:

- Infrastructure for service provision i.e number of terminals and sufficient power backup should be improved. More OPAC terminals need to be provided near the stack area particularly in KU library.
- In both the university should be implemented the new computer system for searching OPAC facility.
- Besides regular training programs on the use of OPAC, on-

site staff assistance is always desirable. Help of library staff will be needed by infrequent users of OPAC.

- The PU library has already made its OPAC accessible through Web. It is suggested that KU should also make the OPAC web accessible (Web-OPAC).

REFERENCES

- Amar Nath, and Aarti Sharma. 2006. Use of online public access catalogue by research scholars in Panjab University: A survey. Library Herald 44(3): 212-23.
- Ariyapala, P.G., and N.N.Edzan. 2002. Foreign Postgraduate students and the online catalogue at the University of Malaya library. Malaysian Journal of Library Information Science. 7(1): 57-67
- Hussain, Akhtar, and M. Massom Raja. 2002. Online public access catalogue: Its development & limitations. IASLIC Bulletin 47(4):26-32
- Kurukshetra University Library [cited 9 April 2010] available from *http://kukinfo.com/library.htm*
- Mulla, K.R., M. Chandershekhara. 2009. Access of Web-OPAC in engineering college libraries in Karnataka: A survey. SERLS Journal of Information Management 46(3): 321-32.
- O' Berien, Ann. 2003. OPACS. In International Encyclopedia of Information and Library Science, ed. Allen Kent, 466.New York: Marcel Dekker.
- Ortiz-Repiso, Virginia, Virginia Bazan, Agnes Ponnsati and Mario Cottereau. 2006. How researchers are using the OPAC of the Spanish Council for scientific research library network. The Electronic library 24(2): 190-211.
- Panjab University Library [cited 9 April 2010] Available from *http://library.puchd.ac.in/*
- Reitz, Joan M. 2007 Online Dictionary of Library & Information Science (ODLIS)[cited 21 April 2010] available from URL: http://lu.com/odlis/index.cfm
- Shiv Kumar. 2011. Effect of web searching on the OPAC: A comparison of selected university libraries. Library Hi Tech News (6) :14-21
- Velmurugan, V Santhur and G. Amudha. 2011. Use of OPAC by the VHSN college users: a study. Journal of Library Indian Library Association 47 (2-3) 37-40.
- Villen-Ruedo, Luis, Josh A Senso and Felex de Moya-Anegan. 2007. The use of OPAC in a large academic library: A transactional log analysis study of subject searching. The Journals of Academic Librarianship [cited 9 May

2010] Available from *http://www.scimago.es/publications/villensensomoyaJAL07.pdf*

- Wells David, 2007. What is a library OPAC. The Electronic Library 25 (4): 386-94.

22

Open Access Journal: A Boon for Internet User Research Scholars

Abdul Jalil
Dr. Sanjay Kumar Singh

ABSTRACT

Recent trends in Open Access publishing is useful to research are discussed. Different types of site and their functions are mentioning in the paper, where the site helps to giving information about the scholarly literature of R & D sector. Research scholar brows needed information and data from scholarly open access journals without any cost or geographical barriers. Data are collected from different types of site. The paper also discussed about what is open access. Research scholars can go through the mention sites. Tremendous growth of literature day is creating space problem to the libraries and information centres. Open access solving the space problem as well as tries to fulfil the five laws of library science. The paper tries to discuss some of them.

Keywords: Open Access initiatives, Open Access Journal, digital contents.

INTRODUCTION

It is library science and IT sector professionals continued process to provide reliable and easily accessible knowledge and information to its browser more and more. This fulfills the Dr. S. R. Ranganathans' five laws of library science. In earlier days professionals tries fulfill it in traditional collection system which takes time and more space in library and information centres. Tremendous growth of literature day by day creating major space problem for library and information centres. Use of internet or web portals to access information solve this type of problem

Access to online journals has been a major tool to academician and research scholars. Generally two types of online journals are available through internet, one is peer reviewed paid journals and other is open access journals. Online journals are considered as major tool for research libraries. Quantity of online journals increases every day. Scholarly renowned publishers converted their printed journal to online journals. Online journals are easily accessible to client libraries and information centre. But all libraries are unable subscribe paid journals, it needs huge amount of money, alternatively open access journals are easily accessible to them.

OPEN ACCESS

Open access to scholarly literature is movement led by eminent organization like the Budapest Open Access Initiative (BOAI), Open Society Institute (OSI), Open software Foundation, etc, which works against all barriers to worldwide information flow and tries to ensure anytime and anywhere information for all available literature, some well known names associated with open access movement are that of Richard Statman, Steven, Harnard, Peter Suber, Linus Torvald etc. The call for open access is basically meant for researchers, librarians, administrators, students, publishers, foundation managers, learned society officers, government officials and citizens.

The open access is the global effort to provide online access to scholarly literature in the field of research and development freely available through internet, especially peer-reviewed journal articles and their preprints. That means the provision of free availability of immediate, permanent access to research results for everyone to use, read, download, copy and distribute to its users.

OPEN ACCESS JOURNALS

According popular encyclopedia "Wikipedia" - "Open access journals are scholarly journals that are available online to the reader with financial, legal or technical barriers other that those inseparable from gaining access to the Internet itself"

Some are subsidized and some require payment on behalf of the author subsidized. Journals are financed by and academic institution or a govt. Information centre those requiring payment are typically financed by many mode available to researchers for the purpose from a public of private funding agency, as part of a research grant. There have also been several modification of open access journals that considering different nature hybrid open access journals and delayed open access journals.

In successively looser senses, open access Journal may be considered to be.

- Journals entirely open access.
- Journals with research article open access.
- Journals aim some research article open access.
- Journals with some articles open access and the other delayed access.
- Journals permuting self archiving of articles.

NEED AND BENEFITS OF AN OPEN ACCESS JOURNAL

It is very much clear that open access has great potential

benefits for the users and their usage. The advantages of open access journals are as follows

Free availability of literature: The availability of literature in open access is fully free. There is no subscription charge.

Unrestricted Access: In open access the readers are permitted to use articles for read, copy, save, print, send, etc., there is no any restriction for its use

License Free: Open access journals do not having any license. These are freely accessible and disseminated

Wider Access: Open access literatures are having wider user than print format. It can be uploaded and download any ware in the world.

Faster Communication : Uploading new articles in open access is takes few minutes. It reaches all over the globe with faster communication to its users.

Less expensive: Publication of open access journals are less expansive.

Authors retain copyright: Articles are published under the Creative Commons Attribution License and can be reused and redistributed as long as they are correctly attributed.

High quality and rigorous peer review: Open access journals run through a thorough electronic peer-review process the same way traditional journals do

Rapid publication: An easy to use online submission and efficient production process enable the immediate publication on acceptance.

Compliance with finder's open access mandates: Articles can comply with open access mandates in the fastest and easiest way. Final articles can be deposited into bibliographic databases and institutional repositories without any embargo periods.

Citation tracking and inclusion in bibliographic databases: Open access journals can be tracked for impact factors and are included in bibliographic databases just as traditional journals.

According to Bhojaraju Gouda and etal, 2008 the beneficiaries of Open Access journals are

Authors: It enlarges their audience and increases their visibility impact of their work.

Readers: It gives a barrier free access to literature they need.

Teachers and Students: It eliminates the need for permission to reproduce and distribute content.

Journals and Publishers: it makes their articles more visible, discoverable, retrievable and useful and attracts submission and Advertising.

Finance Agencies: it increases their returns.

Government: It promotes the democracy by sharing information as rapidly and widely as possible.

Libraries: It solves the pricing crisis of scholarly journals and permission crisis.

Citizens: It gives them access to peer reviewed research.

DISADVANTAGES OF OPEN ACCESS JOURNALS

In case of open access journals author either to need to have a sponsor to pay on their behalf or personally pay the publication fee.

- Some people feel that open Access is unnecessary.
- Some feet that the open Access is to impractical.

METHODS OF ACCESSING OPEN ACCESS JOURNALS

There are two methods for accessing OAJ's. These methods are: Open Access Journal Portals; and Open Access Platforms. These methods act as highly useful access points for retrieving relevant information by the scholarly community. As awareness about Open Access is increasing perceptibly these issues add value to OAJs.

Open access journal portals: The tremendous growth of e-journals has forced libraries to develop means of providing access to these popular resources. Open access journal portal is a method employed by academic libraries to provide e-journal access to their users. There are a number of portals through which open access journals can be accessed. They are discussed below:

Open J-Gate: Open J-Gate is an electronic gateway to global journal literature in open access domain. Launched in 2006, It is a service by Informatics (India) dedicated to the promotion of open access movement of scholarly Journals. Open J Gate indexes articles from 8469 academic, research and industry journals. In that 5674 of them are peer reviewed scholarly Journals. This site is updating every day.

Open Access Journals Search Engine: OAJSE: is an open access E-journal portal of Krishna Kanta Handique State Open University, its head quarter situated at Guwahati, Assam. It has a large number of journals in each field of social science, Humanities and Pure Science. The Journals are arranged in alphabetical order from A to Z. The first one Acoustics and the last one is Zoology. Anyone can browse its articles from anywhere in globe.

DOAJ: The Directory of Open Access Journals covers free, full text, quality controlled scientific and scholarly journals covering many subjects and languages. There are now 8800 journals as on 21st March, 2013 in the directory. A total of 4509 journals are searchable at article level. It covers 121 countries. As of that day 1048660 articles are included in the. DOAJ service. There are 20% of peer reviewed journals are available for accessing. It is having its head office at Lund University Libraries.

DLA: Digital Library Archives is a department in the University Libraries at Virginia Tech, which evolved from the Scholarly Communications Project (SCP) that began in 1989. Its focus is on working with the university community to host its unique born-digital works. DLA enhances online access to the library's unique and rare archival resources. DLA hosts a growing number of faculty archives and VT publications, including Employee of the Week. DLA also collaborates with various universities, for example, to provide a home for the South Atlantic Humanities

Center and to develop and sustain in a distributed digital preservation network through the Meta Archive Cooperative it renamed in the year 2000 Digital library and Archives. It is having online collections such as VT image base ETDs (Electronic Thesis And Database etc.

High wire: High wire now boasts the largest collection of free full-text life science articles in the world, with over several million articles from over 1444 journals, books reference works, and scholarly publications. It is maintained by highwire Stanford university .

J-Stage: The Japan Science and Technology Agency (JST) developed the "Japan Science and Technology Information Aggregator, Electronic" (J-STAGE). The user organizations computerize bulletins of academic societies and research papers with ease and at low cost. Computerized documents can be accessed from anywhere in the world with this system. This project also links up with the National Institute of Informatics (formerly the Ministry of Education National Center for Science Information Systems (NACSIS)). J-STAGE has released 718 journals (344,370 articles), 125 proceedings, ten reports and 42 JST reports by 06 April 6, 2011.

Redalyc: Redalyc is an Open Access electronic library project supported by the University of State of Mexico. It has more than 14,196 IberoAmerican scientific journals with about 174,803 free, full-text articles in pdf format and universal access. Redalyc, also provides the Scientific Journal Index of CONACYT (Consejo Nacional de Ciencia y Tecnologý'a).

HRCAK: HRCAK is the central portal of Croatian scientific journals. The Ministry of Science Education and Sports supports this portal. It is developed and maintained by the University computing center and is based on the idea from the Croatian Information and Documentation Society. Hrcak offers the access to the journals following the Open Access Initiative. It has 244 journals, 4,492 issues, 434 articles without full text and 60,223 articles with full text.

SciELO: The Scientific Electronic Library Online (SciELO) is an electronic library covering a selected collection of Brazilian scientific journals. SciELO site is an integral part of the FAPESP/BIREME/CNPq Project and it is an application of the methodology being developed by the project, particularly the Internet Interface module. The portal acts as an electronic virtual library, providing full access to a collection of serial titles, a collection of issues from individual serial titles, as well as to the full text of articles. The access to both serial titles and articles is available via indexes and search forms .

Bentham OPEN: Bentham OPEN publishes open access journals in all major disciplines of science including engineering, mathematics, chemistry, medicine, life sciences, pharmaceutical science, earth sciences, social sciences and environmental science. Published exclusively online, the journals are available for free viewing via Bentham OPEN's web site.

Open access platforms: Open Access Platforms are those which play an important role in providing links to the information resources on the web. Knowledge of these platforms is essential for fruitful information retrieval. Following are some of the open access platforms.

Cross Ref: Cross Ref is an independent membership association, founded and directed by publishers. Cross Ref's mandate is to connect users to primary research content, by enabling publishers to work collectively. Cross Ref provides a means of linking from bibliographic citation to cited article through the Digital Object Identifier (DOI) system

Open URL: The Open URL protocol has proved to be an even more powerful means of linking library users to electronic journal content. Developed by Herbert van de Sompel, Open URL is a mechanism for linking users to appropriate copies of electronic resources or surrogates of these resources.

Google Scholar: Google Scholar advances the means by which users can access e-journal articles. Scholar restricts its resources to those academic in nature, thus providing an even greater chance of users locating useful content. Google Scholar operates like a federated search service, with the notable exception that Google, not individual libraries, determines what resources are being indexed.

IMPACT OF OPEN ACCESS JOURNALS ON LIBRARIES

The open Access journals and its development being forward the following changing demands on library staff such as:

a. Libraries Can promote the Access of OAJs

b. Library increases its digital resources

c. Library can build specialized automation system.

d. Library can digitize the resources without any copyright problem.

e. Library can preserve OAJ.

CONCLUSION

We believe that this movement is a very good effort that has potential to aid users and professionals with their research and help in extending their knowledge. The journal available through online to everyone to access is a significant improvement for our society's research profile. The open access movement is boon to authors, scholars, researchers etc. the sharing of each other's work with certain ideas will allow more significant ideas to form. We can safely hope that India as well as the world outside will march forward towards the ever increasing horizon of anytime, anywhere access of scholarly literature.

It should concluded that the Government funding agencies should try to make open access to all paid journals for better benefit and search authentic, reliable data for reader. It is relevant that all open access journals are not satisfactory article. So, also it is to be clear that the peer reviewed journals should be make available through open access.

REFERENCE

1. Bhuayan, Hrishikesh: Open Access Journal: A Boon to libraries & Information Centres; ACALA Bulletin, vol. 5 & 6, Dec, 2012. p.36.
2. Bjork, B. C, Gustafsson, T., & Hedlund, T. (2004): The Open access scientific journal: an empirical study. Learned Publishing, 17(3) 199-209.
3. Bjork, Bo-Christofer, Ziga Turk, and Jonas Holmstrom(2005): The scholarly Journal Re-Engineered : A case study of An Open Access Journal in Construction IT , vol.10, p. 349
4. Chakraborty, Sushmita: Open Access resources in Science & Technology Field with Special reference to engineering and Medicine.
5. Charles W. Bailey, R. Open Access and Libraries *www.digital-scholarly.com* (accessed on 15/10/2012)
6. Gopa Kumar, V and Bordol, A.K. : Open Access and institutional repositories: The new scholarly publishing scenario.
7. *www.doaj.com* (accessed on 21/3/2013)
8. *www.wikipedia.org* (accessed on 15/10/2012)

23

Dr. Ganda Singh Punjabi Reference Library: Subject strengths in its collection

Gian Singh

INTRODUCTION

The Punjabi University, Patiala was established on 30th April, 1962 under the State Government Act of 1961. Initially the university started with the objective of developing and promoting the language and culture of the Punjabi people. Over the time has involved into a multifaceted, multi faculty educational institution. The establishment of this university was considered a major landmark in the cultural progress of the Punjabi-speaking people.

The Act stated the objective of the university is "To establish and incorporate a university for the advancement of Punjabi Studies and development of Punjabi language as a medium of instruction or otherwise for the providing instruction in humanistic and scientific subjects and generally for the promotion of higher education and research."

This is the first university in India to be named after the regional language and second in the world, the first being Hebrew University of Israel. It was inaugurated on June 24, 1962 by the great Indian philosopher Dr. R.S. Radhakrishnan, the then President of India. Padam Bhushan Dr. Bhai Jodh Singh, an eminent scholar was the founder Vice-Chancellor of this university. To fulfill the main objective "To promote the Punjabi Language and literature" of Punjabi University, Punjabi Reference library was started with of 2573 book in 1981. This library was renamed as "Dr. Ganda Singh Punjabi Reference Library" on 29th September 2004 in the memory of Dr. Ganda Singh who was an eminent historian of Punjab. It has now a total collection of over 60014 documents as on 28.02.2013. It is subscribing current journals and ten news papers related to its identified areas. During the last three decades, this library has made substantial progress. The collection has been strengthened by purchasing and gratis further the library was organized in manner, which could facilitate and promote its use among students, scholars and teachers. This library has been very popular in internationally apart from its documents collection.

Mr. Hakam Singh the founder librarian remained the head of the PRL. In 1979, Dr. R.L. Mittal took over as Chief librarian and developed the library. Later Mr. H.R. Katyal took over as head of university library. Prof. S.P. Narang headed the library for a brief period. Dr. Devinder Kaur took over as University librarian on 2.21994. On the retirement of Dr. Devinder Kaur, Dr. Jasmer Singh headed the library for a month before joining of Dr. Saroj Bala as head of library on 02-05-2007.

LIBRARY COLLECTION

The collection has been strengthened by purchasing two copies of publications in Punjabi published anywhere in the world and one copy each of the publications on Punjab History & Culture, Sikhism etc. in Hindi & English languages. Collection in Urdu language on Punjabi literature and language, Punjab History and Culture also available in PRL. This library has rich collection on Punjabi language and literature, Punjab History & Culture, Sikh religion. It subscribes 122 current Punjabi journals and 9 Punjabi & 1 English news papers. The private collection of 54 eminent historians, public figures and scholars is the backbone of the library. A complete record of back files of all news papers in Punjabi and back sets of periodicals has been maintained in bound form in a systematic order. General books, Reference books, Manuscripts, rare books, diaries, memoirs, old journals, newspapers, Religious Granths are included in collection of PRL.

SPECIAL COLLECTION OF PUNJABI REFERENCE LIBRARY

Punjabi reference library has given the name 'special collection' for documents which are collected from eminent donors. Where these personal collections of donors has been housed that is special collection section of Punjabi reference library. This is the unique feature that all documents available in special collection section are on Punjabi language, literature, Punjab history, culture and Sikh religion. Special collection including manuscripts, diaries, memoirs, rare books, maps, old journals and news papers, religious granth etc. of literary luminaries and scholars and public men have contributed significantly in building up a strong collection of Punjab history, culture, Punjabi language and literature. This possesses nearly 68,111 prestigious and rare collection of 54 eminent donors. Since January 1996 personal collections of scholars have been housed on second floor of Punjabi reference library building.

The major collections have been received from. Bhai Mohan Singh Vaid, Bhai Kahn Singh Nabha, Dr. Ganda Singh, Dr. Vishav

Nath Tiwari and Manmohan Sehgal have indeed enriched library's treasure. Back volumes of journals, university dissertations, rare books, manuscripts, saroops of Guru Granth Sahib a part of this collection. Recently Punjabi Reference Library collect the 23 manuscripts from museum of Punjabi University. These manuscripts have been housed in Special Collection section. It has now a total collection of over 70,000 documents (as on 07.03.2012). The private collections of eminent historians, public figures and scholars are the back bone of the Dr. Ganda Singh, Punjabi Reference Library. Fifty four donors have donated their personal collections to this library which is valuable treasure. These collections have been organized in a systematic manner. Scholars from all over the country and abroad consult these collections.

GROWTH & DEVELOPMENT OF PURCHASED & GRATIS COLLECTION (1981-2012)

Dr. Ganda Singh Punjabi reference library has total collection 59645 documents as on 31.12.12. In first 2 years, library has collected more documents comparatively other years. In 1992-93 library has collected less document than all other years. Mostly yearly growth of collection is between 1200-2633 documents. In starting year PRL has purchased the more documents all of other times, in its history. Development of collection is regularly continued without any break in any time. We can show the growth & development of purchased & gratis collection by given following table.

Yearly Growth & Development of Purchased & Gratis Collection(1981-2012)

Year	*Annual additions in collection*	*Total Collection*
1981	4506	4506
1982	3779	8285
1983	1969	10254
1984	1301	11555
1985	1736	13291

1986	2633	15924
1987	1727	17651
1988	1387	19038
1989	1215	20253
1990	1323	21576
1991	1548	23124
1992	914	24038
1993	875	24913
1994	2236	27149
1995	1702	28851
1996	868	29719
1997	1860	31579
1998	1772	33351
1999	2860	36211
2000	2165	38376
2001	1383	39759
2002	1473	41232
2003	1196	42428
2004	1709	44137
2005	2221	46358
2006	1551	47909
2007	1707	49611
2008	2062	51673
2009	2138	53811
2010	2210	56021
2011	1755	57776
2012	1869	59645
	Total=59645	

LANGUAGES OF COLLECTION OF PRL

Punjabi Reference Library has collected the documents which are published in four languages by purchasing & gratis. These four languages are Punjabi, English, Hindi and Urdu. But every document published in Punjabi/English/Hindi/Urdu is related with the Punjabi literature and language, Punjab history and Culture and Sikhism. Collection strength of PRL according to above four languages is given below:

1)	Collection in Punjabi Language	54459
2)	Collection in English Language	2656
3)	Collection in Hindi Language	375
4)	Collection in Urdu Language	155

MAIN SUBJECTS IN LIBRARY COLLECTION

There are near about sixty subjects are available in the library collection. All subjects in library collection are related with Punjabi Literature & language, Punjab History & Culture, Sikhism. Library collection including those subjects which are related with social science and science also. Psychology, library science, sociology, Sikhism, Education, Physical education, Punjabi literature and language, English literature, Hindi literature, Law, Music, History and Culture etc. are the main subjects of library collection.

STRENGTHS OF MAIN SUBJECTS IN PRL COLLECTION

Punjabi Reference Library collection includes approximately 57 main subjects. In this library, Punjabi Literature, History and Sikhism are three most important subjects which have major strengths of all other subjects. Punjabi Literature has 28100 documents in the collection. This is only subject which have maximum strength comparatively other all subjects. After Punjabi Literature, the subject Sikhism is secondly important subject which have more than 7800 documents. Computer science, library science, Engineering, Biotechnology, Management, Manufacturing etc are those subjects which have lowest strength in collection. Bound periodicals, bound newspapers, proceeding of syndicates are parts of collection. Two hundred reference books also available in the collection. We can show the strength of the all subjects of PRL collection by given below table.

Strengths of Main Subjects in Collection of PRL

S.No.	*Subject*	*No. of Books*
1	Computer Science	16
2	Bibliographies	30
3	Library & Information Science	25
4	Journalism	106
5	General collection	327
6	Philosophy	197
7	Psychology	387
8	Religion	101
9	Christian	140
10	Hinduism	380
11	Sikhism	7980
12	Islam	100
13	Sociology	900
14	Political Science	205
15	Economics	335
16	Law	350
17	Public Administration	387
18	Education	450
19	Folklore	821
20	Language	600
21	Science	120
22	Mathematics	147
23	Physics	126
24	Chemistry	122
25	Botany	33
26	Zoology	103
27	Medical Science	226
28	Engineering	15
29	Agriculture	105
30	Home Science	120
31	Management	88
32	Biotechnology	60

33	Manufacturing	40
34	Buildings	10
35	Fine Arts	131
36	Music	295
37	Sports	150
38	Literature	575
39	English Lit.	265
40	Danish Lit.	34
41	French Lit.	60
42	Spanish Lit.	36
43	Sanskrit	90
44	Punjabi Lit.	28100
45	Hindi Lit.	713
49	Bengali Lit.	162
47	Marathi Lit.	68
48	Urdu Lit.	94
49	Russian Lit.	312
50	History	3723
51	Geography	126
52	Travelling	150
53	Biographies	190
54	References Books	200
55	Bound Periodicals	4200
56	Bound News Papers	3000
57	Syndicate Proceedings	114

CONCLUSION

This is the unique feature of PRL that every document which available in collection is on Punjabi Literature & Language / Punjab History & Culture/ Sikhism. The major strength in collection is available on Punjabi Literature / History / Sikhism also. Library collection is growing & developing regularly every time without any stop. Library collection has been strengthened by purchasing / gratis. Library has total collection of 59645 documents as on

31.12.2012. This collection includes General books, Reference books, Bound Periodicals, Bound Newspapers and proceedings of Syndicate etc.

REFERENCES

- Accession Registers of Punjabi Reference Library.
- Catalogue /OPAC of Punjabi Reference Library.
- Official Records Regarding Collection of Punjabi Reference Library.
- Periodical Registers & Cardex of PRL.
- Physical counting of Collection of PRL.
- Punjabi University: Annual Reports(2001-2012)

24

Use and Impact of E-Journals on the Users of Panjabi University, Patiala, India

Renu Sharma

ABSTRACT

Punjabi University, Patiala (PUP) library subscribes to a number of electronic journals to satisfy the information needs of its users. The present study is an attempt to find out whether the users of PUP prefers the new format of journals and whether the electronic journals are able to satisfy the information needs of the users. Samples were selected from each category of users comprising of staff members and students for the present study.

Keywords: Electronic journals, Punjabi University, Patia!a

INTRODUCTION

Tremendous developments in ICT in the recent years have

given amazing boost to electronic publishing. As a result the information which is being generated at intense pace from all the directions worldwide for all the themes is now being published in form of electronic journals (e-journals). Anyone with access to a computer equipped with a modem and suitable software can produce and distribute an e-journal through a computer network, thus journal publishing is being democratized. Usually, e-journals are published as electronic equivalents of their print counterparts but recently there is an increase in number of scholarly journals which are being published only electronically. As a result, e-journals have emerged as vital components of information resources of a library and play an imperative role in the distribution of prime information.

E-journals are global information highways, so these are being added to library collections at exponential rates. Libraries are doing extensive work to make e-journals available to their users and keeping them abreast with latest developments in their field of interest. E-journals are accessible either free against print subscription or for a nominal charge along with the print subscription. Access to e-journals is generally provided either by the publisher or through their aggregators. E-journals have provided excellent opportunities to access scholarly information, which were previously beyond the reach of libraries due to geographical constraints. E-journals possess many added features for the facilitation of libraries and its user community.

Punjabi University, Patiala established on April 30, 1962 with the main objective of furthering the cause of Punjabi language, art and literature, Punjabi University has since evolved into the largest University in the state. Its multi-dimensional expansion has not only been quick-paced but steady, sustained and seamless, with each front paving way for the other. The University has achieved a couple of milestones during its move towards furthering the overall development of Punjabi. Having published a record number of over 3,000 titles in Punjabi covering a wide range of areas and establishing a special Punjabi Reference Library, it has taken upon itself the responsibility of catering to the linguistic and cultural needs of the overseas Punjabis.

The Punjabi reference Library has been created to build up a strong collection on Punjab history, culture, language and literature. University's main Library, on the other hand, stocks more than 5,00,000 volumes and subscribes to more than 600 journals. The other characteristics features of these libraries constitute Online Public access Catalogue, database of 2, 00,000 documents, internet facility, current awareness and documentation services, indexing services of newspapers, subject bibliographies, inter-library loan facility, computerized bibliographic and documentation and reprographic services.

OBJECTIVES

Many studies has been carried out in India and abroad which gives information on use of electronic resources by the users of the library. This study will be helpful to the library staff and the authorities of the university to decide whether they have to invest more on the development of electronic collection or to go for an alternative format of journals. The following objectives were framed for the study:

1. To know the awareness of the users towards the electronic resources available in the library.
2. To know the frequency of usage of e-journals.
3. To know the location of using e-journals.
4. To know the purpose of using e-journals.
4. To know which format is more comfortable to them i.e. printed or electronic.
5. To identify the barriers if any which the users has come across while accessing electronic journals.

REVIEW OF LITERATURE

A survey on users of a package of electronic journals in the field of chemistry was carried out by Borrego and Urbano (2007).

They submitted that almost hundred percent respondents preferred PDF format for downloading the e-journal articles than the HTML format. The results provided the opportunity to better understand users' behavior for e-journals and established that this behavior does not vary significantly from that observed in studies undertaken in other geographical contexts. The results showed that there is a strong correlation between the number of articles downloaded and abstracts viewed of a title, so that the rankings of titles by articles downloaded and abstracts viewed are practically identical. Madhusudhan (2008) is of opinion that e-journals perform an increasingly important role in research. His study showed that there is an ever increasing demand for subscriptions of more e-journal titles. There appears to be some need for academics to be provided with training in using e-journals. Majority of the respondents strongly attest to the fact that they need proper training/orientation for searching ejournals. Kaur Baljinder & Verma Rama (2009) found that usage of e-journals has increased due to awareness among the users about the library e-resources and services.

RESEARCH METHODOLOGY

The survey method was selected, as it is one of the most appropriate tools for surveying large population. Structured questionnaire was developed and was used as a tool for data collection supported by the interview. The questionnaire was distributed to all the users covering all departments. Interview was also conducted of the faculties and students in order to get the answers of the unanswered questions. A random sample of 120 users was selected and out of these 105 (87.5%) users completely responded. The data collected were analyzed and results tabulated using percentages and frequencies.

DATA ANALYSIS

Awareness of the Electronic Journals

Table-1

Category of Users	Awareness	
	Yes	No
Staff Members	53 (50.47%)	10 (9.52%)
Students	34 (32.38%)	8 (7.61%)

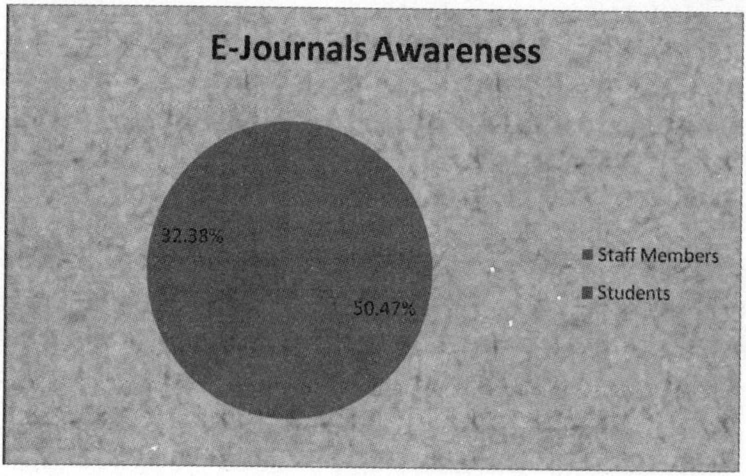

Fig. 1

When asked about the awareness of the electronic journals received under the consortia and the subscribed one. It was revealed from table-1 that, out of 105 users' 60% staff members was aware about the fact that the library is getting access to electronic journal under the UGC consortia plus subscribed resources and they can have an access to this literature from any corner of the campus whereas 40% students were aware about the same.

Frequency of Usage

Table-2

Frequency of Usage	Staff Members	Students	Total
Daily	29	14	33 (31.42%)
3-4 times in a week	18	9	27 (25.71%)
Once in a week	12	8	20 (19.04%)
Rarely	4	11	15 (14.28%)

As far as the usage is concerned 19.04% respondents make the use of electronic journals once in a week. 31.42% of the total respondents use electronic journals daily and here faculty is the major respondent which comprises of 29 respondents followed by students. Whereas 25.71% respondents uses the same facility 3-4 times in a week and only 14.28% respondents uses it occasionally. It seems that it is the faculty who is making daily use of electronic journals because they have well facility in their department to access the same.

Place of access e-journals

Table-3

Category of Users	Department	Library	Hostel	Other
Staff Members	22	28	5	8
Students	2	26	10	4
Total	24 (22.85%)	54 (51.42%)	15 (14.28%)	12 (11.42%)

Table-3 depicts that 22.85% users access the e-journals at their department whereas 51.42% access at the library and only few users i.e. 14.28% users access the same at their hostel. 11.42% users responded other location.

Purpose of using E-Journals

Table-4

Purpose	Staff Members	Students	Total
For Research	40	24	64 (60.95%)
For Class Work	10	10	20 (19.04%)
Keeping up-to-date	13	8	21 (20%)

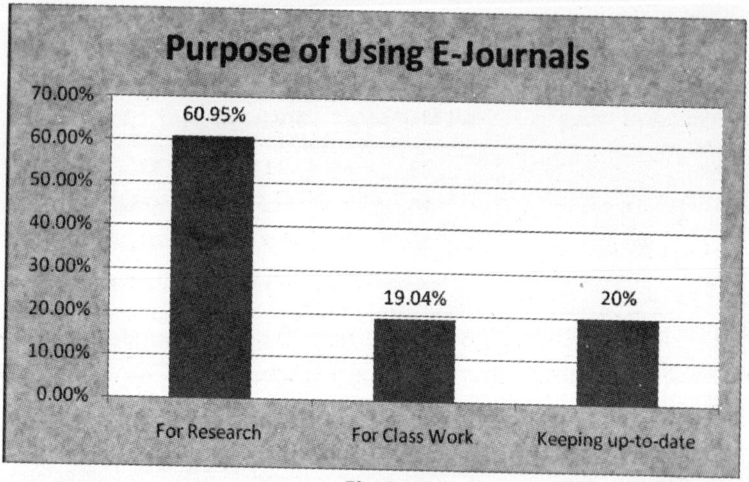

Fig. 2

60.95% respondents are using the electronic journals for just research purpose only followed by 20% respondents are using electronic journals for keeping themselves update with the new information and for research purpose which constitutes 13 staff members and 8 students while 19.04% respondents are using it for class work.

Format Preference

Table-5

Format	Staff Members	Students	Total
Print	28	20	48 (45.71%)
Electronic	35	22	57 (54.28%)
Both (E+Print)	42	32	74 (70.47%)

It is clear from the table-5 responses received from the respondents that majority of the users i.e. 70.47% prefer for both electronic and print format of electronic journal, followed by 54.28% users still preferring for the electronic format were as for 45.71% users prefer the print format.

Problems in accessing e-journals

Table-6

Problems	Staff Members	Students	Total
Lack of knowledge of proper search strategy	11	16	27 (25.71%)
Internet Connectivity	40	14	54 (51.42%)
Difficulty in finding information	12	12	24 (22.85%)

From the responses received it is clear from the table-6 that the 51.42% respondents are facing more problems because of the slow internet connectivity, followed by 25.71% respondents stating that they lack the knowledge of search strategy. Only 22.85% stated that they find it difficult to find appropriate information using electronic journals.

User's Satisfaction

Table-7

Category of Users	Fully Satisfied	Partially Satisfied	Not Satisfied
Staff Members	49	8	6
Students	32	7	3
Total	81 (77.14%)	15 (14.28%)	9 (8.57%)

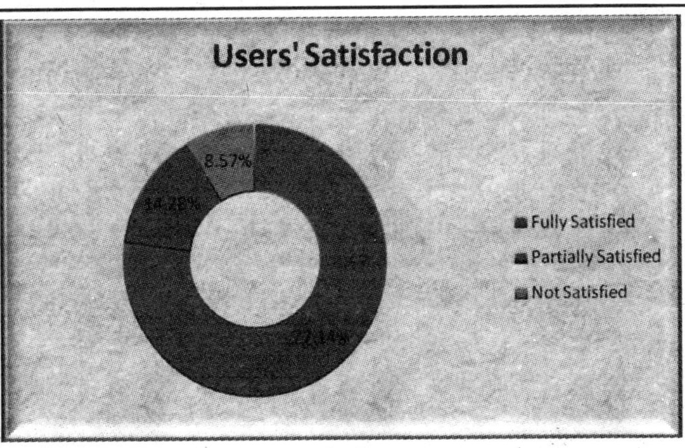

Fig. 3

It was found from table-7 that 77.14% respondents admits that their information requirements are fully satisfied with the electronic journals subscribed by the library, followed by 14.28% respondents are not fully satisfied the resources subscribed by the library can only partially fulfill their information needs whereas 8.57% respondents are not satisfied.

CONCLUSION

The present study reports the use of electronic journals by the users Punjabi University, Patiala. It is clear from the study that younger generation has conveniently adopted the electronic reading culture, but use of e-journals requires some sort of technical expertise. Use of e-journal is very limited because of infrastructural problems. Trends seem that users are gradually getting used to e-journals and libraries stand at a brink of digital information horizon. The only way to keep pace with the bursting of information in all directions is being proactive in form of e-journals, an extensive source of bundled knowledge. So if central library of Punjabi University, Patiala is to go beyond the services of a traditional library and to provide a sound electronic information platform, it is left with little option but to accommodate more and more e-journals. As far as the impact is concerned, electronic journals are really helpful in finding out the appropriate references and is useful to each and every user the only thing that needs to verify that does it really helped the faculties to increase their productivity this can be done by undertaking the citation analysis.

REFERENCES

- Borrego, A & Urbano, C. 2007. Analysis of the behavior of the users of a package of electronic journals in the field of chemistry. Journal of Documentation, 63(2): 243-258.
- *http://punjabiuniversity.ac.in/pbiuniweb/introductionmain.html*
- Kaur Baljinder & Verma Rama. 2009. "Use and impact of electronic journals in the Indian Institute of Technology, Delhi, India", The Electronic Library, Vol.27 (4), pp:611-622.

- Madhusudhan, M. 2008. Use of UGC-Infonet e-journals by research scholars and students of the University of Delhi, Delhi: A study. Library Hi Tech, 26(3):369-386.
- Vasishta, Seema and Navijyoti. 2011. Trends in the Use of E-journals: A Case Study of PEC University of Technology, Chandigarh. Library Philosophy and Practice 2011 ISSN 1522-0222 pp. 1-14.